Every
Moment
Matters

———

How the World's Best Coaches
Inspire Their Athletes and Build
Championship Teams

JOHN O'SULLIVAN

EVERY MOMENT MATTERS

How the World's Best Coaches Inspire Their Athletes and

Build Championship Teams

ISBN: 978-1-7343426-0-4 paperback
ISBN: 978-1-7343426-1-1 ebook

Library of Congress Control Number: 2019919285

Changing the Game Project
60643 Thunderbird
Bend, Oregon, 97702
www.ChangingTheGameProject.com

Cover Design by:
David Miles, Bushel and Peck Books

Interior Design by:
Laura Jones, lauraflojo.com

CONTENTS

INTRODUCTION

WHY COACHES MATTER

A good coach can change a game. A great coach can change a life.
—JOHN WOODEN

The difference between an artist and a coach is that an artist can throw out his work at the end of the day. The coach doesn't get to start over.
—TERRY STEINER

In early 2001, I sat in my office at the University of Vermont. It was a typical bone-chilling winter day and a quiet time of the year for an assistant college soccer coach. The phone was not ringing much. We didn't have any recruiting events to attend, and our players had just returned from winter break and could not start spring practice yet. Then the phone rang.

The call was from a former player of mine from my first coaching job at Cardinal Gibbons High School in Raleigh, North Carolina. His name was Pat, and to this day, he is one of my favorite players I have ever coached. He was hard-working, honest, fiercely competitive, an inspirational leader, and just a great person, both on and off the field. It was amazing to hear his voice and even more exciting that he was coming to visit UVM, where he was applying to medical school.

As we caught up that day, he said something that changed me forever as a coach. "John, I just wanted you to know that studying for the MCATs is really hard, and college was hard, but every time I want to put down the books or give up early when I am working out, I hear your voice," said Pat.

"You hear my voice?" I asked.

"You keep telling me to push a little harder, do a little more," Pat explained. "I keep hearing you say, 'Was that your very best?' So, I pick up my book and study a little more. Or I go back and do another set in the weight room. I just wanted to say thanks, Coach. Because you are still coaching me every day, even though I haven't seen you in a few years."

We finished up our call, and I hung up the phone and took a few minutes to digest what he had said. I shared the story with one of my fellow assistant coaches, and his response was, "That's great; how cool that he called you."

That's not great, I thought. *That sucks. He remembers everything I said and did. He was one of those kids I got along with great and was pretty positive toward. But he had a lot of teammates that I wasn't a very good coach for, that I was downright cruel to at times, I think. What about all of them? For some of them, I was their last coach because they quit.*

When I left the office that day, I went through a rolodex of former players in my head. I was still only twenty-nine and not long into my coaching career, but it didn't take me long to come up with a few names that I had not been a very good coach for. It scared me.

It scared me because in that moment I realized that our words and actions as a coach leave a long-lasting impact. They can stick with a young athlete for the rest of his life. And these moments in which we speak to our athletes are often very emotional, in the heat of an athletic contest, and they occur in public situations in front of friends, teammates, and families.

What we say and do in that moment can make or break them. It can be a moment that builds them up and carries them through tough times, both on and off the field. Or it can be a lingering thought in the back of their mind, saying over and over, "I am not good. I am not enough." In a nutshell, I realized that every action matters. That every word matters.

I realized that every moment matters.

Up until that time, I had spent my coaching career looking for the magic practice session that the great coaches were using. I had spent countless hours filling binder after binder with the Xs and Os of coaching. And what I realized in that moment shook me to the core.

All those sessions, all that sport-specific knowledge was important, but it was not sufficient. There was no magic practice session or set of world-beating tactics I was missing. Yes, that stuff was critical to know, but all that came second to the human side of coaching.

I realized in that moment that coaching was not simply an Xs and Os business. Coaching was a relationship business. My players would not care how much I knew about soccer until they knew how much I cared about them as a person. And in that area, I was falling short.

Fast forward to today, and I am still trying to develop both sides of my coaching game. I am as passionate as ever about finding and utilizing great practice sessions and building a methodology that produces creative, fast-thinking, and resilient athletes. But I am more focused on becoming a better version of me. And I am more focused on reaching every one of my athletes on a human level, getting to know the person and what makes her tick.

I am more focused on a concept that my friend Dr. Martin Toms so eloquently iterates: "You coach a child, not a sport."

Coaching Is about Relationships

This book is different than other coaching books. It isn't about "my winning season" as we so often read about. Many coaches have covered that well. It is not about my losing season either as thankfully some coaches have been vulnerable enough to write about. It is also not a collection of sport-specific *X*s and *O*s. If you can spell *Google*, you can find plenty of practices and training plans these days.

This book is about the human side of coaching and making the most of every moment you have with your athletes. It is about finding your purpose as a coach. It is about the relationships and connections between athletes and coaches, among teammates, and among all the parents and other adults that influence how teams function and perform. It is about creating engaging training sessions that foster enjoyment and love of sport, as well as development. It is a collection of stories, anecdotes, research, and interviews with some of the top coaching practitioners, sport scientists, psychologists, skill acquisition experts, and educators in the world, interspersed with a few of my own stories from nearly three decades of coaching. It will help you coach in a way that allows your athletes to know that you care, so they will care what you know.

Sport has evolved and so, too, must coaches. We need to stop thinking that we are simply transmitters of information about technique, tactics, and physical training. We are so much more than that. We are the architects of an engaging learning environment. We are there to get athletes to stretch themselves and get to a place they have never been—and likely would not get to on their own. To do that, we have to be coached ourselves and never stop learning.

We seem to understand as a society that children have specific needs during the school day. Therefore, we develop curriculums, and our teachers get undergraduate and advanced degrees, partake in continuing education, and have certain standards and procedures to follow in order to provide the best possible environment for the children. At three o'clock, the needs of the child do not change, yet we often turn them over to well-intentioned adults with little-to-no training in child development, education, or psychology—not even a basic understanding of what the child in front of them needs. Often, their only qualification is that they are available. Yet when children are coached by an untrained volunteer, 26 percent of them do not return the following year (as opposed to a 5 percent dropout rate for children who play for trained coaches).[1]

Some coaches say, "I don't get kids these days; I don't know what they want!" Actually, we do know what they want. In her ground-breaking research into what makes sport fun and engaging for children ages eight to eighteen, Amanda Visek of George Washington University discovered that the top five qualities children want in their coach are as follows:

> 1. Respect and encouragement
> 2. A positive role model
> 3. Clear, consistent communication
> 4. Knowledge of the sport
> 5. A good listener[2]

As you can see, the research shows that while kids want their coaches to know the Xs and Os, they also must know that they care and are invested in the child. Many coaches are given information and some training on "knowledge of the sport," but what about the other 80 percent of qualities that matter most? According to studies, of the 6.5 million youth coaches in the United States, fewer than one in five get any training in motivation and communication, the other 80 percent of what kids want from their coaches.[3] Is it any wonder why so many kids quit?

How to Use This Book

The purpose of this book is to help you get a better understanding of who that child is in front of you and what she needs from you to ensure she returns to sport the next season. The goal is certainly not to have you throw out everything you have ever done and start fresh. Without a doubt, if you have picked up this book, you are likely doing many things well. I just want to add to your game.

Imagine if I walked into your practice and told you that everything you were doing was wrong. You would say, "No way! Get out." But if I said, "How about we replace ten minutes of this activity with ten minutes of this one and see how it goes?" You are more likely to say, "Sure, we can try that." That is what this book is all about. Let's add a little to your game and then, over time, add a little bit more. Let's take out the stuff that is inefficient—or may even be hurting your athletes physically or emotionally—and replace it with something better. Then, let's add more when the time is right.

I have divided the book into four parts, and I do suggest reading it (or at least skimming it) all the way through at first. It can also be used as a resource book as you will see that each part has multiple points of entry on specific topics. If you want to improve in a specific area, you can dive right in, and it will still make sense without going back through the entire book. The four parts are based upon four important questions all coaches must ask themselves. They were first written about in my favorite coaching book, *InSideOut Coaching* by Joe Ehrmann. The four sections are as follows:

1. Why do I coach?
2. How do I coach?
3. How does it feel to be coached by me?
4. How do I define success?

Part I is all about finding your why. As business guru Simon Sinek says, "People don't buy what you do, they buy why you do it."[4] It's the same with athletes and parents. When we get down to the nitty gritty of our why, we go on a journey of self-awareness and reflection that sets a solid foundation for our coaching and leadership. In part I, we explore topics such as growing in self-awareness, putting players first, and finding a higher team purpose than winning. You are far less likely to burn out or grow frustrated with the politics and ups and downs of coaching if you have a strong purpose.

In part II, we delve into how we coach. Many of us coach the way we were coached or the way we have always done things. I was guilty of that as well. The problem is that it might not be the most effective way to help your athletes learn or to create an engaging and enjoyable environment. In this section, we will discuss some of the latest research in effective practice design, skill acquisition, how to get transfer from practice to games, communication, building a competitive culture, engaging parents, the difference between coaching boys and coaching girls, and so much more.

In part III, we get into what it feels like to be a part of your team or part of your program. In my research, and in nearly three decades of coaching, I have learned that the best coaches prioritize what it feels like to be a part of a team. The coaches interviewed for this book have won dozens of NCAA titles, as well as World Cups, Olympic medals, and professional championships, and they all believe that getting the feeling right is critical. In this section, we will talk about the qualities of high-performing teams as we explore how to establish core values and standards instead of rules, create a positive team environment, overcome fear and anxiety, build trust, coach your own children, and intentionally create extraordinary moments for your athletes.

Finally, in part IV, I will help you redefine success beyond such ephemeral things such as this season's championship. What does a great season *really* look like? How do you leave a legacy and build the next generation of coaches? How do we stay one step ahead of our competition? And how do we avoid burnout and show up each season refreshed and ready to change lives? The good news is, after reading parts I through III, you'll just need a brief reminder.

But again, start small. Maybe it's a change in practice design. Maybe it's gaining more self-awareness. Maybe it's about building a stronger, more intentional team culture. Maybe it's improving communication or the way you engage parents. This book has all of that and more. Try it out, and if it works, add a little more.

Coaching Is Not a Job; It Is a Calling

If you are reading this book, I hope you realize that I believe coaching is not transactional. It should be transformational. Coaching cannot simply be a job. It must be a vocation, a calling to a place that best suits your skills, your passion, and your ability.

You have taken on one of the most beautiful, powerful, and influential positions a person can ever have. By becoming a coach, you have chosen to work with athletes, both young and old, all of them needing your influence. You have chosen to guide them through the trials and tribulations of learning two beautiful games: sport and life. You are in a position to change their lives forever, not only by making them better athletes but also by making them better people. You are a leader; you are a role model; you are a person who serves your athletes; and you are a person to whom they entrust their physical and emotional well-being.

Never take this responsibility lightly.

Coaching can be one of the most difficult jobs in the world. We work with young athletes in highly emotional and public situations. We keep score, and because of that, our work is often judged week to week, even day to day, based upon the performance of a bunch of kids, how well they play, how much they play, and where they play.

And here is the kicker: every single moment matters. Every time we coach, our words and actions can have a huge impact in the lives of our players, just like my words echoed with Pat years later. Do you still hear the words of your old coaches today? Our influence is never neutral. Our words and actions can stick with our players forever. We don't get to choose which things stick and which ones they forget, so in everything we say and do, we must be intentional.

The world needs great coaches more than ever before. The world needs coaches that realize that every moment matters. The world needs you! And hopefully this book will clarify your path, leading you to become the coach your athletes want and desperately need. Are you ready?

Then let's dive right in.

PART I

―――

WHY DO I COACH?

People don't buy what you do; they buy why you do it.
And what you do simply proves what you believe.
―SIMON SINEK

We spend the vast majority of our time in traditional coaching education learning the tools to run a great practice and coach in the competition. Intuitively, this seems to make sense. Yet whenever I ask a room full of coaches to write down five qualities about the best coach they ever had, knowledge of the sport usually only entails about 10-15 percent of the answers. Instead, they speak about emotional intelligence and the ability to connect. The best coaches have realized that in order to be their best coaching self, they must authentically be their best self. To do that, you need to do the inner work first. You have to know your why. Just ask eight-time NBA champion and current Golden State Warriors Coach Steve Kerr.

Kerr had a fantastic career as a player, winning five NBA Championships with the Chicago Bulls and the San Antonio Spurs and establishing himself as one of the premier three-point shooters in the history of the game. He will be forever remembered in Bulls's history for hitting the championship-winning shot in game six of the 1997 NBA Finals. He also had the opportunity to play under legendary coaches such as Lute Olsen at Arizona, Phil Jackson with the Bulls, and Gregg Popovich with the Spurs. And yet, in 2014, when he was given his first NBA head coaching job with the Golden State Warriors, he had a conversation with another coaching legend that made him realize his preparation for his first head coaching job was insufficient.

Kerr had hit the ground running upon being hired by the Warriors. He spent countless hours planning his offensive and defensive game plans, studying other successful teams, building a video library of innovative game plans, visiting with coaches across multiple sports, and compiling concepts and theories that he thought would work with the Warriors. Then, in August of 2014, he was invited to attend the preseason camp of the defending Super Bowl champions, the Seattle Seahawks, and his whole paradigm shifted.

Kerr had admired the Seahawks from afar and loved the joy, spirit, and camaraderie that was so evident as they demolished the Denver Broncos in Super Bowl XLVIII. He wanted the Warriors to look like the Seahawks. When Head Coach Pete Carroll invited him to spend a few days with the team, Kerr jumped at the chance. He spent two days watching the Seahawks train and prepare for the upcoming season. On the eve of his second day, he sat down with Carroll and had a conversation that, as Kerr explained to us when he was on the *Way of Champions Podcast*, changed his entire coaching philosophy.[1]

"How are you going to coach your team?" Carroll asked Kerr.

Kerr, a bit taken aback, and stammered, "You mean, like, what offense are we going to run?"

"No," said Carroll. "That stuff doesn't matter. You've played forever, and you'll figure out what plays to run and how you want to defend, pick, and roll and all that stuff. I'm talking about what your day is going to look like. What practice will feel like. What are the players going to feel when they walk into your building?"

In that moment, Kerr realized he didn't really have a plan or know the answer. He wasn't sure what practice would feel like, what the culture would be like, or whether the players would enjoy coming to work every day. After playing under some of the best coaches of all time, he had just assumed those things would take care of themselves.

Carroll gave him a homework assignment: "When you get back to your hotel tonight, write down ten things that are important to you. What are the most important things to you, personally, in your life? When you come back tomorrow, we are going to narrow down those ten things to four. Those four principles represent you as a human being."

And then Carroll gave him one final piece of advice, which has stuck with Kerr to this day and is critical for all of us reading this book. "It doesn't matter what values I have or John Wooden had or Phil Jackson or Gregg Popovich," said Carroll. "It's what matters to you because, ultimately, your values have to be reflected in the way you coach. That's what makes it authentic. And if you try to use somebody else's values, the players will see right through you."

When Kerr got back to his hotel that night, he thought long and hard about what really mattered to him. He also thought about what he had witnessed the last few days, from the music blaring during practice to the meticulous preparation and attentiveness at team meetings. He thought about the intense competition in each and every rep of every practice activity and the relentless optimism and interaction between coaches and players.

"That's when it dawned on me," says Kerr. "Pete Carroll had built his team's entire practice routine around the energy, curiosity, positivity, and joy that defined *him*. His team was a reflection of him because every day was based on Pete's values, on what was important to him. And the combination of that wonderful culture and an amazingly gifted roster had helped the Seahawks win the Super Bowl. It all made sense."

Kerr returned to Carroll's office the next day and laid out his four values:

- Joy: after all, they got to play and coach sports for a living, and that should be fun.
- Competitiveness: the goal is ultimately to win a championship, so they must compete.
- Compassion: everyone is suffering in some way or another, and it's up to us to try and help people—no matter what we do for a living.
- Mindfulness: coaches and players who are mindful bring clarity of purpose to the team and perform at their best.

"That's great," said Carroll. "Now you have to build your whole day around those four values." Kerr asked what he meant. "Well, if competitiveness is a value for you," said Carroll, "you guys better compete every day. And if joy is a value, then you better have some fun. And if mindfulness is a value, then you better practice it." Kerr knew he had the final piece needed to build his Warrior culture.

As training camp started, Kerr and his staff set about instilling those values by creating fast-paced, fun-filled practice sessions. Music blared from the loudspeakers. Practices were short and frenetic, packed with information but not drawn out forever. Video sessions were both instructional and educational, with a fair dose of fun. Coaches were not only teachers but were also intentional about connecting with and caring for the players and their families. "We knew it wouldn't happen overnight," said Kerr, "but we felt that over time our players would feel our joy, sense our caring and compassion for them, recognize our competitive desire and our mindful approach to coaching. And hopefully, if we were consistent with that routine, the team would begin to take on an identity that reflected those ideals."

And take on that identity they did. As Kerr so eloquently wrote in the foreword for my good friend Dr. Jerry Lynch's book *Win the Day*, "I'm proud to say that over time, our Warriors team has had wonderful success, mainly because we have had an incredibly talented group. The culture that has taken hold is shown in Steph Curry's joy, in Draymond Green's competitiveness, in the mindfulness of Andre Iguodala, and the compassion of Shaun Livingston and Klay Thompson. It is shown in the brilliantly unselfish play of Kevin Durant, who wanted to be part of a team that connects, cares for, and sacrifices for one another and has forged an identity of his own amongst this wonderful group of players. Ultimately, players determine a team's ultimate success. It is the coach's job to give those players a vision, to develop a routine and a pattern that is meaningful and consistent. And when those things come together, the results can be beautiful."[2]

Those things have come together quite nicely. In Kerr's first five seasons as a head coach, the Warriors have won three NBA World Championships, made five straight NBA Finals appearances, set the single-season record for regular season wins, and established themselves as one of the greatest basketball teams of all time. Joy. Mindfulness. Competitiveness. Compassion.

Those are the four principles that mattered most to Steve Kerr and had been ingrained in him as a person, the four principles that defined his authentic self.

The lesson that Steve Kerr learned that day from Pete Carroll was a simple one: know thyself. Your team and your program should be a reflection of you. Do the inner work first and get to know your why.

So begins our journey in part I of this book.

LESSON 1

"TO BE A BETTER COACH, BE A BETTER YOU"

Do the Inner Work First

To be a better coach, you have got to be a better you.

—JOE EHRMANN

The most powerful leadership tool we all have is our own example.

—JOHN WOODEN

Niagara Falls, New York, can be a wonderful place to spend some time in the summer. The weather is sunny, the scenery is amazing, and, of course, the falls are awe-inspiring. But add in the crowds over July 4th weekend, the insane traffic at the border with Canada, and the stress of coaching in a Region I Championship event, and what you have is a recipe for stress, anxiety, and some pretty poor coaching. Sadly, that weekend back in 2002, I was that poor coach.

My team of sixteen-year-old boys from Vermont was playing our third game of regionals, and having lost our first two, we had already been eliminated from the competition. It was very hot and humid, and our focus and effort come the third match against a very good Virginia team was not what I expected of our group. As the game wore on and the goals piled up, I got angrier and angrier, especially at one of our players whom I will call Steve.

Steve had ability, and he had strength and size, but on that day, he was getting pushed around and not putting in a very good shift in my opinion. As my frustration grew, so did the volume of my angry words at Steve. His teammates noticed it. The parents all noticed it. And certainly Steve noticed it as he withdrew into a shell, afraid to make any mistakes and cowering at every 50/50 ball. I finally blew my top as our opponent scored their fifth goal. I yanked him out of the game with some choice words and basically ignored him as he trudged by with his head down. I didn't care. I wanted players who would compete. In my mind, Steve didn't care about his team, so why should I care about Steve?

A few minutes went by when I received a tap on my shoulder. One of Steve's teammates, let's call him Evan, was a very thoughtful kid who was always connecting his teammates and reaching out to everyone in the group. "Coach," said Evan, "I think you should put Steve back in the game."

"Why would I do that?" I scowled. "He is not even trying hard. He is getting killed out there."

"He is not going to play soccer next year, Coach, mostly because of the way you treat him," said Evan. "That means today is his last game ever with us. He has played with us since he was nine years old. And he is sitting over there feeling terrible, like it is all his fault. We are not going to win this game. I don't think you should have his last game end with him not playing and feeling so crappy. It's up to you." Then Evan walked away.

I turned and saw Steve sitting on the bench with his head down. His friends had their arms around him. A sport he had loved as a boy had been turned into something he loathed as a young man, and I was a big reason for that. In pursuit of winning, I had lost some of my humanity. In that moment, maybe for the first time ever in the heat of competition, I didn't see a soccer player sitting there. I saw a human being. I saw Steve. All the wind went out of my sails. My anger dissipated. And for the first time in my coaching career, I thought to myself, *What the heck am I doing? Steve feels like crap. I am stressed to hell and feel like crap. And none of that is going to change the outcome of this game. There has got to be a better way.*

I headed over to the bench and put my arm around Steve. I told him I was sorry and that I had really let him down. I told him to go finish the game and enjoy himself in his last game with his friends. I grabbed his buddy Evan and put him in as well, allowing two lifelong friends to play their final moments together. I wish I had thanked Evan for his wisdom and courage that day, but I am pretty sure I did not. After all, I was a twenty-nine-year-old coach who was pretty darn sure of himself. But something definitely shifted that day.

I would be lying if I told you that on one hot afternoon in Niagara Falls everything changed forever because that is certainly not what happened. However, I can look at those words of wisdom from sixteen-year-old Evan as a turning point for me, the beginning of a long evolution that still continues today. I realized that before I could try to help my players, I had to help myself. If I was going to be a better coach, I had to be a better me.

There is a very specific reason that this is the first chapter of a book on coaching. It is because, in my experience, both personally and after thirty years on the sidelines and doing coaching education, most coaches never do the inner work at all. We are immediately bombarded with techniques and tactics, with strategies for running sessions, imparting knowledge, and developing winners, yet we are rarely, if ever, told to look inside first. We are told that showing vulnerability and humanity is a sign of weakness. We are told that asking players what they want and need from us is terrible coaching. We become transactional with our athletes.

This is not the path to better coaching. The true path begins when we do the inner work and get to know ourselves, what makes us tick, and figure out why we coach and what our ultimate goal really is. Without this foundational knowledge, without self-awareness, we lack authenticity. And when we are not authentic, our athletes see right through us. So, let's do the inner work first.

This chapter is all about getting to know ourselves and our why. In it, we will look at the following:

- The definition of quality coaching and why self-awareness is a key component
- The difference between reacting and responding to situations
- The tool I use to help coaches and teams understand how they react so that they can train themselves to respond
- A simple exercise to develop your coaching purpose statement

These elements are the foundation for becoming a transformational coach. Let's explore them.

What Is Quality Coaching?

The question, "What is quality coaching?" seems simple to answer at first, at least to the many rooms full of coaches I speak in front of each year. Though few people ever want to shout out the answer publicly, what comes to most of our minds right away are wins and championships. That is certainly the metric upon which we measure our most high-profile coaches. As I write this, the US Women's National Soccer team has just won the 2019 World Cup, and Head Coach Jill Ellis has become the first female coach to win back-to-back World Cups. Her overall record in World Cup Finals is 13-0-1. Yet after winning the 2015 World Cup, the United States crashed out of the 2016 Olympics in the quarterfinal stage. They went from world champions to not even medaling. They then finished dead last in the 2017 She Believes Cup, their most high-profile event that year. As a result, many people called for US Soccer to fire Jill Ellis. After all, if you don't win, you can't possibly be a good coach, right?

The same conundrum faced by US Soccer is faced by many sports organizations every year when it comes to retaining or replacing coaches: if you don't win, are you a quality coach? How does a leader of coaches, whether you are a professional general manager or a high school athletic director, evaluate whether coaches are doing quality work? It was a dilemma faced by Chris Snyder and his counterparts at the US Olympic and Paralympic Committee (USOPC). As Director of Coach Education for USOPC, Snyder is tasked with supporting all the US Olympic and Paralympic team coaches and their staff as they prepare their athletes for Olympic and world championships. He was also tasked with defining exactly what quality coaching was, which was no easy task.

"I would ask coaches, 'Are you a good coach?' and their answer was always, 'Of course, or I wouldn't be here,'" Snyder told me as we strolled around the US Olympic Training Center in Colorado Springs in the summer of 2017. "I would ask them, 'How do we know?' They might answer something like, 'My athletes won six medals at the 2016 Rio games.' So, my follow-up would be, 'So if you don't win any medals at the next world championships, you are no longer a good coach and you should be fired?'" chuckled Snyder. "The answer to that question was always, 'No, of course not.' So, clearly, we cannot define quality coaching simply by wins and losses. It has to go much deeper than that—especially on the junior and developmental levels."

Snyder enlisted the help of Fresno State professor Dr. Wade Gilbert, one of the most highly respected authorities in coach education, and in 2017, the US Olympic and Paralympic Committee released its Quality Coaching Framework to help define what exactly is quality coaching. Their definition is as follows:

Quality coaching is the consistent application of integrated professional, interpersonal, and intrapersonal knowledge to improve athletes' competence, confidence, connection, and character in specific coaching contexts.[1]

In other words, based upon decades of research in education, positive psychology, teaching coaching, and leadership, quality coaching has three components: essential coaching knowledge, athlete-centered outcomes, and contextual fit. We can only assess whether a coach is doing quality work once we assess their specific work in these areas. They are worth defining a bit further for our purposes here.

Contextual Fit

It is quite easy to scour the internet and find numerous sessions or videos of professional coaches working with professional athletes, but do you take those sessions and then use them with your nine-year-olds? Of course not. Gilbert writes that "quality coaching requires the ability to adapt one's coaching knowledge to the specific needs of the athletes and fit the distinctive features of the environment in which one coaches." In other words, it must fit the ages and stages of the athletes you are working with.

Athlete-Centered Outcomes

In the past, we often looked at coaches as conveyors of information, and, thus, all we looked at in judging whether quality coaching was happening was whether athletes were getting technically and tactically better. The Quality Coaching Framework takes that much further and charges coaches with taking a 4Cs approach to athlete outcomes:

- Competence: refining the technical, tactical, and sport-specific performance elements
- Confidence: developing an athlete's self-belief and self-worth,

as well as their resilience and mental toughness
- Connection: building social bonds between teammates, coaches, and support staff
- Character: developing the moral character of athletes—items such as empathy, respect, and integrity—so that athletes are also good role models

Essential Coaching Knowledge

I saved this one for last, even though it is listed first in the Quality Coaching Framework. Gilbert's definition included three components of essential coaching knowledge: knowledge of your sport, knowledge of interpersonal connections, and intra-personal knowledge. In other words, understand your sport, understand how people interact, and know yourself.

One of the biggest transformations in my own personal coaching journey has been the journey of knowing myself or, as Gilbert calls it, intrapersonal knowledge. I am not sure as a twenty-something-age coach I was capable of understanding this, but as I gained more experience and had my own children, I certainly came to understand myself better. And as I did, I believe my coaching improved.

We must know ourselves better because great coaches are authentic. Remember the advice Pete Carroll gave Steve Kerr? We have to be real, or our athletes will see right through us. At the same time, we have to understand that our flaws, be they a quick temper with officials or poor listening skills when communicating with our athletes, are not excuses to behave a certain way. Knowing ourselves will help us to take the time to respond appropriately with our athletes, instead of reacting instinctually. And great coaches do not react; they respond.

Don't React. Respond!

In his book *Above the Line* about the 2014 Ohio State football National Championship season, Head Coach Urban Meyer lays out a simple equation: E + R = O (Event plus Response equals Outcome). In every competition, whether you are an athlete or a coach, there will be numerous events. There might be bad calls, funny bounces, and missed assignments. All of these events have an influence, but as Meyer stresses, it is our response to those events that is a far greater determinant of the outcome than the events themselves. We do not control the events, but we do control our response. Sadly, many athletes and coaches fail to respond. They react instead. And there are good reasons for this.[2]

In the 1990s, Italian researchers stumbled upon a class of neurons in the brain that fire not only when an individual performs an action but also when that individual witnesses another perform an action. They call this mirror processing. This is why we yawn when we see others yawn and flinch when we see someone stub a toe. Do you ever smile when you see someone smile? These reactions are governed by your mirror neurons, which allow you not only to simulate the actions of others but the emotions behind those actions as well. Researchers have used fMRI technology to test the effect of emotional attachment on brain function, and the results are extraordinary.

When you are coaching your team's game, watching a loved one participate in an athletic contest, or even watching your favorite college football team play on Saturday, you are actually using a different region of your brain to judge a pass interference call or judge offside than you would in a neutral situation. The neutral decision-making areas of your brain actually disengage, and you use your inferior parietal lobe (IPL). The result: your brain reacts as if *you* were the one performing the action. This is why both parents and coaches can completely lose it at the games they are highly invested in. Our brains react as if *we* were being fouled or having a goal unjustly called back.

The same mirror processing that governs our behavior is also why teams feed off of each other's energy, often either peaking and dominating together or sulking and giving up at the same time. Team emotions are contagious, both in a positive and negative way. This is our natural reaction, but as we all know, sometimes our reaction is not so helpful.[3]

Our reaction to various events is largely driven by our personality. When psychologists talk about personality, they are referring to individual differences in characteristic patterns of thinking, feeling, and behaving. Personality describes our instinctual behaviors and our default comfort zone. It dictates how we react to certain situations. For example, I tend to be an "act now, ask questions later" type of person. I don't tend to give things much thought or detailed planning. As a result, I am not always a good listener or very perceptive of how my actions might affect those around me. At times, this may provide the exact right behavior at the exact right time. Other times, it can be very ineffective. I am sure there are a few former players and referees I have crossed paths with that might agree.

The idea that we each have personality tendencies has been around for thousands of years. From the Chinese in 2000 BC to the ancient Greeks (sanguine, choleric, melancholic, and phlegmatic) to twentieth century psychiatrist Carl Jung (thinking, feeling, sensation, and intuition), people have been studying personality tendencies. You may have taken a personality assessment at your workplace, such as Myers-Briggs, DISC, Strengths Finder, or others. Far too many personality "tests" make outlandish claims about their effectiveness and convince people that their personality is their fate. There is no science to back many of these claims up. Many assessments of personality type are not always strongly predictive indicators of personality. However, I do believe that if those assessments are used in a way to help people understand their tendencies in behavior, communication, and other areas in order to stimulate discussion and personal reflection, they can have great value. More on that in the activities section below.

What is far more important than personality is character, for our character provides the opportunity to respond. Character is the combined result of our training, our morals, and our values. It is a collection of our culture, life experience, and education that shapes the way our brains work. Character is all about self-awareness and being cognizant of how we tend to react so that in certain situations, we can take a deep breath and respond appropriately. A simple yet effective way to understand the difference between personality and character is to picture an iceberg. What you see above the water line represents our personality, that which causes us to react, and the much larger mass below the waterline represents our character, that which enables us to respond.

Coaching education should be about developing your character so you can make the right decisions at the right times. Do you make the correct tactical adjustment when you need a goal with five minutes left in a game, or do you spend that time getting angry at your players and the referee? Event plus response equals outcome. We control our response and exert even more control when we are aware of how we may react in certain situations. As Joe Ehrmann says, "To be a better coach, you have got to be a better you." Part of being a better you is the ability to control your reactions and responses.

Know Your Why

As part of knowing themselves, coaches need a purpose, advises Wade Gilbert. They need a "why" and a deep reason for coaching. "A strong sense of coaching purpose should act as both a pull and push for coaches," writes Gilbert. "It should serve to inspire coaches (pull) toward their vision and goals. It should also motivate (push) coaches to hold themselves accountable to the same high standards they set for their athletes."[4]

In the classic *Alice in Wonderland*, the Cheshire Cat advises Alice, "When you don't know where you are going, any road will do." This applies to coaching as well. Without a clear purpose and acknowledgment of your why, your coaching becomes haphazard. When you coach to win a league championship or a national title, your coaching can become transactional as your pursuit of the goal tramples everyone—including your athletes—in your way. But when you start with why and clearly define your purpose for coaching, the why becomes your compass.

One of my favorite writers, Seth Godin, shared a tale on his blog about a Nepalese Ghurka rifleman who escaped from prison in World War II:

> A Ghurka rifleman escaped from a Japanese prison in south Burma and walked six hundred miles alone through the jungles to freedom. The journey took him five months, but he never asked the way and he never lost the way. For one thing he could not speak Burmese and for another he regarded all Burmese as traitors. He used a map and when he reached India he showed it to the Intelligence officers, who wanted to know all about his odyssey. Marked in pencil were all the turns he had taken, all the roads and trail forks he has passed, all the rivers he had crossed. It had served him well, that map. The Intelligence officers did not find it so useful. It was a street map of London.[5]

As Godin concludes, even if you have a lousy map, the right compass will get you home. Coaches need a compass. That is why many coaches find it helpful to come up with a well-defined purpose statement. In the following section, you will have an opportunity to develop your own.

Two Activities to Develop Self-Awareness and Define Your Coaching Purpose

Take the Equilibria PDI Assessment

At Changing the Game Project, we use an assessment with our coaches and teams called the Equilibria Personality Diversity Indicator (PDI), which uses four colors (E-Colors) to help people understand their tendencies and explain the tendencies of those around them. Equilibria began in 2004 in the oil and gas industry and has a tremendous record of improving safety in dangerous and highly stressful jobs. Today it is used by schools and sports teams, as well as many other industries, and has a huge impact in helping promote inclusion, diversity, and understanding among groups.

Through workshops and the online assessment tool, Equilibria has collected hundreds of thousands of data points around communication, recognition, leadership, and more that resonate strongly with the participants in our workshops and others across a variety of industries. We have found that it is an incredibly powerful tool for facilitating self-awareness, building trust, and defining a team's mission, vision, and values. I have seen many athletes and coaches have "aha" moments in terms of understanding themselves and the individuals on their teams, and I have used these moments to stimulate some great discussion on inclusion, diversity, teamwork, leadership, and more.

Why do I use Equilibria? I find it very easy to understand and apply, and my teams do as well. Plus, in my first conversation with founder Lewis Senior, he said, "Our personality is how we react. It is a very small part of who we are. Our character is how we respond. We use the PDI to train people to understand their tendencies so they can respond, not react." This made a lot of sense to me as I wrote about above. Equilibria has four basic E-Colors that describe the different personality tendencies:

- Red: the doer or director
- Yellow: the socializer/engager
- Blue: the supporter/relator
- Green: the thinker/analyzer

We all have all four E-Colors in us, and we train ourselves to draw upon all of them at different times, regardless of which colors represent our personality tendency. For example, my E-Colors are predominately

Red and Yellow, with high percentages of both. I tend to be decisive, action oriented, and a good social connector. I get things done. When I overplay these strengths, they turn into potential limiters, and I become impatient, a poor listener, and a poor planner (just ask my wife). The more aware of this I have become, the more I can see opportunities to plan a little more, to listen instead of sharing my opinion, and to recognize that just because I said it, it does not mean they heard it.

Go to www.EquilibriaInSports.com or download the E Colors app on your phone and take the assessment. It only takes about fifteen minutes to complete. It will give you a basic assessment of your personality tendencies, strengths, and potential limiters. You will also better appreciate how you might disrupt teamwork for others and how they might disrupt teamwork for you. You will gain insight into how to approach difficult conversations with athletes and parents and how to intervene in these situations more effectively. Have your team take the assessment as well; I think it will be insightful.

I also encourage you to find or schedule a workshop in your area as you will gain a much deeper understanding of the E Colors and how they work. Finally, while not as fun and interactive as a live event, you can take a workshop online through Udemy (https://www.udemy.com/succeed-with-personality-diversity/). Just remember that your personality is not your fate and discovering your E Colors is not an excuse for poor behavior or a reason to discriminate or exclude others. It is simply the first step in the self-awareness process so you can stop reacting and start responding.

Develop Your Coaching Purpose Statement

I first came across the idea of writing a purpose statement in Joe Ehrmann's classic *InSideOut Coaching*. Ehrmann uses the analogy of the sailor who cannot navigate simply by studying the wind and the waves. He writes, "You have to set your sights on a port, a lighthouse, some WHY, the purpose that keeps us centered and focused on honoring the high calling of being coaches." Ehrmann began to develop his why standing at the graveside of his brother Billy and recalling the trauma he had experienced as a boy and an athlete at the hands of transactional and bullying coaches and adults. As Ehrmann searched for the meaning of his own life, he realized that a lot of his issues were around warped concepts of masculinity and success. As a result, his why evolved into the following statement: "I coach to help boys become men of empathy and integrity who will lead, be responsible, and change the world for good."[6]

Everything Joe Ehrmann does is guided by that purpose statement. It is his compass and the touchstone for every action he takes. It is highly personal and tied to how he wants to use sports to change lives. It should not be your statement; it is his and his alone.

Personally, my purpose statement has evolved over the years, along with my coaching. While it was not well defined as a young coach, my actions told the world that my purpose was to win as often as possible to prove my significance to the world. It was highly transactional, and kids that didn't help me win caught the brunt of my anger, stress, and anxiety over not winning. Today, thankfully, it has evolved into the following: "I coach to build a lifelong love of activity in the children I mentor and to use the power of sport to intentionally develop character and transform lives for the better."

For me, it means that I try to coach the person, not the sport. It means I try to give my athletes what they might not be getting elsewhere, be it discipline, high expectations, or an adult who simply believes in them. It means that I teach them to work hard and to deeply invest in what they are doing, even at the risk of coming up short of their goals. It means that I model passion and enjoyment. It is hard to encapsulate all that into a concise sentence, so I reserve the right to always revise this statement as my insight evolves.

If you think you need a compass to keep you on track, I challenge you to come up with your own coaching purpose statement. Make it personal. Make it authentic. Let it evolve over time. For now, though, finish the following sentence starter: I coach …

Summary

Even if you have a lousy map, the right compass will get you home. I believe it is the same in coaching. The environment in which we coach—and the messages we get from popular culture and the plethora of misguided, transactional coaches in youth sports today—can provide a pretty lousy roadmap for how to train and develop not only great athletes but better people as well. To be a better coach, we have to look inside first and become a better version of ourselves. To do this, we must

- Understand the components of quality coaching so we can make the shift from transactional to transformational.
- Gain a deeper understanding of our tendencies and default behaviors so we can train ourselves to respond, instead of react, in appropriate ways.
- Come up with a coaching purpose statement that becomes your compass, even when the world around you provides a lousy map.

The journey to becoming a better version of yourself is a never-ending one, and it provides a wonderful model of self-improvement for your athletes to follow. And since it is a long journey, there is never a better time to start than today. Good luck.

LESSON 2

"YOU COACH A PERSON, NOT A SPORT"

Be an Athlete-Centered Coach

You have to ask one fundamental question: who is in front of me?
—KRIS VAN DER HAEGEN

You coach a child, not a sport.
—DR. MARTIN TOMS

One of the greatest advantages in sports is being the home team. There are environmental advantages as your opponent may be sleeping in a strange bed and eating different food. He may be struggling with a different time zone, travel fatigue, and even oxygen deprivation (for instance, teams that travel to play in La Paz, Bolivia, must adjust to its 11,000-foot altitude). There are also psychological advantages, such as the crowd influence on competitors, referees, and officials. The home team advantage has been statistically proven true in many sports, especially in the sport of soccer. That is why the year 2000 was such a disaster for Belgium men's soccer, the co-host of the 2000 European Championships.

Heading into the event, Belgium had high hopes, which were bolstered after defeating Sweden in the tournament's opening game. Successive losses to Italy and Turkey saw the Belgians finishing in third place in their group and failing to advance to the knock-out round. Meanwhile, their tournament co-host, the Netherlands, was playing an exciting brand of soccer, defeating eventual champion France in group play and advancing to the semifinals before exiting in a penalty shootout.

As their northern neighbor celebrated, Belgium's fans were in mourning, and the sport's leadership faced a critical moment. Soccer was the country's most popular sport, and yet they were the sixty-sixth ranked team in the world. According to Kris Van Der Haegen, currently the Director of Coaching Education for the Belgium Football Association, this was the perfect moment to get the people around the table and ask a very important question: "Why can't we compete with Turkey?"[1]

Van Der Haegen and his colleagues knew they needed a total reboot from youth to senior levels of the sport. Success on the senior level would start with improving the experience for children in the sport. They knew they needed to improve coach education, but before they decided what to teach the coaches, they had an even more important task. They had to get very clear on who the game was all about in the first place. "The main actor of the process is the player," says Van Der Haegen, "not the coach, not the team, but the individual player. And if the main actor of that process is the player, then it's very easy to understand that, in children's football, we have to do what children like because they are at the center of everything we do. They want to play football in their own way and not in the way that adults want to play football."

To improve results on the senior level, Belgium had to start with improving the game for their youngest players. To do so, they decided that coaches must understand the needs, values, and priorities of the human being standing in front of them, chomping at the bit and ready to play. Or, as Van Der Haegen puts it, "You have to ask one fundamental question: who is in front of me? Look at the characteristics (of the player) and then adapt the environment to fit with those characteristics. If these two things don't fit, you are wasting your time."

This essential question led to a major reboot for Belgium soccer, a systematic change that has had dramatic results and provides a great example of the successful implementation of an athlete-centered sporting environment, as opposed to a coach-centric environment. You coach a person, not a sport. This realization is a game changer. It will allow you to connect with more of your athletes, and it will inspire them to perform at even higher levels.

In this chapter, we will dissect the importance of creating a person-centered environment and why it matters. To do so, we will cover the following:

- What a person-centered/athlete-centered environment looks like
- How Belgium's youth development transformation has driven senior team success and what it can teach us about our own programs
- A coaching self-assessment to ensure you are creating an athlete-centered environment
- A quick exercise your athletes can complete that will help you get to know them better

When you ask yourself, "Who is in front of me?" and you build your coaching and teaching around the needs of that person, you will find that it transforms your coaching. For many years, I did not care much who was in front of me. Today, I cringe at the thought of coaching that way as I see the tremendous difference this change of approach has made, not only for my athletes but also for the enjoyment I get in coaching. I think you will, too.

What Does an Athlete-Centered Environment Look Like?

Great coaches understand that coaching is a relationship business. They know that the sport-specific knowledge matters but is not sufficient. It is 10-20 percent of what you do, and the other 80-90 percent is all about the person in front of you. Every one of those people has unique needs, and the better you understand them, the more you can inspire them to perform well. When I proposed this idea to Steve Kerr from the Golden State Warriors, he agreed and shared his own personal story about a career that was mostly spent as a reserve player. "When you're not playing and you're sitting on the end of the bench, you just don't feel valuable," says Kerr. It's an empty feeling, one that he experienced first-hand. He is very attuned to this as a coach. "What can you do as a coach to engage those guys? You can't play them all the time. You can play them…you can throw them out there once in a while and keep them engaged. But it takes more than that. It's conversation. It's an understanding of that player's career. We have fourteen guys on our team; every one of them has his own unique set of circumstances. And it's my job to understand what those circumstances are."

Kerr continued, "When I think about Steph Curry, I immediately think about all the people who are demanding his time. And I think, *I've got to find a way to help Steph simplify his life and get some rest.* And when I think of the fourteenth man on the team, I think, *That guy's career is on the line, and he is desperately trying to stay in the NBA. He needs my help and my advice.* So, that's a totally different job than managing stuff. But I better understand that concept because that's my job." This is the essence of athlete-centered coaching.[2]

Today's "win at all costs" youth sporting environment is often not conducive to creating an athlete-centered learning environment. The emphasis on results, promotion, and short-term success is far more likely to result in what researchers call an autocratic or coach-centric emphasis. In such environments, coaches are likely to use a one-size-fits-all approach and view their athletes as a collective group with the same exact needs. As such, knowledge transfer becomes one directional—coach to athlete—and not collaborative. It usually results in explicit learning environments where skills are broken down and accuracy is valued over discovery. Athletes are told what to do and when to do it and are expected to follow coaching instructions exactly. There is no deeper understanding of concepts and no ownership of the goals or outcomes as they all belong to the coach. Long term, athletes become so dependent upon coach input that they stop thinking for themselves.

In contrast, an athlete-centered environment is one in which the learner takes center stage. He is an active participant in the decision-making, creating not only more autonomy but also an understanding of the actions and behaviors that lead to improvement. Coaches in athlete-centered environments become facilitators and learn to question athletes in order to help them understand concepts and skills at a deeper level. They allow the time and space for athletes to develop at their own pace and put the goals of the athletes and the team at the forefront. They take the time to get to know the athlete as a person, just like Steve Kerr does for his team. This promotes an environment where athletes gain self-awareness, make decisions, explore creative solutions, and assess choices with the coach acting as a facilitator—not the autocratic dictator. Athlete-centered coaches view the team as a collection of people with individual needs and individual developmental timelines and, thus, focus on serving the needs of all those individuals within the team concept. This is hard to do but definitely worth the effort.

Coaches that are masters at this athlete-centered approach are fantastic at asking the right questions, instead of giving the "right" directions. Instead of explicitly telling an athlete what she did wrong or how her decision could have been better, they might ask questions such as:

- What did you see in that situation?
- How did that feel when you passed it that way?
- Did you notice any other options available to you?
- Was that the best time to play that pass? Why or why not?
- What did we do in the moments that we were having success?

These are all questions in which the coach may be looking for an answer that is "more right" than others, but she does not have a cherished outcome and avoids framing the question in a way that produces a single "correct" answer. The athlete-centered coach allows her athletes to discover solutions, to take notice of their environments, and perhaps even come up with solutions that the coach herself did not see. She recognizes that athletes who are able to discover solutions in training are far more likely to use them in competition. *(GOLD)*

Athlete-centered coaching requires letting go of your ego and accepting that sticky learning is not always quick learning. It requires recognizing that today's result is not a great indicator of learning and development if the outcome is a result of coaching influence, not athlete discovery. Whether you are coaching at the grassroots level, like most of us, or coaching professionals, as Kris Van Der Heagen or Steve Kerr do, this athlete-centered approach is highly effective. Plus, your athletes will love you for it as it develops their competence, ownership, and connection with you and with each other.[3]

The Belgium FA Transformation

The Belgian FA reboot began in earnest immediately after Euro 2000. Van Der Haegen and his colleagues thought back to their childhood experiences, where often they were doing endless drills and isolated technical work while wondering if they would get the chance to actually play the game. Many coaches never let them play actual games and instead dangled a scrimmage as a carrot that they might get to if they covered all the "important stuff" first. A whole generation of kids signed up to play but rarely got to. The leadership of the Belgian FA knew they had to change the coaching mindset to that of an athlete-centered coach.

Van Der Haegen started with his own club. The first objective was to remind coaches their primary job was to help the kids fall in love with the game. "If you can make them love the game, then you can teach them the game," he reminded his coaches. "But if you don't help them love the game, they won't learn the game. And how can you help them love the game? By maximizing situations of game time in the training sessions." After all, it's why they signed up in the first place.

Belgium soccer's leadership also knew that many of the world's best players developed on the streets, playing pick-up games out from under the watchful eyes of adults. Great players needed environments where they would feel free to dribble and try creative things and where there were no referees or joystick coaches telling them what to do and making decisions for them. "You have to let them be free and then observe them and help them if it's necessary," says Van Der Haegen. "And if not, let them discover because they are more intelligent than you think they are!"

The Belgian FA began the revamp by scrapping traditional five vs. five games for younger children and instead played two vs. two with a goalkeeper at ages five and six. They played six-minute games with the players each doing a half in goal and a half on the field. This format promoted dribbling and allowed players who might never score a goal in an entire season to score five or six every weekend. Fields were set up in a ladder format, and after each game, the winners moved right, and the losing team moved left. Within a few games, all the players competed against others of similar ability. Everyone was scoring goals, winning games, and having fun. Everyone, that is, except the parents in the beginning.

"I remember at my home club," chuckled Van Der Haegen, "some of the parents said, 'Kris, you're crazy. What are you doing? Football is a collective game, and you're making them play one vs. one and a goal-keeper.' And I said, 'Yes, football is a collective game—but only when they are teenagers and adults.'" He understood that for five-year-olds, it was about dribbling and scoring. Yet in the eyes of many, the sport's leadership was destroying the game.

The Belgian FA decided that kids would play small-sided format games through age thirteen and only then play full eleven vs. eleven matches. They decided to eliminate all tables and standings from the game until the under-fourteen age. They ensured 50 percent playing time for every player by changing the game from two halves to four quarters and mandating that there were no subs except for an injury during each quarter. Every player on the bench at the end of one quarter must play the next one. They allowed children who were late physical developers to get a doctor's note and play down a year with children of similar developmental age. They mandated that practices must be a minimum of 70-80 percent games-based and not isolated technical sessions. They made the sport all about the needs of the child.

"You cannot ask adults to do what children do, so don't ask children to do what adults like to do," says Van Der Haegen. "If you put a child of five or six years old on the bicycle of an adult person, the child will look at you and say, 'Are you crazy?' Yet, we do this in sports all the time. We ask them to play eleven vs. eleven or eight vs. eight at a very young age, but they are not able to do it. We have to adapt the game to what they are, who they are, how they think, and how they want to play. And then the magic will happen."

The magic is definitely happening in Belgium. According to FIFA, the world soccer governing body, as of the writing of this book, Belgium is the number-one ranked men's soccer team in the world and has moved into the top twenty on the women's side for the first time in their history. It all started with the philosophy of putting the athlete first and taking a personal approach, instead of a one-size-fits-all approach, to coaching. It started with answering one simple question: who is in front of me?

Three Activities to Become a More Athlete-Centric Coach

Take a Self-Assessment

In the following self-assessment tool, rate yourself on a scale of one to five in each of the following areas. And if you are brave and your athletes are old enough, have them rate you as well.

Coach-Centered Behavior			**Athlete-Centered Behavior**	
Instructs athletes			Seeks athletes' solutions	
1	2	3	4	5
Team needs/goals			Collection of individual needs/goals	
1	2	3	4	5
Winning/results			Development of athlete/person	
1	2	3	4	5
My way or the highway			Creativity/self-awareness promoted	
1	2	3	4	5

Now, tally up your score and divide by four. The higher your number, the more athlete-centered your coaching is.

_____ + _____ + _____ + _____ + _____ = _____ /4 = _____

Get to Know Your Athletes Better

Third-grade teacher Kyle Schwartz knew that if she could connect better with her students, she could be a better instructor for them. She knew that many of her students and their families were affected by poverty, divorce, hunger, and many of the issues that cause children to struggle or act out in school. As a result, she decided to ask them to complete a simple activity. She asked them to finish this sentence: I wish my teacher knew…

The results astounded her. Some were funny, and some broke her heart. All provided insight into her students and allowed her to better create a safe and supportive classroom and to connect with her students by knowing their unique stories. She shared her insights, and soon a worldwide movement called #IWishMyTeacherKnew was born.[4] When I read Schwartz's book, I thought to myself, *Why aren't coaches doing this?* So I decided to give it a try as well. And the things I learned blew me away.

I learned about kids who were going through divorce and others who had a parent with cancer. Some let me know they only wanted feedback in private, and others said they don't like being first in line to demonstrate. Others urged me to keep pushing them because, even though it didn't always look that way, they appreciated it. As a result, at my talks, I urged coaches to have their athletes complete the following sentence: "One thing I wish my coaches knew about me that would help them coach me better is …"

As of the writing of this book, I have been asking coaches to do this for three years. I tell coaches to instruct their athletes *not* to write about things that are obvious, like, "Help me get faster" or "Help me work on my left foot." We instruct the kids to share something that we would likely never know unless they told us. Three years later, I have heard stories from coaches about abusive situations and family illnesses. One coach even tearfully told me how this activity actually saved a player's life as she was contemplating suicide because her family was homeless and living in their van. The coach intervened and got the player counselling help, and the team stepped up and rented a house for the family until the parents could find jobs. We both had tears in our eyes as he told me this story and speculated that if he had never done this activity, she would have never shared this with anyone.

So, coaches, go ahead and give this one a try. Have your kids complete this sentence and see what you can learn. You won't regret it.

Conclude Your Player Meetings with the Magic Coaching Question

Karch Kiraly was voted the top volleyball player in the world for the twentieth century and has continued to enjoy success as the head coach of the US Women's National Volleyball Team. He is always growing and stretching as a coach, and one of his greatest characteristics is how he concludes every player meeting. He concludes his player meetings with a simple question: "How can I be better for you?" Imagine what it would do for your coaching and the connection you have with your athletes if you asked the same question at the end of every player meeting you had.[5]

Summary

To coach more effectively, it is critical to understand who is in front of you and then build an environment that suits the needs, values, and priorities of the person being coached—not solely the person doing the coaching. In order to do that, you must

- Understand the critical components of a person-centered/athlete-centered environment and build them into your coaching practice.
- Create your own version of the Belgium FA transformation and revamp your offerings for your youngest athletes to suit their needs.
- Take the coaching self-assessment to ensure you are creating an athlete-centered environment.
- Ask your athletes to finish the sentence: "One thing I wish my coaches knew about me that would help them coach me better is …"

- Conclude your player meetings with the question, "How can I be better for you?"

Great coaches are athlete-centered and person-centered. They recognize that if they connect with the individual and if they coach the person and not the sport, they will reach more of their athletes than by taking a one-size-fits-all approach. Good luck.

LESSON 3

"THE GOAL IS TO WIN; THE PURPOSE IS SOMETHING MUCH DEEPER"

Pursue a Higher Purpose than Winning

The goal is to win. We play, plan, and prepare to win every game that we put kids in, but that's not the purpose. The purpose is something much deeper; it's the reason why the game exists, which is the human growth and development of students and connecting them to caring adults in their learning community. Without the awareness and without an understanding of the deeper purpose, the default is automatically going to be, "Did you win or did you lose?"

—JODY REDMAN

Willie Cromack was frustrated. The Vancouver, British Columbia-based youth soccer coach was tired of the "win now' mentality he was seeing in his son's soccer games. As a former collegiate soccer player, he knew that his young players needed the adults in their lives to be patient and give them time to develop. He knew that creativity would only happen if his players did not fear making mistakes and if they were able to take their eyes off the "did we win" mentality and focus on the process of improving. He also noticed that the first question out of many parents' and coaches' mouths after a game was, "Did you win?" and how that one question often took the focus off development, creativity, and patience. Cromack knew there must be a better way.

After college, Cromack had taken a break from playing soccer to run the family bike shop. During his time at the shop, he became heavily involved in charity bike rides, raising money and awareness for causes ranging from cancer to education to homelessness. Some of these rides lasted a few hours while others took weeks. Cromack noticed something about the participants in his charity rides. They were motivated by something that gave them the energy and motivation to complete daunting rides. They focused on a purpose much higher than winning the race, such as raising money by completing a feat of endurance and perseverance. Most important, simply by completing their goal, they won.

Upon finishing their events, Cromack saw bikers with great pride in their accomplishments, in the completion of a journey and in the fulfillment of a dream, regardless of whether they finished first or last. As he told me, "This experience showed me the trials that people would go through to make a difference on the planet and for people they loved." Then Cromack thought to himself, *Why can't we do this with my youth soccer team?*

Cromack, like many youth coaches who are focused on long-term development, took the field each and every week preaching technical play. His nine-year-olds were working on passing out of the back and playing to feet instead of just kicking the ball away. He challenged players to beat opponents one vs. one and, if they failed, to try again. And as he did this, his team lost games to teams that kicked it over the top to the fast kid. They lost to teams that had their goalkeeper kick the ball as far forward as possible, instead of rolling it to a defender and trying to play. They lost to teams that were more concerned with today's result than the development of a future player.

Cromack struggled to convince his team parents to be patient. He struggled to convince opposing coaches of the need to teach and play the game correctly and that today's scoreboard meant little in the long term. He needed his team to play for a purpose higher than winning. In other words, he needed to find a way to introduce the charity cycling ethos into youth soccer. So, Cromack started Play Better.

Play Better is an online giving platform that can be run through a simple phone app. Teams create a team page that handles all the administration of charitable receipts, collects reward donations, and allows supporters to leave comments or compliments for players or the team. Cromack found external donors to pledge money that coaches could use to match team donations if goals were met. As he describes it, "It's like a benevolent team Facebook page!"

Play Better serves to change the "goals, wins, and rewards" mentality by helping players, coaches, and parents support the process more than the immediate result. "By refocusing the 'goals and wins' to something developmentally sound," says Cromack, "and rewarding those achievements with a bigger external motivator, like a charitable cause, we alter the culture immediately."

Cromack decided to try his idea out on his son's soccer team first and soon realized that many of the families were being dramatically impacted by cancer. He invited the players to make a difference by reaching developmental metrics that would reward them with donations to help fight cancer. If they played one hundred passes, they raised a certain amount of money. Two hundred passes? Even more money.

The results were immediate for the team. The players loved it. The parents endorsed the higher purpose because they saw their kids learning on and off the field. Everyone involved felt the culture shift. "The key was that we attached meaningful technical development goals to a reward," says Cromack. "They were never just made up. They were directly related to what would make the boys better players. The results were better players, a better environment to learn in, and overall learning that went beyond soccer."

By setting technical goals, such as passing back to the goalkeeper twenty times, Cromack's team started playing better without ever speaking about winning. "The idea of attempting to win the game is never taken away. Winning simply finds its rightful place in their brains: important but not more important than the world and their own development."

The biggest difference Cromack has seen is in the fearlessness of the players and the willingness of parents to let their kids fail and learn. He has seen more players try to nutmeg an opponent, be creative in a tight spot, or have the courage to hit the killer pass. All of these might earn a small donation for charity. "You tell me," says Cromack, smiling, "could you yell at your son or daughter if they make a mistake trying a nutmeg in order to support a local charity? Or if they mishit a pass when their intention was to connect the pass on behalf of eradicating a disease? Impossible. You don't have a heart if you can still be annoyed. You may be a tad frustrated, but the bigger picture prevails for parents, players, and coaches!"

What has been most surprising to Cromack and other Play Better participants is how it has changed the culture of the games for all involved, even the opponents and referees. One of the Play Better teams had an anti-bullying group as their chosen charity. They presented their opponents a pink wristband before their game and then went out and played. The referee for the game was blown away by the positive environment both on the field and the sidelines. He hadn't seen anything like it. After the game, he told Cromack it was his easiest game to referee in years. Two weeks later, he donated all his refereeing fees for the season to support the anti-bullying cause.

Play Better is an example of a team having a higher purpose than winning. When you have a higher purpose, whatever it may be, it becomes your compass that keeps you pointed in the right direction—no matter what obstacles are thrown in your way. You can have some outcomes that you hope to achieve, but you must be driven by a higher purpose than winning, and you must be focused on the daily process of getting better. Erin Quinn, three-time NCAA champion lacrosse coach and current athletic director at Middlebury College in Vermont, put it very succinctly for me: "Great leaders and teams are outcome aware but purpose and process driven."

The next few pages are all about developing teams that are outcome aware but purpose and process driven. Perhaps you coach a youth team and can use a platform such as Play Better. Or perhaps you coach a collegiate or high-school-age team and results are required to keep your job. It does not mean you cannot pursue a higher purpose than winning. In fact, if you want to sustain your success, you must follow that path. Over the next few pages we will

- Take a deeper look at a college soccer program that exemplifies this philosophy, whose men's and women's teams have won a combined sixteen NCAA titles since the year 2000.
- Learn from a World Cup and twenty-two-time national champion coach about the importance of having a higher purpose than winning.
- Discuss the difference between developing performance character and moral character.
- Look at how an outcome aware but purpose and process driven philosophy has turned around an entire youth sports program in Wisconsin.

Having a higher purpose than winning is about having a team compass that keeps you pointed in the right direction. It can help you have a tremendous season for your nine-year-old soccer team, and it can help you win more NCAA Championships than any other collegiate soccer programs.

The Messiah Method and "The Carolina Way"

Michael Zigarelli is a professor of leadership and strategy at Messiah College, a small Christian college located in Mechanicsburg, Pennsylvania, about twelve miles from Harrisburg. The school is known for its liberal arts education and its evangelical Christian faith. In the sports world, it's also known as the standard bearer for excellence in both men's and women's soccer. Since the year 2000, the Messiah College men's soccer team has won eleven NCAA Division III Championships, and the women's team has won five titles. Messiah holds the distinction of being the only NCAA soccer program to win both the men's and women's title the same year, a feat they have accomplished four times. It is this consistent excellence that intrigued Zigarelli and led to his 2011 book *The Messiah Method: The Seven Disciplines of the Winningest College Soccer Program in America.* (And they had only won a paltry eleven combined titles at that point.) When I first spoke to Zigarelli, I was fascinated by what he called "Discipline #1: Pursue a Higher Purpose than Winning."

"Anytime a group is unified in purpose, they are going to be stronger," Zigarelli told me. "You are going to be stronger if you are working together, have the same mindset, have the same aspirations, and have the same mission. This is obviously a Christian university, and the players are treating this experience as an opportunity to honor God in all they do; their soccer is a worship experience for them. But unity is a driving principle, and there cannot be any tolerance for a lack of unity, just as there is no tolerance for a lack of fitness or a lack of fundamentals."

At Messiah, the relentless pursuit of excellence and playing to a standard is a principle and mindset, even a lifestyle, that transcends and positively affects everything they do. It affects their relationships, their career, their coaching, and their leadership. According to Zigarelli, it elevates them to become a better human being. "This is a leadership and people development factory," he says. "This is a place where your child becomes a better man or a better woman, not just a better athlete. Athletics is a platform and a means to a greater end. There is a higher purpose than winning."[1]

A 2010 letter from Messiah women's coach Scott Frey to his players encapsulates the higher purpose perfectly:

> If at the end of your career all you can say is, "I was a National Champion, and we won a lot of games," then I'd say it wasn't worth the time or energy. But if you can look back and say, "I learned a lot about myself. I did things I never thought possible, both physically and psychologically. I made the most important and lasting friendships of my life. I've learned that helping others and seeing them succeed at something is better than it happening to me," then it is, without question, worth all that you do.

The higher purpose Frey writes about here, which is echoed in the work of Messiah men's coaches Dave Brandt and Brad McCarty, is a common characteristic among all of the top coaches I have met on my coaching journey and interviewed for the *Way of Champions Podcast*. Cindy Timchal, an eight-time NCAA champion and all-time winningest lacrosse coach, talks about it. Nancy Stevens, the three-time NCAA champion and all-time winningest college field hockey coach talks about it. And Anson Dorrance, a World Cup winner and twenty-two-time national champion soccer coach speaks about as well. Each coach has his or her own way to describe and bring this higher purpose to life, but it is a critical part of success.

For example, Dorrance has created "The Carolina Way," a legacy that each player is a part of and is asked to contribute to. North Carolina women's soccer is a tight-knit family, with the alums mentoring current players and everyone striving to leave the jersey in a better place. If his team reaches a national final, he will stay up most of the night prior to the game and write a personal letter to each of his seniors outlining their contribution to the program. He will give his seniors a copy of each letter and send them out of the locker room. Then he will read each letter to the remaining players and ask them to go out and compete for their teammates who are playing their final collegiate game. The tears will flow, and a steely resilience will settle across the Carolina team.

To date, North Carolina has played in twenty-four national finals. The Tar Heels have won twenty-two of them. Dorrance credits that tremendous winning percentage in the biggest game of the year to those senior letters. "How is it possible to have a better winning percentage in the national championship final than the rest of the year?" he asked me. "I genuinely know that it's because every kid on the roster was playing for something that was emotionally important to them and for something beyond themselves. They were playing for a higher purpose than winning."

Regardless of the ages and stages of your athletes, they should be competing for a higher purpose than winning. It is not my place to tell you or your team what that purpose should be. However, you do need one that fits the age and sporting context of your athletes. One higher purpose that transcends gender and ages is character development, which, as we have discussed in lesson 1, is an essential component of quality coaching. And to do that, we first have to understand that there are two types of character to be developed. Our job is to develop both.

Performance vs. Moral Character

We often hear people exclaim that sport develops character, but that is only partially true. Sport naturally develops what we might call *performance character* traits. These are traits such as grit, resilience, and self-discipline. These are what researchers call "willing values," the mental, emotional, and behavioral attributes that drive performance in an achievement activity. In most cases, participation in a sport will, to some degree or other, draw out these attributes and present opportunities to develop them.

There is another type of character, though, which we refer to as *moral character*. These are the traits needed for ethical behavior and functioning within a society, such as integrity, respect, and caring. Doing a handstand or throwing a fastball does not develop these traits. Only coaches who intentionally focus on them will develop moral character in their athletes. And sadly, this intentional character development has gone missing in many youth sporting environments.[2]

As part of their InSideOut Initiative, former NFL star Joe Ehrmann and former coach and athletic director Jody Redman are engaging with schools and encouraging coaches to put the development of moral character on equal footing with performance character. Research has shown that elite-level athletes often score higher in qualities such as ruthlessness and callousness. Yet in school and youth sports, this is a problem.

"Studies show that the longer you play and the higher levels you attain, the more morally and ethically callous players become. There is something leukemic in American sports, and it is damaging the healthy development of our girls and boys," says Ehrmann. He and Redman, with the financial support of the NFL, are on a crusade around the country to shift this paradigm. They are convinced that education-based athletics is about connecting kids to caring adults and that coaches are supposed to build relationships that focus on social-emotional development, with winning as a byproduct. "Why do we even have high school sports if they are not education-based?" asks Ehrmann. "I think there needs to be a realignment in America. We have social contracts in this country. I think for a long time there was one for sports where sports was going to be a tool to help guide and nurture boys and girls into adulthood. I think that contract is broken."

Redman agrees. "If we're going to evaluate coaches solely on their win-loss record, then it's our responsibility to tell them that and really not function under this guise of, 'Well, we're education-based.' If we are education-based, then what are those other factors that we want coaches to focus on besides just the physical aspects of the game? A coach can want to perform in a way that develops a student's capacity to be a better person, but unless there's support for that and unless the community that they're functioning in values something more than just the outcome on the scoreboard, then really coaches are forced to focus on winning."[3]

We coach in a performance-driven society, and for many of us, our community and our leadership will pay lip service to moral character when all they really want is more wins than losses. Some of us may be lucky enough to coach in a truly athlete-centered, education-based organization. Even then, we will face parents and community members who are willing to compromise a lot of moral development in order to win. That is why we need to know our why, as we covered in lesson 1. And that is why both athletes and coaches need a higher purpose than winning. "I think coaches burn out not because of the hours or the excessive time away from families or sacrifice," says Ehrmann. "I think they burn out because they're not coaching toward a purpose high enough to justify the sacrifices that they make."

A Case Study in Transforming Your Youth Sports Program

When you drive through Appleton, Wisconsin, you know you are in America's heartland. It is a typical, small Midwest city, with the Fox River flowing through downtown and people who are full of that Midwest charm I came to love in my years living in Michigan. Appleton was also typical in that many of its residents and their children were caught up in what I call the "race to nowhere in youth sports," that race to the bottom to do more and more at younger and younger ages. Kids were flocking to travel teams, and the recreational, in-town leagues were struggling to field teams. Families were frustrated with local youth sports, and children were disappearing from youth sports programming at a rate that even native Appletonian Harry Houdini would have trouble conjuring up. But a few years back, all that began to change.

Nate Baldwin became the Youth Sports Programmer for Appleton

Parks and Recreation in 2015 with a goal to transform the program. Baldwin was a lifelong athlete who remembered fondly his childhood days of playing season after season of different sports at local parks, competing with and against his friends and neighbors. He had witnessed the slow drain of children and families from local programming, pulled in by the allure of "travel teams" and "serious competition" at ages when many of the participants could barely spell the name of the sport they were playing. Appleton Parks and Recreation was typical of many local youth sports organizations as they faced declining numbers across their four major sports: flag football, soccer, baseball/softball, and basketball.

Baldwin wanted to change this. He wanted to grow his programs; he wanted to have better coaches who, in turn, would develop better athletes. He wanted to deal with fewer parental behavior issues and play his part in building a healthier community. These were all outcomes that Baldwin was convinced he could achieve. But he knew that outcomes could not be his focus if he wanted to get there. He needed to be purpose and process driven.

"The first thing that struck me was how willing a typical park and recreation sports program was to be the 'fall back' option in the community," lamented Baldwin. "We were willing to be the program families settled for if their children either weren't talented enough or financially fortunate enough to participate with an elite/travel program, who all had a big, vocal, and strong presence in this part of the state. I believed my first order of business was to basically stand up for the benefits we provide to the community, to define our values, define our philosophy, and boldly position those qualities as the reason to *actively choose* our program over the competition."

Baldwin and his staff undertook a year-long program of listening to and understanding the needs of the community. They interviewed staff, parents, and current and former participants in their programs. They looked at the research provided by organizations such as The Aspen Institute's Project Play Initiative, Changing the Game Project, and others. And then, they set out to define who they were and what they stood for by outlining four core values for their programs:

1. Inclusivity: Appleton Parks and Recreation had a place for you, regardless of your skill or background.

2. Intentional skill development: Appleton Parks and Recreation would help players get better at sports through structured lesson planning, coach training, and frequent feedback during the season to help coaches and players get from point A to point B, from week to week, and from season to season.

3. Family balance: Appleton Parks and Recreation would establish reasonable time commitments to allow kids to be kids, enjoy family dinners, get their homework done, and enjoy free play; ask for reasonable financial commitments that didn't artificially increase pressure or expectations; and offer a season length that allowed a child to pursue other interests and other sports without guilt.

4. Promoting lifelong enjoyment of sports: Appleton Parks and Recreation was committed to making the youth sports experience so positive and encouraging that every child would want to make sports a part of their life, regardless of whether they chose to pursue the activity competitively or not.

Next, Nate and his team began the process of relentlessly sharing these values, educating coaches and parents, and holding people accountable for upholding them. They let the community know that Appleton Parks and Recreation was something to be actively sought out, no longer just a fall-back option. They said, in essence, "This is how we do things here. If this is not a good fit, we understand. Perhaps it's not for you." And by the fall of 2018, the results were staggering.

When Nate Baldwin joined Appleton Parks and Recreation, their four main sports had the following participation numbers:

- Youth baseball/softball: 452
- Youth soccer: 836
- Youth basketball: 235
- Youth flag football: 119

When Baldwin joined us on the *Way of Champions Podcast* to report on their progress in Appleton in October of 2018, he reported that participation numbers in their four major sports were up a staggering 60 percent. The numbers were as follows:

- Youth baseball/softball: 864 (91 percent increase)
- Youth soccer: 1062 (27 percent increase)
- Youth basketball: 518 (112 percent increase)
- Youth flag football: 190 (60 percent increase)

Overall, the programs had increased from 1,642 kids to 2,634. It turns out that this type of programming was exactly what people were looking for. "It shows that kids still want to play, and it shows that families still value a positive sports experience, dictated by core values that make sense, match their family values, and promote the overall health, well-being, and development of their children," says Baldwin. "These families have embraced it wholeheartedly with their participation and their enthusiasm to share it with their friends, family, and neighbors."

The transformation of the program has also had some unexpected benefits as well. Parent sideline behavior has improved tremendously, with Baldwin noting that whenever a staff member sees an incident brewing, other parents usually step in and tone it down before the staff member has a chance to intervene. But the greatest unexpected benefit has been in the coaching ranks.

Baldwin, like many youth sports directors, had been told that if you ask volunteer coaches to commit extra time to training and implementing curriculums and practice plans, they would refuse to coach or quit. But he has found exactly the opposite. In 2015, he had eighty youth soccer teams, and twenty-eight of them had no one volunteer to coach. He and his staff had to pick up the phone and call each family trying to find anyone willing to run the team. In the fall of 2018, he had only eight vacancies on 117 teams. "It is so rewarding and positive that coaches can't wait to sign up again," said Baldwin. "And most of our training is not about technique and tactics, just about our philosophy and the role we expect our coaches to play. It gets them fully invested and makes them partners in this process."

Most important for Appleton Parks and Recreation, they are seeing a shift in the role of sports and what participating families see as the value of sports in their children's lives. "We put so much pressure and so much attention on those four years of high school sports," said Baldwin, "and what we are saying is, 'Look beyond those fleeting four years. What do you want for your child after they are done? Do you want this sport to still bring enjoyment and value to your child's life? Do you want your kids to coach their own kids one day or to officiate?' We do so much damage if we forget that sports are supposed to be about lifelong enjoyment and participation." That is a higher purpose than winning on a programmatic level.[4]

Activities to Establish a Higher Purpose than Winning

Establish Your Coaching Purpose Statement

Even though this chapter is about having a collective team purpose that goes beyond results, if you have not already done so, please refer back to lesson 1 where we discussed establishing your personal coaching purpose statement. I give examples of both Joe Ehrmann's and my own personal coaching purpose statement. It begins by completing this sentence: I coach …

Without your personal foundation, it is difficult to have the patience and persistence to stick to a collective one.

✳ *Help Your Team Discover Their Higher Purpose*

If you have a young team, perhaps check out Willie Cromack's work at www.goplaybetter.com. He will even give you twenty dollars for signing your team up. If you have a high-school age or older team, I suggest a team book club. Three of my favorite books for helping teams find their higher purpose are

- *The Hard Hat: 21 Ways to Be a Great Teammate* by Jon Gordon;
- *Legacy: What the All-Blacks Can Teach Us about the Business of Life* by James Kerr; and
- *Wolfpack: How to Come Together, Unleash Our Power, and Change the Game* by Abby Wambach.

In lesson 12, you'll learn more about establishing a strong team culture based on this purpose.

Summary

Programs that establish a track record of continual excellence have one common trait: they play to a higher purpose than winning. For schools such as Messiah College, the purpose may be religious in nature; while in other programs, it may be involvement in community service, working with children with disabilities, or establishing a big brother/big sister type program. To find your team's higher purpose, I recommend the following:

- Pay close attention to programs such as Go Play Better, Messiah College, and UNC women's soccer and learn from them.
- Understand the difference between developing performance character and moral character and be sure to intentionally teach

moral character in your program.

- Reach out to people such as Nate Baldwin and Willie Cromack and discover how an outcome aware but purpose and process driven philosophy can turn around your program.
- Establish a book club and help your team consolidate around a higher purpose than winning.

Good luck!

PART II

HOW DO I COACH?

Coaching is an art form,
but there's no reason it cannot be informed by science.
—DR. MARK WILLIAMS

Coaches need to stop seeing themselves as transmitters of information
and start seeing themselves as architects of an
optimal learning environment.
—DR. JOE BAKER

The town of Sitges, Spain, lies about thirty-five kilometers south of Barcelona on a piece of the most idyllic Mediterranean coastline you can imagine. It is backed by the mountains of the Parc Natural del Garraf and features beautiful beaches, cobblestone alleys, and beachfront mansions that makes you want to kick back, relax, and think long and hard about living there someday. It is no wonder they call it the St. Tropez of Spain.

About half a mile south of the iconic Iglesia de San Bartolome y Santa Tecla, the beach is swarming with blue-shirted soccer players buzzing along skillfully in the sand, all the while laughing, giggling, and clearly having the time of their lives. And looking over this beehive of activity, proudly smiling, is the man responsible for these players. He is American Todd Beane, founder of TOVO Academy.

TOVO is the brainchild of Beane. The name is short for the Dutch phrase Total Voetbol, a testament to a style of play synonymous with Beane's late father-in-law, Johan Cruyff, the legendary international player for the Netherlands, as well as an iconic player and coach at FC Barcelona and Ajax Amsterdam. To say Beane has lived the dream life for an American soccer coach would be an understatement. Beane was a collegiate player at Dartmouth College, had a short stint as a professional player in the United States, and then decided to pursue his passion for education. He received his master's degree from Stanford University and then set out to teach across the globe. It was at an international school in Central America that he encountered one of the big problems with education.

"I sat in a staff meeting talking about policies and procedures for the upcoming school year when one of the teachers blurted out, 'This stuff would all work perfectly if there were no students here,'" chuckled Beane. "And we all laughed, but it got me thinking about how many schools are set up more as people management and not learning environments. If we get the learning right, all else follows. But when you establish institutions one hundred and fifty years ago, set up for one purpose, and then everything advances, you are stuck with a structure and an antiquated system."

In 2002, Beane received a call from a friend in Spain saying that Johan Cruyff was looking for someone to work on a project with him in Barcelona and would Todd be interested. There is arguably no more influential figure in world soccer than Cruyff, in terms of how he played the game, how he coached the game, and how he thought about developing players and organizations. As such, it was a no brainer for Beane.

"Of course, being a passionate player and fan, I didn't really think twice about that, and I packed my bags and moved to Spain," Beane told me. "When we speak about football, Johan was a man of great vision, a man of great integrity, very romantic in his ideals about the way the game should be played. Staying true to that vision was something I watched him do time after time, and I always admired that about him. Sitting in a room with him, watching him work at Barcelona and at Ajax, mapping out a vision of what it is supposed to look like, was a great honor."

Subsequently, Beane married Cruyff's daughter Chantal and kept working on projects with the Cruyff Institute, and upon his father-in-law's passing, he founded TOVO. His goal was to put forth a methodology that honors Cruyff's vision of the game and combines that with his own background in pedagogy and education. The central philosophy of TOVO is "Players First."

Beane recalled a story about travelling to Amsterdam with Cruyff to work with his boyhood club Ajax. The club had become so focused on marketing, management, and revenues that it had lost sight, in the eyes of Cruyff, of its primary purpose: developing players. And they intended to change that by flipping the organizational chart on its head. "When we looked at the organizational chart, footballers—the players—were not even on the chart, and yet this is an institution that supposedly is developing capable players," lamented Beane. "So we flipped it; we created a 'footballers first' mentality and put them first on the chart. And if we put them first, who else has to be there? Trainers, nutritionists, groundskeepers, those in humble service of the players. Things like marketing and the board members come much further down. And by putting players first, we create programs with great continuity and coherency for our children to develop."

This "players first" ideology became the founding philosophy of TOVO's 3 Cs approach: to develop a player's cognition, competence, and character. Beane believed that developing top players meant giving  them the technical and tactical skills, the ability to think quickly and creatively, and the character to be resilient, disciplined, and a good human being. "I mean, what's the alternative?" asked Beane. "Win at

53

all costs? Not develop players? Not develop character? Develop irresponsible people? The idea sounds ludicrous. The idea that a player isn't provided the support and advocacy to develop themselves as a person is ridiculous."

Beane set about writing up the foundational principles of TOVO by compiling all his thoughts and wisdom gleaned from working alongside Cruyff and other great leaders. He combined that with his years in education and coaching, neuroscience, pedagogical research, and more to come up with his 3 Cs approach. He wanted to come up with a methodology that would allow every coach to create a more engaging and effective environment than he had grown up with. He knew players needed less isolated practices and non-game-related activities and instead needed environments that were cognitively faithful to the game environment. "The game, in its entirety, is complex, and we need to develop players who can problem solve and execute with technical precision but also with the dedication and resilience required," says Beane. "To pretend that we can pick out one or two things and piece it back together on Saturday is ludicrous, and we know better, and we shouldn't be doing it. It disturbs me that we are still doing it with what we know about learning and skill acquisition and applied environments."

What Beane has developed is a methodology and a way of coaching that puts the athletes' needs first. It is a way of doing things that is faithful to the physical, technical, and cognitive demands of the sport he is teaching. It is research based. I am not saying that coaching the same way you have been coaching for the last twenty years is not working at all, nor am I saying that if you are a soccer coach, Beane's methodology is the only effective way to coach. But you do need a methodology and a sound foundation for how you coach. What I am asking you to consider is this: is the way that I coach the most effective way I can take what I know and transfer it to my athletes so that they can actually learn it and apply it in game conditions?

54

"Sometimes in sport we are too insular," says Beane, shaking his head. "We have the same coaching conventions and conversations over and over with the same people. We need to step out and look at talent development from a much broader scope and learn from people outside of sport who are mastering the craft of advocacy for children in a way that maximizes their potential. That can be a classroom teacher, a musician, a tech guru, a parent. The knowledge that we need has to also come from beyond sport."

Great coaches are innovators. They never stop learning; they never stop honing their craft; and they are always looking both inside and outside their sport for information they can borrow and use with their own teams. The beauty of coaching is that it is not just a science. It is an art, which means that you get to take this great information and make it your own. You must be your authentic self, just like Steve Kerr is with the Golden State Warriors and Pete Carroll is with the Seattle Seahawks. But base your authenticity not upon ignorance or resistance to change but upon curiosity and adaptability. Be firm in your principles because they represent your authentic self. But be flexible and adaptable in your methods and your practices because the sport you coach is always evolving and so must you.

How do we know that the practices we have developed and the methodology we are following is working? First, we ensure that it comes from trusted, age-appropriate resources. Most every sport-governing body across the globe has released a curriculum. In the United States, our Olympic sports call it the American Development Model (ADM). In Canada, they call it Long Term Athlete Development (LTAD). Professional clubs have their own versions as well. If you are following one of these, hopefully it is research based and built upon sound principles. But there is one more clue you have to look for, something that happens right in front of you, every single day. In the words of Todd Beane, "Learning and fun. Fun and learning. I can't say that enough. When you see a child fully engaged, laughing and enjoying the experience while learning, those are the environments we need to create."

Do you want to know how to create this type of environment? Then, as they say in Sitges, "Vamonos!"

LESSON 4

"YOU CAN'T PRACTICE IN THE 'KIND' WORLD IF YOU COMPETE IN A 'WICKED' ONE"

Turn Technique into Skill and Create an Effective Learning Environment

Context isn't noise; it's a signal.

—ANDREW WILSON

The intelligence has to be on the field, not on the sideline.

—TODD BEANE

I t is often said that hitting a baseball thrown by a Major League pitcher is the hardest task in sports. Even a fastball with little movement, thrown ninety-eight miles an hour, is not only scary but also extremely difficult to hit. The ball has a three-inch diameter while the bat, at its widest, is 2.75 inches. A batter has less than a half second to decide whether to swing. Throw in a rising or sinking pitch or a variety, such as a curveball or slider with both horizontal and vertical movement, and the task gets even harder. You might think that if you made the ball significantly larger and slowed down the delivery of the ball it would be easier to hit. You would be wrong if the pitcher was no longer a Major League pitcher, with a traditional overhand throwing motion, and was, instead, Olympic softball pitcher Jennie Finch.

In February 2004, a few months prior to gaining national acclaim by winning the Olympic gold medal with Team USA, Finch was invited to be a coach in the annual Major League Baseball Pepsi Challenge softball game. As the players got to know her and took a few swings against her in batting practice, they soon came to realize that hitting a bigger ball thrown between sixty and seventy miles per hour from a mound only forty-three feet away—the equivalent of a ninety-five mph fastball—was no easy task. In fact, making any contact at all was nearly impossible. So, in the game's fifth inning, with the American League All Stars trailing nine to one and National League slugger Mike Piazza at bat, the American Leaguers called Finch into the game. Her teammate Aaron Boone took off his glove and laid down with his head on a base to take a nap. A few others left the field to get a drink. And the bemused crowd watched as Finch promptly struck out Piazza and Brian Giles to end the inning. Post-game, players lined up to take a crack at Finch, and one by one they left the batter's box shaking their heads. She struck out every batter. Only one, Tim Hudson, even managed to get a bat on the ball.

In 2004 and 2005, Finch went on to host a segment for Fox Sports' *This Week in Baseball* and travelled around the league, interviewing various players and promptly striking them out. Many of the game's most accomplished hitters could not even get a bat on the ball. One, feared home-run-hitter Albert Pujols, was so exasperated by Finch that he exclaimed afterwards, "I don't want to experience that again!"[1]

So, how is it that the best hitters in the world, with some of the most perfected swings in the world, were made to look mediocre, even though the object they were trying to hit was bigger and moving slower? The reason is simple: learning to be a great baseball hitter and learning to be a great softball hitter are two very different tasks, even though the basic technical element of swinging a bat to meet a ball is nearly the same. Hitting a Major League pitch is not about reaction time or having quicker reflexes. The human body cannot react quickly enough to actually hit a fastball. It is about the ability to perceive what is happening with the pitch, anticipate the movement of the ball, and time the swing to arrive at the same place and time as the ball. This chain of perception and action must be nearly automatic because the ball arrives so quickly there is really no time for thought during the pitch. Great baseball hitters have spent thousands of hours learning to perceive and anticipate pitches thrown from a certain distance with a certain motion. They may have done swinging practice and hit balls off a tee, but to become Major League hitters, they had to practice hitting within a specific context. Finch's underhand delivery was not something they had seen or practiced. Hitting overhand baseball pitchers did not prepare them. Hitting off a tee certainly did not. When it came to trying to hit a larger ball thrown at a slower velocity with a different delivery, everything was out of context, and the hitters were out of luck.

Hitting a baseball—or, for that matter, shooting a hockey puck or heading in a cross in soccer—is not simply a technique performed in isolation. It is a skill developed over thousands of hours of practice—but not just any practice nor the simple repetition of isolated technique. Complex motor skills, especially in sports where the environment is constantly changing and where multiple factors influence the competition, are best learned in context. In fact, as Jennie Finch has proven to many Major Leaguers, they are only learned within the context of the dynamic environment. If the behaviors and actions required in a game are different than what is happening in practice, then the behaviors you see in training will not necessarily emerge in the game. As researcher Andrew Wilson, an ecological psychologist at Leeds Beckett University, says, "Context is not noise; it's a signal. We are learning how to skillfully interact with a dynamic environment, and behavior emerges in real time from the information we gather."[2]

There are two types of learning environments according to researcher Robin Hogarth: "wicked" worlds and "kind" worlds. A "kind" world is a world with strict rules, accurate feedback, and easily quantifiable results. Think chess. The feedback you receive links outcomes directly to the appropriate actions and judgements. Simply by repeatedly engaging in the isolated activity the participant learns and improves. A "wicked" learning environment, according to Hogarth, is much more dynamic. Patterns are far less repetitive, and feedback is hard to come by, often delayed, and inaccurate. The rules and environment are in a constant state of flux and require far more experience in order for a participant to see patterns emerge and successfully interact on a consistent basis with the environment.[3]

For the vast majority of sports, our athletes operate in a "wicked" world. The environment is in constant flux. They never play the same exact pass or take the same exact shot twice, and they have opponents influencing their actions. The question we have to ask ourselves as coaches is this: do our practices mimic a wicked or a kind world? Because if we compete in a wicked world but practice in a kind one, our athletes will struggle to transfer what they have done in training to the game environment.

In this chapter, we will explore what effective teaching looks like so our practices will mimic the competition environment and the learning will transfer to the game. To do so, we will cover

- The difference between technique and skill;
- Making your teaching sticky: how to add interleaving, spacing, desirable difficulties, and quizzing to your coaching;
- Convincing the athlete, the parents, and yourself that learning is taking place; and
- Not stealing the reps from your athletes.

Unless your training sessions mimic your competition environment, very little transfer takes place. Unless your training situations have the requisite elements that mimic the environment our athletes are competing in, you may be teaching, but your athletes are not doing much effective learning. There is a lot of research available on how to create the most effective learning environment for our athletes, but oftentimes it is hard to find such environments and even harder to understand how to create them. This chapter is my attempt to make it a little more palatable and a lot more applicable to your coaching.

Developing Skill, Not Simply Teaching Technique

Travel to most any youth soccer field in the United States, and you will see the following elements: children standing in lines or dribbling around a coned area, each with a ball, endlessly repeating a technique such as a drag-back turn. They then progress to two lines, ten yards apart, and the players pass to the opposite line and follow their pass to the end of that line. After a water break, the players line back up and pass their coach a ball. He then lays it off square for the child to shoot on goal. The player retrieves her ball and gets back in line. Rinse and repeat.

Ask that coach, "Did you have a good practice today?" and he will likely say, "Yes, those kids got five hundred touches, and we practiced dribbling, passing, and shooting." Ask the parents eagerly observing, and they might feel the same: "It was great! These kids really need those touches because in the game, they cannot dribble, pass, or shoot." I used to think that as well. Today I would ask those parents and coaches a better question: "How many decisions did they make today?"

Sadly, the answer to that question is likely, "Not that many." In spite of getting five hundred touches, the vast majority of those touches took place in the absence of any decisions, defenders, or direction, elements that are required to connect the practice environment to the game conditions in a dynamic game such as soccer. You may be developing technique, but you are not developing skill because those are two very different things. And without skill development, transfer does not take place. These are elements worth explaining.

I realize some people might argue semantics here, so here is how I define these terms: a *technique* is the ability to perform a physical task while a *skill* is the ability to deploy it in the competition environment. One thousand touches with no connection to the game would be like hitting one thousand balls off a tee in baseball; you might become a better swinger, but it won't make you a better hitter. One thousand pitches from an overhand pitcher will not prepare you to face Jennie Finch. One thousand isolated touches a day will give you the technique, but without context in your training, those touches will not develop the skill to play the actual game.

Far too many coaches think skill is the aggregation of various techniques that are then applied in a linear fashion back into the competition. That fundamentally misunderstands the fact that skill is something that requires context to develop. You cannot separate it from context. You need problems to be solved in order to develop skill. In a practice with no game-like activities, with no defenders or direction to force decision-making, there may be technical development, but there is very little skill development. And without skill development, there is no transfer.

Transfer is the ability of a learner to successfully apply the behaviors, knowledge, and skills acquired in a practice environment to the competition. If the training environment does not mimic those game conditions or if it poses decisions and scenarios that are not encountered in a game, then transfer does not occur.

"Transfer does not happen often," says Andrew Wilson, the researcher from Leeds Beckett I mentioned in the beginning of this chapter. "It is spectacularly task specific. If you learn to perceive a task in one dynamic environment and that environment does not exist in the game, then transfer will not occur. It only occurs when the dynamic principles overlap." Wilson uses the example of passing in soccer. Two players passing a ball back and forth may be working on locking their ankle, placing their plant foot correctly, and following through so that the ball is hit in the right direction with the right pace. But that is insufficient preparation for passing a moving ball between moving defenders to a moving teammate in the exact space he needs to receive it at exactly the right time. "Behavior emerges in real time for the information the athlete is given," says Wilson. "Context governs transfer."

This is not to say that there is never a time to teach specific movements to one child with one ball. But why would you gather as a team to work alone? Would this group time not be better spent working in groups and working on the dynamic elements of the game, leaving individual work for kids to do at home? Shouldn't the vast majority of your training sessions be focused on actual transferable skills and not simply technique? I certainly think so, and the research seems to back it up.

Todd Beane, whom we met on the beach in Sitges, Spain, in the introduction to part II, hears the argument all the time that you must teach technique before you can teach skill. He sees no reason to separate technical training from true skill development. "Four things have to happen in milliseconds before you receive the ball," says Beane. "What we train is how you can master time and space before you receive the ball so you can execute with efficacy." Beane sees the game of soccer as a constantly repeating series of actions. Players must

- Perceive the situation.
- Conceive of possible solutions.
- Decide on the best solution.
- Deceive their opponent, if necessary.
- Technically execute their pass, shot, or dribble.
- Assess their choice and prepare for the next play.

"Cognition has been divorced from so much of the training I see," says Beane. "The thinking player is to be valued, and we need to train it and bring out the potential of every player and every person. Our kids here go home, and everyone will say, 'OMG! You have become so much better technically.' But if they find an extra meter of space, they find time, and any extra time increases the likelihood of technical execution. So, yes, we do ball mastery work, but we do it within the context of the demands of the game in a cognitively faithful way."

Kris Van Der Haegen and his colleagues in Belgium have followed a similar approach. "Repetition, repetition, repetition of technique is not the best way to prepare players," says Van Der Haegen. He recognizes that players have to read the game and make decisions, so in training sessions, this is what you have to simulate. They have to be aware of space, time, and opponents. You see a lot of training sessions with exercises where they do a passing exercise and then shooting, but there are no opponents," says Van Der Haegen. "But I've never played a game without opponents."

Regardless of the sport, context always matters. I have written a lot here about highly dynamic sports such as soccer, hockey, or lacrosse, but creating proper context is not limited to those sports. For example, certain elements of golf may be "kind," but things such as course conditions, weather, and a golfer's own stress and anxiety are all conditions that make golf more of a wicked sport than one might think. Hitting fifty seven-irons in a row off the same lie to the same target does not mimic anything a golfer does when playing the course. Even in swimming, lane selection, water temperature, and competition anxiety are elements that we can attempt to replicate in training in order to better prepare our athletes for a competition.

To sum up, if we want our athletes to learn deeply and deploy what they have learned more effectively, the research tells us that we must build learning environments that represent the competition. Have you ever wondered how to do that? Here is what I have learned about how to build the best training environment for my athletes.

How to Build a Sticky Learning Environment

Think about going to the weight room to work out and build strength. If you add no weight to the barbells, you are not going to improve very much—and you certainly are not going to improve very quickly. We add resistance because that will help us develop and grow. For Trevor Ragan of *The Learner Lab* podcast, we need to think of the weight room when we are training our bodies and our brain. "The brain, in many ways, is like a muscle," says Ragan. "We know we need some weight to build a muscle. The ninth and tenth reps, when we're really fighting and struggling, that's not the most fun feeling in the world." Skill development is just like the weight room, says Ragan. It doesn't always feel good. "Helping them understand that it's okay to be uncomfortable might help people spend a little more time in a learning zone."

Ragan is deeply immersed in the science of motor learning and skill acquisition, and he consults with organizations ranging from the Cleveland Indians of Major League Baseball to Microsoft and the United Nations. He is great at explaining science in a way that we all can understand it. "In order to grow and get better, we have to operate at the edge of our abilities and a little out of our comfort zone," says Ragan. "It's not only okay to struggle with something, it's kind of necessary. It's sort of the price of admission that you have to pay to get good at something."

There are certain researched-based principles that help coaches and teachers incorporate the appropriate amount of struggle and stretch into our sessions. The most approachable book on this topic is Peter Brown's *Make It Stick: The Science of Successful Learning*. I will not do sufficient justice to this book nor the decades of research in a few paragraphs here, but there are a few concepts that are critical components of sticky learning that we can all apply to our training sessions.

Interleaving

There is a lot of bad advice given to both athletes and coaches when it comes to learning, but perhaps the worst is "repetition, repetition, repetition." Brown calls this the myth of massed practice. "Most of us believe that learning is better when you go at something with a single-minded purpose," says Brown. "Faith in focused, repetitive practice of one thing at a time until we've got it nailed is pervasive among class-room teachers, athletes, corporate trainers, and students. Despite what our eyes tell us, this faith is misplaced." The faith is misplaced because, in the short term, we can see and feel ourselves improving. But those gains are short-lived. "If learning can be defined as picking up new knowledge or skills and being able to apply them later," writes Brown, "then how quickly you pick something up is only part of the story. Is it still there when you need to use it out in the everyday world? The rapid gains produced by massed practice are often evident, but the rapid forgetting that follows is not."[4]

Massed or blocked training is repeating the same exact technique over and over—think hitting fifty reps in a row with your seven-iron or practicing the same soccer move without opposition fifty times in a row. The science tells us that when we block our training, with each subsequent repetition, our brain devotes less energy to going through the process of solving the problem before us. For example, I saw Dr. Tim Lee, a leading researcher in this space, demonstrate this to a crowd of golf coaches with a simple math problem. He asked them to come up with the answer to the following multiplication problem: what is 21 x 14?

Coaches went through the problem in their heads and slowly hands came up as they came up with the answer. Finally he called on a raised hand. "294!" shouted the coach. "Correct," said Lee. "How did you come up with that?" The coach went on to explain how he went through the process of multiplying 21 x 10 and then 21 x 4 and then adding them together.

"Ok, next problem," said Lee as he advanced his slide. The next problem came up: what is 21 x 14?

The audience chuckled, and someone shouted triumphantly, "294!" We all laughed, and Lee asked us about the process we went through to come up with that answer the second time around. We didn't. We already knew the answer. "This is similar to what the brain does when we block our practices," said Lee. Every time we repeat the same exact motion, we devote less time to going through the process. We shout out the answer, and this slows down learning as it allows the brain to divert its attention away from the skill you are trying to develop.

Research demonstrates that interleaved training—solving different math problems instead of the same ones repeatedly—promotes mastery and long-term retention when compared to massed practice. Interleaved training mixes and matches various techniques and skills, usually in a game-conditioned setting. Many practitioners call it "repetition without repetition." The main reason is that interleaved learning engages different parts of the brain. Neuroimaging has shown that motor skills learned from massed practice seem to be consolidated in areas of the brain used for cognitively simple and less challenging motor skills, what we might call factual knowledge. Interleaved learning is consolidated in areas associated with learning higher-order motor skills and provides conceptual knowledge, an understanding of when and how to deploy a skill in relation to its environment. Writes Brown, "The varied and more challenging practice demands more brain power and encodes the learning in a more flexible representation that can be applied more broadly." In other words, if you want to be able to call upon it more readily, it needs to be learned with more struggle.

If you are an ice hockey coach, for example, instead of doing an entire practice on skating or passing, you would incorporate multiple elements into your session. USA Hockey's ADM is excellent at this, setting up six stations on a sheet of ice and having players learn something new at each one. In the short term, athletes may experience a feeling of frustration and think, *I was just getting good at that, and we moved on.* But in reality, the interleaving of these skills trades short-term satisfaction for long-term learning, and next week the hockey player will retain more of the previous week's session than if he had only worked on one aspect of his game. This frustration can be an obstacle, though, and we will speak more about that below.

Spacing

One of the advantages of interleaving your practice is the concept of spacing. The power of spacing your practice, or spaced repetition, has been demonstrated repeatedly in research since 1885, and studies have shown up to 40 percent retention improvement when spacing versus cramming your learning. The basic concept is this: after learning a new skill or idea, learners should give themselves time to forget so that the brain, when presented with this material in the future, must struggle to recall the skills it learned previously.

Spaced practice should be combined with retrieval practice as it forces the brain to create new connections and form relationships between material. Covering crossing and finishing in soccer, for example, can consist of various components, such as shooting with the feet, heading, clipping or bending a ball, running in the box, timing, and a slew of other things. To cover all these day after day will work somewhat, but spacing out the components and helping your players search for connections between the material will produce more sticky learning.

Let's say you do a crossing and finishing session working on patterns of movement. Instead of repeating that session the next day, wait two weeks, set up the activity, and see if they can replicate the same movements without you cueing them up too much. Force them to struggle to recall what was covered. The optimal timing between practices varies. For material your athletes are less familiar with, shorter spacing is more effective, and where an athlete is more familiar with the material, longer spacing can be more effective. In general, though, the best time to reintroduce a topic is right at the point where they are about to forget it.[5]

Desirable Difficulties

Interleaving your practices and spacing them out are successful learning strategies because they produce what researcher Robert Bjork calls "desirable difficulties." First coined by Bjork in 1994, the concept of desirable difficulties is one all coaches can wrap their heads around. (Yet, in the experience of many coaches, far too many parents cannot.) The term refers to learning a task with a considerable but not overwhelming amount of struggle. In other words, we want to make learning more challenging, frustrating, and slower in the short term in exchange for long-term gains. When they achieve one level of mastery, we must immediately up the ante and ask them to do a bit more. This type of teaching can be frustrating for athletes as they never seem to actually "get it" in practice. It can be frustrating for parents watching their kids struggle. Yet, the research demonstrates it is far more effective than allowing them to repeatedly accomplish a technique or concept they have already mastered.

In one research example, the baseball team at Cal Poly State University in San Luis Obispo, California, was split into two groups of hitters. These were already highly experienced NCAA players, and they agreed to do extra batting practice twice a week following two different protocols. One group did the usual hitting practice, taking forty-five pitches evenly divided into three sets of fifteen. They hit fifteen fastballs, then fifteen curveballs, then fifteen changeups. This, as we explained above, is a massed practice. The second group hit forty-five randomized pitches, and the hitter never knew what pitch was coming. In other words, practice was interleaved. You can imagine what this looked like in practice.

Hitters in the first group hit the ball progressively better during each practice as they knew what pitch was coming and were able to anticipate the ball and time their swings with each subsequent pitch. They saw consistent improvement throughout each session. The second group, as you can imagine, struggled more. They did not know what was coming. They did not seem to anticipate or swing as well as their teammates in the massed practice. They did not seem to be developing the same proficiency as their massed practice teammates. They may have even grown a bit frustrated. If this was a youth baseball practice, you can imagine the parents on the sideline cheering on their massed-practice son as he drove ball after ball into the outfield, while the interleaved parents wondered why their kid was so bad at hitting. Perhaps they even had a word with the coach about throwing their son some better pitches to hit.

The Cal Poly baseball team continued these extra practices twice a week for six weeks, and when their hitting was assessed at the end, they had very different results. The group that had interleaved their practice, hitting forty-five random pitches every session, displayed greater improvement than their teammates who knew what pitch was coming for those last six weeks. Throughout the six weeks, the group that struggled each session, which to the untrained eye—and perhaps even in their own minds—was not improving, was actually improving faster than the group that was smashing the ball all over the park. Their struggle traded short-term success for long-term benefits.

As Brown writes, this study demonstrates two familiar lessons about learning. First, desirable difficulties require more effort and seemingly slow down apparent gains. They may feel less productive in the moment, but they make learning stronger and more enduring. And second, as we will speak about at the end of this chapter, illusions of mastery can be very attractive for coaches, parents, and even the athletes themselves.[6]

Quizzing

The concept of standardized testing in schools has rightfully been panned for its overemphasis on teaching to the test and its de-emphasis on actually educating students. But sadly, one important concept of sticky learning has been swept up in the anti-testing maelstrom, and that is periodic quizzing. "If we stop thinking of testing as a dipstick to measure learning," writes Brown, "[and] we think of it as practicing retrieval of learning from memory rather than 'testing,' we open ourselves to the use of testing as a tool for learning."[7] The research is very clear that active retrieval strengthens memory, and the more difficult the retrieval practice, the better the learning. Luckily, in sports, we have two ways in which our athletes are quizzed.

The most obvious way they are quizzed is within competition. This is the opportunity for an athlete to demonstrate what he has learned well and what still needs work. That is why within competition it is important for coaches to not joystick their players around the field or court. It is OK to ask them questions. What do you see? Where else could you be? But if all you are doing is telling, you are giving them the answers to the quiz. You are not forcing them to recall the material you covered in practice.

I love playing controlled scrimmages in practice against an opponent, where the coaches do have the opportunity to make a stoppage and correct something and perhaps paint the picture on a bigger field, but we must recognize that scenario as one in which we are teaching and not testing. If we can be patient enough to see the scenarios we have been working on emerge, we can watch how our athletes handle those situations. We are allowing them to retrieve the material and will see if they have actually learned it.

The second scenario is to check for learning in practice by setting up an activity or game that we have done in the past, rolling out the ball, and letting the kids play without cueing up what you are looking for. If you have been working on spacing when your team has the ball, for example, do the players find ways to create width and depth, and do they help their teammates do the same? Or is it back to being all bunched up? It is so easy in this scenario to gather the players and say,

"Remember last week when we worked on spacing? What did we talk about doing?" They shout out, "Get wide … Stretch the field … Don't get in the same passing lanes as teammates!" And you say, "Good, let's see it!" But in reality, you just cued up all the answers for them. What if you just roll the ball out and see if they can recall those things on their own? Wouldn't this be a better indicator come game time whether they can replicate proper spacing? I know I certainly struggle with this as it is gratifying to cue it up for them, see them do it well, and then pat myself on the back for being a great teacher. But I have no idea if they have actually learned something. Give your athletes a quiz and try not to give them the answers immediately beforehand. It's a great way to teach and an even better way for them to learn.

Convincing the Athlete (and Her Parents) That Learning Is Taking Place

Jump on your social media account and before long you are sure to find a few "knowledge hacks" and strategies for improving your baseball swing or taking twenty strokes off your golf game in just seven days. Yet in 2007, a study by the US Department of Education laid out the actual learning strategies that could be backed by science, and that extremely short list contained spacing, interleaving, and testing. In other words, the most effective learning strategies, as backed by actual evidence, demonstrate that long-term learning is often the least obvious in the short term. When you fill your sessions with desirable difficulties, such as interleaving and spacing, and when you stand aside and watch athletes struggle to recall what they have learned, it is not always pretty. Your athletes may be looking to you to solve their problems, and oftentimes their parents are expecting you to solve them, too. "We don't pay you to just sit there on the sideline while they lost!" I have been told in the past. But I know better, and now you do, too.

You know that learning slow and learning with struggle is effective long-term learning, just like those Cal Poly baseball players hacking away at random pitches. Your athletes and their parents may want to see immediate results, like those Cal Poly hitters who knew a grooved fast-ball was headed their way. That dichotomy might be reflected in your evaluations, just like it was for some professors at the United States Air Force Academy.

At the Air Force Academy, every student is required to complete three math courses, beginning with Calculus I. An algorithm randomly assigns twenty students to classes so that each section has students with varying levels of standardized test scores and high school grades. In each subsequent year, the students are once again randomly reassigned to Calculus II and then higher-level math and engineering classes. Test-grading for the classes is also standardized by the Academy, so no professor can skew the outcome by being an easy grader. Two economists decided to compile data on over ten thousand cadets who had been taught calculus by 421 different professors over a ten-year period. They wanted to see whether early calculus success, as defined by grades and student evaluations on professor effectiveness, would be a good indicator of performance in later, higher-level math and engineering classes. The results were stunning.

As you might imagine, there were certain professors that had a stronger impact on student performance on the Calculus I exam and also got rave reviews from their students. There was another group that were judged quite harshly by their students, and, not surprisingly, many of those students did not do as well on the end-of-term exam. But when the researchers looked at how the students did on future math and engineering classes that required Calculus I as a prerequisite, they were shocked.

The professors whose students did best in the short term were not nearly as successful at promoting long-term results for those students. As the researchers wrote, "Professors who excel at promoting contemporaneous student achievement, on average, harm the subsequent performance of their students in more advanced classes." One professor, who ranked dead last of the 421 professors in terms of long-term student performance, was ranked sixth overall in student evaluations and seventh in student exam performance. The professors who promoted a deeper understanding of the material, and actually set their students up for long-term success, were punished on their student evaluations for it.[8]

In another study, researchers found that learners believe they are learning more when they participate in blocked practices. Robert Bjork found in one group of students that 80 percent were convinced they had learned better in a blocked practice activity, whereas test results demonstrated that 80 percent of them had actually learned more by interleaving. Learning deeply means learning slowly, and for most learners, it does not feel as though they are learning. As David Epstein writes in *Range*:

> Desirable difficulties like testing and spacing make knowledge stick. It becomes durable. Desirable difficulties like making connections and interleaving make knowledge flexible, useful for problems that never appeared in training. All slow down performance and make performance suffer, in the short term. That can be a problem, because like the Air Force Cadets, we all reflexively assess our progress by how we are doing right now. And like the Air Force Cadets, we are wrong ... Before our eyes progress reinforces our instinct to do more of the same [but] the feedback teaches the wrong lesson. Learning deeply means learning slowly. The cult of the head start fails the learners it seeks to serve.[9]

Coaches, we live in a world where everyone is seeking that proverbial head start and where early specialization and overcoaching are prevalent. It is a world where too many coaches and parents are chasing after short-term results and joy-sticking their players around the field in order to get them. But we have to remember that slow learning is deep learning. The intelligence must be in the field, not on the sideline. We must trade short-term results for long-term development and educate our parents and athletes as to why we are doing it. Take the long view.

Don't Steal the Reps

Trevor Ragan from *TrainUgly.com* loves to use the example of a weight room and a spotter to explain the importance of patience in the learning process. If the weightlifter did the first three reps and then began to struggle, he might want a spotter to help with the next few reps. But he would not want the spotter to grab the bar and do the next seven reps for him. "We can all agree that scenario will not make you stronger or any better at doing squats," says Ragan. "Stealing the reps does not help in the weight room." Yet head to most sporting venues and you will see parents and coaches yelling instructions from the sideline—essentially stealing the reps from their athletes. If we can agree this won't help in the weight room, why do we think stealing reps helps on the sports field?

In my experience, I meet many coaches who think they are being the metaphorical spotter. They think they are guiding the young athlete toward improvement, that by fixing his positioning or yelling the correct decision to make they are promoting development. In reality, in many cases, they have stepped in and taken over the bar. They are doing the heavy lifting, and the athlete has his autonomy and decision making stolen from him. That is stealing reps. According to Ragan, there are four things to look for in a great learning environment:

The brain is like a muscle. We need some struggle to grow; you will not get stronger if all you do is five-pound dumbbell curls day after day. You need to add weight. You need stretch. You need desirable difficulties. It means putting our athletes in the learning zone. If we always intervene and solve problems, we will get short-term improvement but miss out on long-term learning.

Growth takes time and patience. We don't just do one set of push-ups and expect big results. We don't eat healthy for one meal or one day and realistically expect to lose ten pounds. It takes time, reps, and patience to build a new skill. Progress is slow and steady, and sometimes there are regressions, but if we stick with it long enough, growth happens.

We don't learn by watching someone else do it. To see the results, the athlete needs to do the work, not simply watch others get all the playing time or practice reps. Kids need to get meaningful playing time. Skills are developed by actually doing them, getting the reps in, making mistakes, assessing, and trying again. Every young athlete needs practice reps, and every player needs game time.

We can improve any skill if we do the work. Of course, we all cannot master every skill or be the best athlete in our given sport, but everyone is capable of improving. People learn at different rates and at different times, but given enough time and an optimal learning environment, people will eventually learn. It takes focus, effort, and time, but any skill can be learned and improved upon as long as we create an environment that keeps our athletes engaged and with a growth mindset.

Great coaches don't steal the reps from their athletes, just like great spotters do not steal the reps from someone doing squats in the weight room. Take a step back, allow your athletes to succeed or fail, and let each of their reps become teachable moments. Again, this is not to say there is never a time to coach from the sidelines, but choose your timing and your words wisely.

Activities to Help Your Athletes Learn Deeply

Turn Up the Dial of Representativeness

Representative task design is a framework for assessing whether practice tasks simulate key aspects of the specific competition environment an athlete is about to participate in. The more practice represents the competition environment, the more likely it is that skills will transfer. Ian Renshaw, a senior lecturer at Queensland University of Technology in Brisbane, Australia, has spent decades teaching and researching skill acquisition, coaching, and sport psychology and is one of the leading proponents of representative design and what is called a constraints-led approach to coaching. He and co-authors Keith Davids, Will Roberts, and Daniel Newcombe have recently released a new book titled *The Constraints-Led Approach: Principles for Sports Coaching and Practice Design*, which is an overview of this approach. In the future, they plan to release sport-specific books that will help coaches design and implement better practices.

In this approach, a coach adds constraints to the tasks the athletes perform, the environment they perform in, and to the individual themselves in order to make a desired behavior more likely, without explicitly asking for said behavior. The goal is to get the athlete to self-organize and generate solutions to the problem being presented. The higher the degree of representativeness that those constraints create, the more likely the solutions and skills being developed in practice will transfer to the competition.

Renshaw and his colleagues paint a great picture of how to make our sessions more representative. They advocate thinking about a dial with a range of one to ten. The higher the number, the more representative your activity is. Hitting a baseball off a tee may be a one, and hitting a pitch from a Major League pitcher in the bottom of the ninth with two outs and the bases loaded may be a ten. Everything else falls in between. If you rate each activity in your sessions on this dial, you can determine whether the learning is likely to transfer. "The question to ask when you have less-representative tasks," Renshaw told me when we chatted about his book, "is how can I make this one a three? How can I add constraints so this three becomes a five? We cannot always practice at nine or ten, especially with new learners, but you can't always have the dial at one either."[10]

So take a crack at this. Write out your next practice plan and rate each activity in terms of how well it represents the dynamics of the competition environment. Does it have a nice progression? Does it fit the level of the learner? Is it too easy or too hard? And most important, is the dial turned up enough so that transfer will actually occur? If not, you need to rewrite that practice.

Ask Questions Instead of Giving Answers

Instead of telling your right defender to pinch inside or step up, ask her, "Where should you be right now?" Instead of yelling "shoot" or "pass," say nothing and allow your athlete to make the decision and assess her choice. Then maybe you ask, "What problem were you trying to solve? What did you see there that made you play that pass? Were there any other options? Do you think one of the other options was a better choice?" Help them discover the answer by guiding them through the process, rather than giving them the answer. If you help them start to see the "why," they will eventually pick the right how.

Use the Competition as a Quiz

Competition should exist to measure progress and see what your athletes have learned. If you do not give them the space to explore and make mistakes, how will you ever know if they have learned something? This does not mean no coaching is allowed, but keep it to a minimum and recognize if your coaching during competition is of the "promoting learning" or the "problem solving" kind.

Ask Them Three Great Learning Questions

Post-practice or competition, there are three questions that are always appropriate and helpful in framing a balanced assessment of the performance and where to go next:

- What went well?
- What needs work?
- What did you learn from today that you can work on in practice in order to improve?

If you help your athletes see the good and the bad of their performance and help them formulate a plan for moving forward, good things happen.

Let Your Athletes Teach Each Other in Practice and at Halftime/Timeouts

If you have been working on a pattern of play, have your athletes be the ones to set it up and rehearse it instead of the coaching staff. At timeouts or at halftime of your game, let the athletes—instead of just coaches—speak up about what is working and what needs to change. Develop thinking players.

Be a Model Learner for Your Athletes

If you want your athletes to embrace the process, approach challenges with a growth mindset, and not fear making mistakes, then you do the same. The great UCLA basketball coach John Wooden once said, "The most powerful leadership tool we all have is our own example." Nowhere is that statement more relevant than in your ability to model the mindset of a lifelong learner for your athletes.

Summary

One of our biggest challenges as coaches is to educate our parents and our athletes that learning is taking place, that struggle is good, and that learning slowly will help them win the race to the correct finish line. Another struggle is to give up control of the athlete and simply take control of the environment. We can create an environment in which the player is encouraged to do the right things rather than being explicitly told what to do. The environment must encourage the behaviors we want to see. To do that, we must incorporate the best, evidence-based principles into our own training and then educate everyone we work with on why we do it the way we do it. To do so, we must

- Develop skill, not simply technique, and remember context is not noise; it is a signal. Our training sessions should have a cognitive element, lots of decision-making, and should mimic the match conditions.

- Interleave instead of mass our practices. Do not replicate the same technical activity fifty times in a row. Instead, mix and match, add defenders, direction, and different constraints that compel athletes to focus—not go to autopilot mode.

- Space out the learning and revisit topics at an appropriate time to force our athletes to retrieve previously learned information.

- Engage in periodic "quizzing" in order to check for learning and understanding, both through competition and replaying certain activities or games in practices without explicit instructions on what you are looking for.

- Embrace the desirable difficulties and teach our athletes to do the same, even though that may hurt our evaluations in the short term.

- Refrain from stealing the reps from our athletes. Be patient; let them try and fail; teach them to embrace the struggle; and remind them any skill can be improved given enough time.

The evidence that slow learning is sticky learning is quite clear in the research; it is not as clear in the moment. And that is why we must engage and educate our parents so that they understand why we are doing this. It is tough to see your child struggle and lose game after game, and we cannot just simply say, "Because I said so," when asked why it is happening or why we are training our athletes a certain way. I am not saying this will be easy, but it is necessary. Creating a great learning environment in coaching is one of the most important things we do as coaches.

LESSON 5

"GREAT ON PAPER, S#!% ON GRASS"

Build an Engaging and Effective Practice

Too many ideas are great on paper, but shit on grass.
—KRIS VAN DER HAEGEN

Show them where to look, not what to see.
—JOHN KESSEL

O
n July 7, 2019, the US Women's National Soccer Team won its fourth World Cup. Over twenty million households watched the team defeat the Netherlands, two to zero, in the final and saw purple-haired Megan Rapinoe take honors as top scorer and top player at the event. They saw the fleet-footed Rose Lavelle weave and spin her way through helpless defenders to score the winner and then let out a tremendous roar from her knees as her teammates mobbed her. Perhaps they watched Crystal Dunn and Becky Sauerbrunn snuff out attack after attack, Tobin Heath carve through defenders, or saw goalkeeper Alyssa Naeher save a penalty kick to preserve their two to one semifinal victory over England. Regardless of the

defining moment in the tournament, I can guarantee one thing: tens of thousands of little boys and girls were inspired and asked their parents, "Can you sign me up for soccer?"

Now, picture their first practice come August. Their well-intentioned coach, Coach Bill, welcomes his aspiring young players to the session. They are ready to dance through defenders and score goals and make diving saves, but Bill has other ideas. He hasn't had much training as a coach or working with young children, and he cannot find the PDF he was handed at the coaches' meeting where he got his bag of cones and balls. The league director was grateful to have enough coaches and was not going to ask them to actually do any coach training.

Coach Bill had played some soccer in high school, so he figured he could do some of the same stuff. As a bunch of seven-year-olds stare up at him, eagerly awaiting the first game, Coach Bill sends them off to run a few laps. After they are done, they stretch, which seems weird to the kids since they never stretch before they play at recess in school. Then, they get in lines and do repetitive drills. After all, this is how Coach Bill's high school coach did it.

"Are we going to scrimmage, Coach?" asks Jenny. "I want to play! I want to be Megan Rapinoe!"

"Not until we learn all our techniques, Jenny," smiles Coach Bill. "If we have time at the end, maybe we can play." The look of dejection on Jenny's face is palpable as she gets back in line. The minutes tick by, and Coach Bill blows the whistle for the end of practice.

"But we didn't get to play a game!" exclaims Jenny.

"Maybe next time," says Coach Bill. "We have a lot to learn."

Week after week, these eager kids show up, hoping to play the game and emulate their heroes. It is, after all, the reason they signed up for soccer. And week after week, Coach Bill emulates his old coaches, doing endless repetitive drills, lecturing the kids, and having them stand in lines and run laps when they don't listen—just like his old high school coach. Each subsequent week, a few more kids don't show up, and by season's end, only five or six kids are at practice.

"I don't think I want to play soccer next year," says Jenny to her mom as she walks away from the final practice. "It just wasn't that fun. We never get to play."

Given the fact that in many countries across the world, participation numbers in youth sports have either flatlined or are dropping, I will make a bold claim here: Jenny's experience is not a unique one. Many children are inspired by a flash of brilliance or a team, such as the US national team, that captures a nation's attention and inspires a generation of kids to try a sport. And sadly, a few years later, many of those children no longer play because they had their own version of Coach Bill: well-intentioned but poorly trained and unwilling or incapable of delivering the type of experience that gets kids to sign up again next year. As Australian high-performance coach Wayne Goldsmith says, "The only athlete that cannot get better is the one that isn't there." Sadly, many are not there for very long. Around the world by the age of thirteen, around seventy percent of athletes have quit organized sports. This needs to change.

Chances are, if you are reading this book, you have had some formal coaching education or have been involved in coaching for a few years. Sadly, much of what you learned in your initial coaching education years ago, or by searching for activities online, is either outdated or not age-and-stage appropriate for the kids you are coaching. To quote Goldsmith once again:

Ask dentists what are the five most important things they should be learning, and you would naturally expect that the bulk of what they are learning would be those things. Ask a car mechanic and I would expect that the bulk of what they learn would be those fundamental attributes of a great engine mechanic. They are given the most important skills to succeed in that role. When I ask coach educators what are the five most important qualities of their best coach, they will list off things like caring, engaging, respectful, passionate, and inspiring. Then I ask them to open their text and point to those parts of their coaching education manual. They will find things like a molecular diagram of Adenosine triphosphate or a paragraph about proprioceptive neuromuscular facilitation. That is all important stuff but I really think a lot of our problems happen because our coaching courses are not teaching coaches what is most important. We are not teaching them how to coach.[1]

In the last chapter, I wrote about the research on how people learn and how to make that learning stick. This chapter is all about designing and facilitating a great practice for your athletes, based on that research. In my experience, far too many practices are, as Kris Van Der Haegen from the Belgium FA said in the opening quote of this chapter, "Great on paper, but s#!% on grass." They are well-intentioned and may contain some effective activities or ideas, but taken as a whole, they are less than the sum of their parts. They do not effectively engage the learner; they do not effectively create transfer from the training field to the competition; and ultimately, they drive children out of sports.

In this chapter, we will discuss the following items:

- Running a "less but better" practice
- Focusing on age-and-stage appropriate learning
- Letting the game teach through whole-part-whole
- The role of free play in learning
- Golden Threads and CARDS for effective practices

It goes without saying that running effective practices is a critical component of coaching. In these next few pages, I will provide you with some evidence-based ideas and solutions for improving your sessions and more effectively engaging your athletes. Let's go!

Running a "Less but Better" Practice

Oftentimes, in preparing our training sessions, we act like amateur golfers. Inexperienced golfers step up to the tee box, grab the driver, and hit it as far as they can. Then they go find the ball, pick out a club, and do it again, eventually reaching some part of the green, taking a few putts, and walking off with their double bogey. An experienced golfer, on the other hand, begins at the end. She knows where she wants to putt from, so she works backwards and thinks, "If I need to hit it to that part of the green, what club do I want to hit it there with? And if I want to hit a nine iron to that spot, what club do I need to hit off the tee so I can hit a nine iron to that spot?" Then she selects a club and hits her tee shot.

Many coaches design practices like the amateur golfer. They pick a favorite activity and then another, regardless of whether they are related or not. They assign each of them an allotted time and then hope they have enough time and a theme at the end to play a game with some semblance of learning evident. They begin at the beginning, instead of the end. As a result, many of their practice activities have little connection from one stage to another; they lack measurable objectives in terms of what they want to accomplish; and their athletes never fully understand, "Why are we doing this?"

A better approach to planning your sessions is to begin at the end. When planning, instead of simply thinking about a few of your favorite activities, ask the following questions:

- How do we want to play?
- What are my learning objectives for this session that will build toward how we want to play?
- What activities do I need to use to accomplish this?
- How can I organize it and teach it so my players will love it?

- How can I integrate our team values into this session so I can tie it to our higher purpose?

If you answer these five questions in order, you will create a far better session than simply throwing together a few haphazard activities and hoping to find time to scrimmage at the end. And one of the most important things you can do, especially when answering the first three questions, is take a "less but better" approach.

There is a phrase in German, "weniger aber besser," which translates to "less but better," and I think this is a great idea to keep in mind when planning your sessions. Less but better simply means doing fewer things but doing them really well. One of the biggest issues I had as a young coach was that my practices had too much content. In my first high school head coaching job, I was constantly trying to cover so much that my training sessions went too long, followed no logical pattern, and never gave my players any idea where we were going, why we were doing it, or when practice would end. In my mind, I had so much to teach, but for my athletes, it was too much.

Today, when I plan not only my single-practice sessions but also my multi-week training cycles, each of them has a more specific objective, a "less but better" approach. In the words of author Stephen Covey, "The main thing is to keep the main thing the main thing." I do blend multiple technical and tactical topics together; after all, soccer is a dynamic sport, and we have to be careful that we carve it up in the right places. I also cover multiple topics over the space of a few weeks' cycle, but I do so in a way that gives each session an objective. At the end of each session, I keep a notebook in which I record observations on the session, answering these four questions:

- Did we accomplish our objective today?
- Were the activities appropriate and organized, or should I have used different ones?

- Did the players have a great time and train hard?
- Did we talk about our values and how they drive performance?

This post-practice assessment, usually in the car or immediately following the session when it is fresh in my mind, creates a record for what we have covered and what sessions my players enjoyed the most. It allows me to decide whether the activities were appropriate or need to be altered in a future session and whether I need to send a quick note to them via email in case I forgot to cover something. Finally, if we are struggling with an aspect in a game, I can go back and see if we really covered it well and covered it recently or if we need more sessions on those topics.

Is My Practice Age-and-Stage Appropriate?

In January 2018, I was speaking at the Professional Golfers Association Global Youth and Family Golf Summit in Orlando, Florida. Over two hundred and fifty golf instructors, many of them working with young children, had come together to learn from an amazing lineup of teachers in psychology, motor learning, mindset, and more. It was one of the best speaker lineups I had ever seen, and I was a kid in a candy store, ready to settle in and take notes as Dr. Stephen Norris came to the stage to speak about the recently completed PGA American Development Model for golf. Norris has worked in numerous countries and multiple sports designing age-and-stage appropriate guidelines for coaches.

"Take a look at your seat right now," said Norris. "Is it the right size for you? Does it fit your body and your legs well?" He smiled. "Imagine if we were sitting in a kindergarten classroom today, with tiny chairs and tiny desks so that your knees banged against the seat in front of you. How enjoyable would that be?" We all chuckled.

"That is what we often do to kids. We don't put kindergarteners in big chairs and huge desks, yet we ask them to play on big fields with adult rules. And then we are shocked when they are uncomfortable and don't want to come back. That is why we need age-and-stage appropriate developmental models."

In the United States, the US Olympic and Paralympic Committee, in conjunction with each sport national governing body, created the American Development Model in 2014 in order to help American sports develop their own age-and-stage appropriate models.[2] Largely based upon principles of long-term athlete development and quality coaching best practices (see the work of Istvan Balyi and Canadian Sport for Life), the ADM's goal is "to promote sustained physical activity, athlete safety, and age-appropriate development with the aim of creating a positive experience for American athletes across all levels of sport." Every sport governing body is required to develop their own sport-specific model based upon five stages of developing athletes:

- Stage 1: Age 0-12, discover, learn, and play
- Stage 2: Age 10-16, develop and challenge
- Stage 3: Age 13-19, train and compete
- Stage 4: Age 15+, excel for high-performance *or* participate and succeed
- Stage 5: All ages, thrive and mentor

The ADM is obviously a big-picture overview for American sports, but we can learn from these overarching principles as we build our own specific sports environments. The key principles of the ADM are as follows:

- Universal access to create opportunity for all athletes
- Developmentally appropriate activities that emphasize motor and foundational skills
- Multi-sport participation

- Fun, engaging, and progressively challenging atmosphere
- Quality coaching at all age levels

The overall goals of the ADM are to increase the entire athlete pool and create better athletes with transferable skills across sports, ultimately building a generation that is passionate about sport and will transfer that passion to their own children. It is about training coaches to use child-centered activities in practices and competition environments so that we do not have a generation of young athletes playing games that are far too complex to understand or played on fields and courts that are too large for the participants. Nearly every country has their own version of the ADM, and most of them are sport specific, so my advice to you is to look for your own sport's recommendations and guidelines.

The biggest challenge we face as coaches when it comes to creating appropriate environments is to resist the temptation to take something we see professional coaches doing with professional athletes and think we can use that with our own kids. Perhaps we can modify it, but it is very easy to take snippets we see on television or a coaching clinic and then add them into our sessions without understanding context. Sometimes it works, but often it is too complex to be effective. For decades, we have done this with the size of our competitions, by playing eleven vs. eleven soccer or full ice hockey with very young children. We add in complex rules and then get frustrated when the children don't space out appropriately or understand things like offsides or zone defenses.

"When kids play eleven vs. eleven on a big pitch and you film the whole game with a drone, you will see that they never play on the whole field," says Van Der Haegen from Belgium. "All eleven players are never involved. So they will also play on a zone that's much smaller and where about six, seven players are involved. And if you then check how few times many players touch the ball, then you will understand why a lot of players won't develop because you can't develop if you don't touch the ball. Because if that were the case, you should be able to develop by playing PlayStation."

Challenge yourself to create age-and-stage appropriate practices and advocate that your competitions are appropriate for the age and ability of your players. Also, take notice that there is a range of ages per stage as different children grow and develop at different times. Not all twelve-year-olds are created equal, if you know what I mean. When my daughter was ten, for example, she played basketball in a local league. The team that practiced before us was two years younger and shot on modified-height baskets. My daughter and her teammates would show up and start shooting, and I would observe good technique and a decent success rate. Then, sadly, the modified baskets would be removed because someone had decided that girls in fifth grade needed to use ten-foot-high rims. All of a sudden, shooting technique went out the window and was replaced with two-handed heaves as the girls struggled to even reach the rim with their shots. Success rates plunged, and all I thought to myself was, *Is the person running this league even watching these girls play?* The answer was probably not. Because if he was and he cared about the kids, there was no way he would allow them to keep playing on full-size courts and hoops. Were *some* ten-year-olds capable of shooting on those full-height baskets? Of course they were. But not the *majority* of them, especially the ones who were less physically developed. We must put a stop to this.

Let the Game Be the Teacher:
A Whole-Part-Whole Approach to Practice

When I began my soccer coaching journey, I was frustrated by the way US Soccer instructed coaches to build their practices. We were told to start small, one child or two per ball, and then build to larger, more complex activities before finishing with a game. I tried this at first, but I found that it looked great on paper but did not work in the real world. If you have ever coached young children, you know what I mean. They don't all show up on time. They show up in various states of readiness. They do not need a warm up. And if you start with a small activity that needs lots of explaining, as each subsequent child shows up, you end up explaining the activity multiple times. The kids who show up late have little incentive to hurry across the parking lot as they certainly did not sign up to stand in lines. They showed up to play.

I have always believed that a whole-part-whole approach or, as it is sometimes called, play-practice-play, is a far better method—especially for children twelve and under. Whole-part-whole essentially means to let them play a game first, break it down to a teachable component in the middle, and play again at the end. This solves multiple issues. First, it does not matter when kids arrive as you only need two to get your first game started. Once your numbers get big, you can break into multiple games. Children tend to run across the parking lot and harass their parents to get them to training on time when you play first. And, playing first does wonders to work off the excess energy that tends to come along with young children who have been sitting in a classroom all day and were handed a sugary snack on the drive to training. Plus, they signed up to play the game, and it's easy to make sure that they get plenty of game time when they start and end with some sort of game.

There are those that disagree with this approach, arguing that you have to start small and build to larger concepts, but that line of thinking demonstrates a misunderstanding of the difference between technique and skill as we discussed in the last chapter. This is not to say that we cannot use breaks in the action to do some fundamental movement or stability exercises or a few reps of an isolated technique, but they can be interleaved with the games. You can also modify games, such as attacking and defending multiple goals or altering the shape and size of the field. And you can also do some coaching during these early games, focusing on the theme of your training session so that you are already drawing attention to the topics you are going to cover that day.

Thankfully, US Soccer and many other sporting governing bodies are now recommending a whole–part–whole approach to practices, especially for our youngest athletes. As children get older, they certainly need more movement and flexibility/stability in the beginning of training in order to prevent injury, but even professional soccer players play rondos, and basketball players do shootaround activities, albeit not at full speed. Just think about it this way: the kids are there to play, and the more playing you do, the more engaged they will be. The game is a wonderful teacher.

The Role of Free Play

Ted Kroeten is on to something in St. Paul, Minnesota, and you can tell from the smiles on the faces of the hundreds of kids frolicking around the facility run by Kroeten's organization Joy of the People (www. JoyOfThePeople.org). Some of the children are playing a competitive soccer game on an indoor turf field while others have quite a match on an inflatable field with bouncy walls. Older children are intermingled with younger ones, "teaching" them how to play, dominating the games but not in a way that discourages the younger kids from participating. Joy of the People is all about free play, and Kroeten has found that many children, sadly, no longer know how to get a pick-up game going.

Kroeten is a highly experienced soccer coach and player, and when he started Joy of the People, he thought he would squeeze in time for free play amongst all the skill training and deliberate practice. Luckily his board of directors forced him to prioritize play. Over the past decade, he has seen his first participants grow into incredibly skillful and creative players, with a group of U19s recently winning the National Championships in futsal. He has seen players leave his program for more formal clubs and quickly return because they have lost the freedom to improvise and be creative. He has seen children raised in more structured environments come to Joy of the People and, at first, struggle with the lack of rules, discipline, and adult instruction. Over time, though, he has seen the smile return to their faces as they start playing with joy again.

We hear a lot in sports about the importance of deliberate practice: focused improvement through repetitive activity, continual feedback, and correction and the delay of immediate gratification in pursuit of long-term goals. What has gotten lost for so many children, especially with the demise of the neighborhood pick-up game and the overscheduling of our children, is simple play. Researcher Jean Cote calls this *deliberate play*, which he defines as "activities such as backyard soccer or street basketball that are regulated by age-adapted rules and are set up and monitored by the children or adults engaged in the activity. These activities are intrinsically motivating, provide immediate gratification, and are specifically designed to maximize enjoyment."

Play instills a passion and a love of sport. Play builds all-around athleticism. Perhaps most important, play stimulates brain development. It hastens the growth of the brain centers that regulate emotion and control both attention and behavior. Play inspires thinking and adaptation, promoting creative problem-solving and conflict resolution. It allows children to build their own games, define their own rules, and develop the cognitive skills that are needed, not only for athletics but also for every aspect of life.[3]

In a recent conversation with Kroeten, we got off on a fascinating tangent around creativity and play. Kroeten introduced me to the work of Stephen Krashen and his research on language acquisition. Krashen has found that there are two phases of language learning, acquisition and structure. In the acquisition phase, where learners get a variety of comprehensible input through being immersed in the language or through music and media, the learners gain fluency. Learning is unconscious. Once structure is added and the learners are taught about rules, laws, skills, and techniques, learning becomes conscious. The learners gain accuracy, but the acquisition basically stops. Kroeten equates this to how players learn a dynamic game such as soccer. During the acquisition phase, we want to provide the least amount of structure as possible so the learner will create, try new things, and play without fear of making a

mistake. Later, when we add structure, we can bring about accuracy.

The problem is, we all too often focus on structure and accuracy first and then try to coach the creativity back into them later on. It does not work. "When we teach youth sports in this country, we pretty much focus on the rules, laws, skills, and techniques," says Kroeten, "and we don't give any time to the joy and love of play. Only in acquisition can we really improve and become fluent. What we have seen is that when kids move out of acquisition to a local super club, they seem to plateau. They have not put enough time in acquisition."

Kroeten is not opposed to coaching and structure but believes we need more time to let the kids play before adding too much structure and accuracy to their games. In his research, most of the best players have had a lengthy acquisition phase before they have added extensive structure. And that is why we need to create an environment where kids can simply play, both within our practices and by being encouraged to pick up a ball outside of practice. "Acquisition builds fluency, and structure builds accuracy," says Kroeten.

"When they are kids, they just want to play," concludes Kroeten. "They don't want reviews. They don't want rewards. If a competitive game is too much, they will naturally drop down a level to a less competitive place." As the kids get older, they still want fun, but fun changes. It becomes doing the things that they are good at. Yet what Kroeten has also discovered is that when we introduce free play, it can only have one goal: enjoyment. "If you try to do free play to improve and get better, it will not work," says Kroeten. "It can only be for one reason, and that is enjoyment. You have to let go of performance in order to really grow from play, and once you do that, when you go into a performance, you do very well. In that performance you are now playing the game instead of fighting or working the game."[4]

Our society has devalued play to such an extent that many children no longer value it anymore. This is incredibly sad. I meet many children who struggle to organize a pick-up game or select teams, set up a game, and play. I have tried to run "Free-Play Fridays" at different organizations, and attendance is generally poor. If I run "Skill Development Fridays," they are packed. We have lost sight of the tremendous value of free play, and we need more situations where coaches provide a safe environment but then step back and let the kids enjoy themselves. We need more organizations to educate their parents on the value of these environments. We need fluency before accuracy, and that comes through free play.

Golden Threads and CARDS: Two Great Approaches to Training Design

Our job as coaches, especially youth coaches, is to prepare our athletes for the future of our sport, not necessarily the present. For some children, the future might simply be to get them to come back next week or next season. If we are working in a high-performance sport and our athletes are identified as potential international or professional performers, we are preparing today's twelve-year-olds for the game ten years from now, not for the game today. And as we know, sport is constantly changing, with tactics, strategies, sport science, and psychology always evolving and pushing the boundaries of sport. The question we then face as coaches is this one: how can I prepare today's young athletes for tomorrow's reality if I do not even know what that is?

Two organizations out of the UK have come up with unique ways to think about and design engaging practices that keep your players coming back and speed up mastery. Both provide us with examples to follow when designing our own sessions. The first of these was designed by Great Britain Field Hockey, and they call it the Golden Thread. The goal of the Golden Thread is to provide hockey coaches with a framework of the essential elements of a great practice session, and its application goes far beyond field hockey. They believe that fun, game-like activities are a far better tool than endless repetition of technical drills. The goals for each child in a session are

- To feel involved;
- To have lots of touches of the ball and play small-sided games;
- To score lots of goals, achieve tasks, and increase fun and enjoyment;
- To understand winning isn't crucial, to let everyone play; and
- To adhere to simple rules.

In order to accomplish this, the Golden Thread advises coaches that each session contain the following five elements:

- Lots of fun
- Loads of touches
- Stretch (operating on the edge of their comfort zone)
- Constant decision-making
- Looks like the game

Coaches are advised to be positive and encouraging, create an enjoyable and relaxed atmosphere for the players, and incorporate these five elements.[5] This may seem obvious, but think back to many practices you participated in as a young athlete. Think about many sessions you have witnessed—or perhaps even ran as a coach. Were these elements an integral part of the session, or did you have more important stuff to do?

Remember above, when I wrote we are developing players for a game that will be played ten years from now, not simply this weekend? This was the reality that the England Rugby Union high-performance staff faced in 2011 as they plotted the future of the sport in the UK. The working group included sport scientists, psychologists, and coaches, such as Head Coach Stuart Lancaster and U18 Head Coach John Fletcher. They were tasked with identifying and developing players for a way of playing that might not even exist today. They needed to build adaptable players who possessed skills and behaviors and were ready for whatever the game threw their way. In the words of Fletcher,

"We tried to future-proof the game." The approach they came up with is now known as CARDS and has taken hold not only in rugby but across many sports in the United Kingdom as well. I believe it is a very relevant way to look at your own practice planning as it provides five essential elements that are not only desirable in today's player but will also be desirable in the future as well.

In order to prepare for both the present and the future of the game, the England Rugby Union staff identified five characteristics that every player should possess and every coach should work to develop:

- Creativity
- Awareness
- Resilience
- Decision making
- Self-organization

"The best environment I have seen for player development is the playground," says Fletcher who, along with his former England assistant coach Russell Earnshaw, now runs a mentorship group for coaches called the Magic Academy where they stress a creative, child-focused approach to learning.[6] "On the playground there are never blowout games; the kids reshuffle the teams and make it competitive. There is a lot of inclusion, and there is a lot of exploration. Coaches have to be comfortable with that and understand that a lot of learning happens when things do not go well."

Regardless of how the sport evolves, Fletcher and Earnshaw are convinced that players who possess the qualities outlined in CARDS will be prepared for the game. They will be problem solvers, capable of doing the unexpected, fearless, and resilient in the face of adversity. They will be adaptable when tactics and strategy change and capable of adjusting to an opponent during a match. "The CARDS approach," says Fletcher, "gives every conversation about player development an anchor."

Earnshaw elaborates on that point. "It has also liberated coaches in a way," he says. "I am sure you have seen coaches become overwhelmed with the technical and tactical—other people's anchors—but this approach gives you more freedom and lets the players take more responsibility. Plus, coaches have to model it, so we have to be creative and develop ourselves as well."

I have found in my own coaching that taking this CARDS approach has been very helpful in my practice design. I can look for and allow space for players to organize activities and positions and come up with solutions for problems. They are given time to push through moments of stretch and difficulty, and players are allowed to learn through creative successes and failures. Each session is a blending of these skills and an opportunity for coaches to look for CARDS behaviors. "We still have our principles of how we want to play," says Fletcher, "and then we have CARDS, which are the skills and behaviors we feel are most important. We don't do them in isolation. We blend them together and reward these behaviors, and each player might have a specific behavior that they are focused on that day."

Activities for Designing Better Practices

Start a Coaching Journal with All of Your Sessions

Develop the habit of recording your training sessions in a journal or online resource where you can reflect on each session immediately afterwards. Ask the following questions when designing your training sessions:

- How do we want to play?
- What are my learning objectives for this session to build toward how we want to play?
- What activities do I need to use to accomplish this?
- How can I organize it and teach it so my players will love it?

- How can I integrate our team values into this session so I can tie it to our higher purpose?

At the end of each session, record your answers to the following questions:

- Did we accomplish our objective today?
- Were the activities appropriate and organized, or should I have used different ones?
- Did the players have a great time and train hard?
- Did we talk about our values and how they drive performance?

Use your journal to map development and refer back to it to make sure you have covered relevant topics and to remember how your athletes responded to those sessions. My training journals are some of my most effective tools I have in player development.

Use a Whole-Part-Whole Approach to Session Design

Especially when working with younger children, let them play first, teach a concept, and then relate that concept back to a final game. Make sure most of your session looks like the game.

Find Days for Free Play

Remember the goal of free play is enjoyment, so learn to step back and let them play. This is where you will see a lot of the CARDS behaviors emerge.

Grab Some Coaching Challenge Cards from the Magic Academy

This is an actual deck of challenge cards, and a coach can select one before the session and be challenged to coach creatively. It might say, "Make only three coaching points the entire practice" or "Video/mic yourself for training and observe what you learn." The deck has challenges for before, during, and after sessions and can definitely get you out of your comfort zone. They even have challenge cards for your players as well. Check them out at www.themagicacademy.co.uk/.

Summary

Surfing the internet and observing top coaches working can be a great place to gather materials for our own coaching sessions—but not always. If we want to run evidence-based, engaging sessions that develop our athletes and keep them coming back for more, our practices must have the following characteristics:

- They must be age-and-ability appropriate for the athletes we are working with. Your country and your sport likely has a long-term athlete development model that is based upon research and best principles of coaching. Start there and build your sessions appropriately.

- They must develop the type of characteristics that are desirable, not only in today's athlete but also for the athlete of the future. To do that, use the Golden Thread to be sure your session has the right components and take a CARDS approach to make sure every session includes opportunities to develop creativity, awareness, resilience, decision-making, and self-organization.

- And finally, don't forget what it was like to be a young athlete. You signed up to play the game, not stand in line. So, take a look at the whole-part-whole approach and create the time and space for free play. I believe you will find that it is a far better method for creating engaging, athlete-centered sessions.

Remember, it does not matter how good your practice looks on paper if it is lousy on grass. So, create dynamic, engaging training environments for your athletes, and they will be begging to come back for more.

LESSON 6

"WIN THE DAY"

Don't Show Up to Win; Show Up to Compete

Champions behave like champions before they're champions: they have a winning standard of performance before they are winners.

—BILL WALSH

What we can do as coaches is just love our players, have them compete as hard as humanly possible, and have joy in the process.

—CINDY TIMCHAL

The year was 1995, and Cindy Timchal knew a little something was missing from her Maryland Terps women's lacrosse program. Timchal had already established her reputation as a top coach at Northwestern University, and in 1992, her second year as head coach at Maryland, the Terps had won the second NCAA title in program history. They had come agonizingly close in subsequent years to winning another title, and Timchal knew that to become more than a one-time champion, something had to change. That something was not simply wanting to win a championship. Everyone they played wanted to win. They needed a competitive advantage, an identity and a way of doing things day after day that led to continual improvement and an edge that would see them through any situation. They had to take the focus off winning a title and turn it to something that would be within their control. They had to start, in her words, "Winning the day."

"You don't become a championship player or team simply by wanting to win," says Timchal, who currently coaches at the United States Naval Academy. "You step out onto the field every single day that you have an opportunity to practice and get better to win the day and to play as champions. When the whistle blew, we wanted to win, but it was more than that. We wanted to really prove how hard we work, how tough we are, how much we work together, and how much we love each other. And by doing that, the scoreboard should reflect all that love that we have for each other on the field."

Timchal, along with her assistant coach Gary Gait and sports psychologist Dr. Jerry Lynch, knew that they needed to find a way to compete every single day at every single moment. They knew that winning would be a byproduct of these marginal gains, compounded daily, and if they could create that type of culture and recruit players who would thrive in such a competitive atmosphere, the wins would take care of themselves. Their own practices needed to be the most competitive part of the week. Their own scrimmages needed to be the toughest games they played all season. They could not rely on their opponents to raise the bar; they had to raise it in house.

And raise the bar they did. From 1995 to 2001, the Maryland Terps women's lacrosse program won every single NCAA Championship, tying John Wooden's Division I record for consecutive championships at seven. "It's tough work, holding people accountable," says Timchal. "Holding your own teammates accountable isn't easy. It's not easy to demand of each other. We get players to buy in to the culture, how hard they work, and for something that is far greater than themselves. We may come up short. But we, in our hearts, know that we've put it all out on the line and given it all we've got, so we can walk away feeling like okay, no regrets. There's zero regrets when you create a culture of giving to each other."

Timchal and her staff raised the bar by creating a "win the day" culture in the Maryland lacrosse program, one she has since replicated at the Naval Academy, which in 2017 became the first female team from a service academy to reach an NCAA Final Four. To date she has over five hundred wins and eight NCAA titles. She creates a culture that sets high daily standards and forces players to show up focused, engaged, and ready to compete. There is a high level of technical and tactical knowledge being passed on, without question. But there is something much more than that. They show up to compete, while others show up to win. And that makes a huge difference.

This chapter is all about creating a competitive, "win the day" culture in your program. To do so, we will cover three basic principles:

- Don't show up to win; show up to compete
- *Sisu*, the Finnish word for continuing to act in the face of repeated failures and extreme odds
- *Kaizen*, the principle of marginal gains and continuous improvement

Here we go!

Don't Show Up to Win; Show Up to Compete

In a 2009 story in *Esquire* magazine, then USC Football coach Pete Carroll was asked about his unorthodox energy and way of coaching. He told a crowd of program supporters that after being fired by the New England Patriots in 1999, he decided to study legendary UCLA basketball coach John Wooden. Wooden, of course, is known for being the quintessential winner, but he didn't win his first championship until his sixteenth year of coaching. That's when it hit Carroll. "It hit me just like I got punched right in the forehead! Once (Wooden) got it, he just nailed it. Once he figured out what was right for him, how to engineer his program in the way that best exemplified his philosophy, nobody could touch him. He wins nine of the next eleven championships, and then he retires, just goes off into basketball heaven. How beautiful is that?"

Carroll continued, "I asked myself: What is my philosophy? What is my approach? And I came up with the thought that if I was going to describe me, the first thing I'd say is I'm a competitor. Just one simple line: I'm a competitor. That's my whole life since I was three, four years old. I tried to beat my big brother in every game we played. All of his friends would just laugh at how hard I'd try. I'd be fighting and scratching and crying and whatever it took, from the time I was a little kid. Reading Wooden, I realized, if I'm gonna be a competitor, if I'm ever going to do great things, I'm going to have to carry a message that's strong and clear, and nobody's going to miss the point ever about what I'm all about."

Next, Carroll explained to the assembled crowd that he was inspired by Jerry Garcia, front man for the Grateful Dead. "Jerry Garcia said that he didn't want his band to be the best ones doing something. He wanted them to be the only ones doing it. To be all by yourself out there doing something that nobody else can touch—that's the thought that guides me, that guides this program: We're going to do things better than it's ever been done before in everything we do, and we're going to compete our ass off. And we're gonna see how far that takes us."[1]

If there was a way to teach winning, a secret formula, don't you think everyone would teach it? Of course they would. But there is not. What people like Pete Carroll have figured out is that you don't show up to win. You show up to compete every day, and the winning eventually takes care of itself. As Dr. Jerry Lynch and I teach the teams that we work with, those who show up to win are:

- Focused on outcomes;
- Focused on uncontrollables (officials, weather, opponents);
- Tight, tentative, and tense; and
- Lacking confidence because so many things are out of control.

Showing up to win is *not* a performance enhancer. It harms your performance because you lose sight of the process. On the other hand, showing up to compete means a player is

- Focused on the process and all the little things it takes to get better;
- In control of the controllables and responding appropriately to everything as it happens;
- Calm and relaxed; and
- Playing with increased confidence.

Showing up to compete is *the* performance enhancer. It increases confidence because you have turned all your attention onto the things you control and off those things you cannot control. And the more often you show up to compete, the more marginal gains you make.

Sisu and the UNC Competitive Cauldron

In his book *Atomic Habits*, author James Clear recounts the story of the Winter War between Finland and the Soviet Union in 1939 and 1940. On November 30, 1939, the Soviets invaded Finland, dropping bombs on the capital of Helsinki and plunging Finland into World War II. Four hundred and fifty thousand troops marched upon the Finnish border, and six thousand tanks and four thousand planes bore down upon the vastly outnumbered and outgunned Finns. But while the Finns only had thirty-two tanks and 114 aircraft, they had something the Soviets did not: *Sisu*.

As Clear writes, "*Sisu* is a word that has no direct translation, but it refers to the idea of continuing to act even in the face of repeated failures and extreme odds. It is a way of living life by displaying perseverance even when you have reached the end of your mental and physical capacities … It is a type of mental toughness that allows you to bear the burden of your responsibilities, whatever they happen to be, with a will and perseverance that is unbreakable. It is the ability to sustain your action and fight against extreme odds. *Sisu* extends beyond perseverance. It is what you rely on when you feel like you have nothing left."

Fighting in brutally cold temperatures and outnumbered nearly three to one, the Finns wore down the Soviets, who, by March of 1940, had suffered three hundred and fifty thousand casualties, forcing them to sign the Moscow Peace Treaty, ending their advance against Finland. "We will all face moments when our physical and mental resources feel tapped out," writes Clear. "There will always be times when we are hammered with failure after failure and are called to find a fire within. And perhaps even more frequently, there will be many moments when we want to achieve something, but it feels as if we face incredibly long odds. In those moments, you have to call on your *Sisu*."[2]

I love this concept of *Sisu* as it applies to creating a "win the day" culture. How many of our teams want to achieve something great, but we face extremely long odds? That happens all the time. Everyone wants to win at game time on Saturday. But does your team want to win and do the things it takes to be successful six months prior to Saturday, to show up again and again and create such a high standard that the results take care of themselves? This is when we have to find that fire within and create a place where, even on their bad days, our athletes are still competing at a very high level.

The University of North Carolina women's soccer program has their own version of *Sisu*. They call it the competitive cauldron, and it has led to unprecedented success. Under Head Coach Anson Dorrance, the Tar Heels women's soccer program has won twenty-two overall national titles and twenty-one NCAA Championships. His teams have won over one thousand games, and many of his former players are amongst a who's who of women's soccer history. But to understand the true legacy of excellence Dorrance has established at North Carolina, one only needs to read a quote from another all-time great coach. In an interview with *Football News Magazine* in 1997 about UNC football's top-ranking, legendary UNC Basketball Coach Dean Smith was asked what it was like having another UNC program other than basketball ranked number one. "This is a women's soccer school," said Smith. "We are just trying to keep up with them."

At UNC, Dorrance and his team of coaches and graduate assistants make everything competitive and record the results of every activity, from one versus one games to fitness tests and full-field scrimmages. Everything is posted on a bulletin board for everyone to see. There is no hiding in the UNC women's soccer competitive cauldron. One way Dorrance has found to up the ante is by creating competition among what he calls the "small societies" in a team.

"I went on a tour of this fabulous facility in Argentina," Dorrance told me. "One of my favorite moments on the tour was to go through their main lobby area, and they had a great world championship coach by the name of Cesar Luis Menotti, and they had a quote from him that said the greatest teams in the world are teams where the field is riddled with collections of small societies. I asked my interpreter what this meant, and he was telling me that the way you form a great team is by the relationships that each of the people on the field have with each other."

Dorrance loved this idea and seeks to build those relationships by creating competitions between the small societies on his teams. "The left side of my team will play the right side of my team. The front line will play against the defense. We pair offensive midfielders with their defensive midfield counterparts. You can set up all these battles where you're forming these societies, and, for us, the chemistry between all these different platforms and small groups can have the biggest impact on our success on the field."

One of the greatest representatives of the competitive culture Dorrance seeks to create at Carolina was April Heinrichs. The 1986 graduate was a two-time national player of the year and also captained the US Women to the 1991 World Cup Championship. She later coached the US Women to the 2004 Olympic gold medal. The thing about Heinrichs that Dorrance loved was her competitive nature. "April Heinrichs, for me, was the consummate competitor, and I loved her," gushed Dorrance. "I loved everything about the way she competed. She competed without remorse, and that was the culture I wanted to build, basically collections of Heinrichs just competing like there's no tomorrow, which improves everyone." This is the key for Dorrance. When Heinrichs was a freshman at UNC, some of the upperclassmen complained that she was relentless and wondered what he was going to do about competitive nature. In Dorrance's mind, he had an idea. "All I was thinking was, *What are we going to do about her? How about we clone her!*"

Dorrance also realized that in order to create a culture of relentless competitors, he also had to protect a player like Heinrichs. "I always pointed to her as an example of the way I wanted all of them to compete. If we value the competitive firebrand of a player, then we have to protect them because they're not going to be the players that are going to be universally embraced in most cultures. We have to protect these extraordinary competitors and then try to get the culture to be more like them. My model in those early environments when we were shaping the US national team was Heinrichs because she was ruthless in the most positive way. She wanted to win everything. It wasn't like there was a huge talent disparity between her and everyone else. We had some phenomenal players back then, but the quality that she brought every single time was she was going to win, and then all of a sudden you have these collisions between all of these great competitive personalities."

Timchal has had her share of Heinrich-type competitors over the years and continues to create the "win the day" mentality at the US Naval Academy. Timchal uses what she calls the "never, nevers," a concept that she and Lynch came up with years ago and he wrote about in his recent book aptly titled *Win the Day*. The "never, nevers" are as follows:

- Never give up, no matter what the score or situation.
- Never lose confidence by focusing on outcomes. Focus on controllables instead.
- Never let an opponent defeat your spirit, identity, or culture.
- Never be afraid of mistakes or losing as they are the greatest teachers.
- Never try to go too big; instead, do all the little things well over and over.
- Never fail to respond to a mistake with IPR (immediate, positive response).
- Never whine or create drama unnecessarily.[3]

"Win the Day," writes Lynch, "means coaches and athletes control what they can and let go of outcomes and results ... it is about the physical, emotional, spiritual, and mental preparation and doing the little important things brilliantly in the present moment, rather than the big things marginally in the future. It's all about 'what's important now' (WIN)."[4]

Kaizen and the Aggregation of Marginal Gains

In August 2004, the New Zealand All Blacks rugby team was down and out, thrashed by South Africa forty to twenty-six and reeling from their elimination from the TriNations Tournament championship. The team management, along with leading players Richie McCaw and Tana Umaga, settled into a three-day leadership meeting to right the ship. They did not discuss tactics and technique so much as they discussed the culture of the All Blacks and the need to put a stop to the excessive drinking and partying that was dragging the group down. The three-day meeting was later called by coach Graham Henry the most important three days of his career, for in those three days the group was specifically talking about a word that would lead to a period of unmatched success in world sport: *kaizen*.

The word *kaizen* is a Japanese word for "change for the better" and has become synonymous with the idea of continuous improvement. For the All Blacks, "Kiwi Kaizen" was the relentless pursuit of getting 1 percent better in one hundred different ways. From sleep to nutrition to how they select players and whom they invite into their culture, the All Blacks recognized that pursuing small gains in many areas would compound over time. They recognized that fighting back the instinctual drive to focus on outcomes and to be completely focused upon the process instead was the path to righting the ship.

Finally, they recognized that doing all the little things day after day, month after month, would aggregate. Small improvements are not necessarily noticeable on the day or over a week, but over time they become big things. By the same token, taking it a bit easy one day or training without focus or intensity will not break your team. But over time, those 1 percent declines start to add up as well, and pretty soon there is a massive gap between those who sought 1 percent improvement daily and those who allowed themselves to be less than the best version of themselves.

This is what we mean when we speak about the aggregation of marginal gains. In the words of author James Kerr, "Marginal gains are 100 things done 1 percent better to deliver cumulative competitive advantage." So, how have those marginal gains worked for the All Blacks? Since 2004, they have become the first ever back-to-back World Cup champions (2011 and 2015) and won 92 percent of their games heading into the 2019 World Cup, where they fell in the semifinals. *Kaizen* makes a difference.

The idea of marginal gains has become a popular one lately. It is all about accountability and the willingness of coaches and teammates to hold everyone accountable to the same standards that drive those 1 percent gains. Many people do not like to be held accountable or called out when they are not bringing 100 percent focus or effort. But when you don't make those tough coaching decisions or you look the other way, it sends a message. That which you don't condemn you condone. And people take notice when you let your best player give less than his very best or choose not to call out a top performer for a poor attitude. Changing behavior and making marginal gains is not easy, and it takes a lot of time. That is why the quickest way to do it, and the only way to do it, is to do it every day.

Activities to Establish a Competitive Culture in Your Program

Use Shorter Duration, Higher Intensity Activities

One of the things many of the top coaches I have spoken to have told me is that far too many teams go too easy on the hard days and too hard on the easy days. When they are recovering post competition, perhaps practice should be at a 50 percent maximum physical exertion as your marginal gains that day are to rebuild muscle and prepare for the hard days ahead. When they are fully recovered and three or four days out from a match, training should probably be 100 percent exertion if you are going to stretch your athletes physically and technically. Yet too many teams don't go all out on the hard days and go too hard on the easy ones. And pretty soon, every day turns into a 75 percent exertion, which is not a way to optimize performance. You never train at a high enough intensity to truly improve, and you never train at a low enough level to recover. You coast along, never stretching and never fully recovering, and eventually those who do it right pass you by.

In the fall of 2018, I conducted a coaching clinic with Garga Caserta, the strength and conditioning coach for the Portland Thorns of the National Women's Soccer League. The Thorns were the 2017 league champions and in 2018 fell in the championship game. One of the secrets to their success and continuous improvement, believes Caserta, has been shorter duration of higher intensity activities. When Head Coach Mark Parsons was hired in 2015, he sat down with Caserta and showed him video clips of how he wanted to play. They were clips of a high tempo, high pressing style that would require a high level of fitness and athleticism. Parsons also knew that you could not roll out a ball and play eleven vs. eleven for sixty minutes on day one and expect that level of intensity. So, they started small.

Their first full-sided matches of pre-season would last four minutes. Four minutes! But in those four minutes, Parsons would demand a level of intensity that was extremely high. Once they could play at the requisite level, they would stretch the games to five minutes and so on. Now, of course, a ninety-minute soccer game has ebbs and flows, and you cannot play at the same intensity level for ninety minutes as you can for four, but the idea was that he wanted them to feel what their highest level of exertion felt like. He wanted to stretch them and ensure they did not hold back. Play four minutes the right way and you earn the right to play five. Play intensely for five minutes and you earn the right to play six. I have found this to be a very effective way to up the intensity level of my practices: short durations of high intensity games. When players know that games are not infinite, it creates urgency and effort.

Play "Last Goal Wins"

I also like to play games where it's "last goal wins." That way, even if a team is up two or three goals, they cannot just coast to the finish line, and the team that is losing still has a chance to pull it out. This creates situations where winning groups learn how to manage a game and see it out, and losing teams learn how to throw numbers forward and fight till the end. Throw in a couple of iffy "refereeing" calls from the coach as well and you can create more game-like adversity and intensity as well.

Establish Your Team Values and Your "Never, Nevers"

Come up with your own list of "never, nevers," similar to Navy lacrosse, and build team values and a culture that promotes relentless competitiveness (see lesson 13 for more on this).

Summary

If you are going to take your athletes to a place they have never been before and won't get to on their own, then you are going to have to create a culture and an environment where they are going to compete like crazy, just as coaches such as Pete Carroll, Cindy Timchal, and Anson Dorrance have. To do so, try the following:

- Don't show up to win; show up to compete and let the winning happen by itself.
- Teach them about *sisu* and the need to be unrelenting, even in the face of extreme obstacles.
- Establish your own "never, nevers" for your program.
- Teach them about *kaizen* and how continuous, small improvements add up over time into huge gains.
- Start small and compete at a very high intensity over short periods of time, gradually building the length of those activities once your athletes are able to compete at the requisite level.
- Manipulate the games and add adversity through bad officiating decisions or "last goal wins" games to keep them competing until the end.
- Ensure your team goes hard enough on the hard days and easy enough on the easy days.

If you want your team and your athletes to compete successfully on game day, then they must compete like crazy in training. Help them consolidate around an identity that makes practice their hardest days of the week. Compete like crazy, and see where that takes you.

LESSON 7

―――――

"MAKE YOUR ATHLETES FEEL INVALUABLE, EVEN IF THEY ARE NOT THE MOST VALUABLE"

Create a Positive, Inclusive Environment

Many coaches look at children as empty vessels needing to be filled instead of young people with amazing potential and intelligence to be stimulated and tapped into.

―HORST WEIN

A great coach can make his or her athletes feel invaluable without them being most valuable.

―ORIGINAL SOURCE UNKNOWN

om Farrey has been around the world a few times covering sports. As a reporter for ESPN and the author of *Game On: The All-American Race to Make Champions of Our Children*, he has covered sports on all levels, from Pop Warner to the professional ranks. He helped create *ESPN.com*, appeared on multiple award-winning broadcasts of *Outside the Lines*, and has won two Emmy awards for his work. But perhaps no work he has ever undertaken is more important than the initiative he started in 2013: Project Play.

Project Play is a program sponsored by the Aspen Institute's Sport and Society initiative, and Farrey is the executive director. Its aim is to bring together leaders and create resources to reinvigorate community sports and provide access to quality sporting activities to all children, regardless of age, ability, and financial means. Their work has moved the needle in a few short years and brought together luminaries such as Michelle Obama, Kobe Bryant, Billie Jean King, and organizations such as Nike, the US Olympic Committee, nearly every sport governing body, and other leaders in the athletic space. The goal is to reimagine youth sports, specifically for children age twelve and under.

Through countless trips, numerous panels and meetings, and multiple national conferences, Farrey and Project Play have highlighted the need for major reform in youth sport, yet he still felt something was missing. He was looking for a true model program or, better yet, a country that was doing it right. He travelled to Australia, Canada, France, Germany, Cuba, China—you name it—and still they all fell a bit short. Then, in early 2019, Farrey went to Norway.

"Imagine a society in which 93 percent of children grow up playing organized sports," wrote Farrey in an article in April 2019 for *The New York Times*.[1] "Where costs are low, the economic barriers to entry few, travel teams aren't formed until the teenage years—and where adults don't start sorting the weak from the strong until children have grown into their bodies and interests. Then, the most promising talents become the most competitive athletes in the world, on a per-capita basis." It sounds like a utopia—and a far cry from the youth sport system many of us are familiar with. But that is what is happening today in Norway.

Farrey's trip was inspired by Norway's performance at the 2018 Winter Olympics in South Korea, where the nation of only 5.3 million people won thirty-nine medals, more than any other country in the history of the Winter Olympics (for perspective, the USA finished fourth in the medal count with twenty-four). How was it that such a small nation could produce such extraordinary results on the biggest stage? What Farrey found was that competitive success starts at home, on the community level, with a simple philosophy: "Joy of Sport for All."

In 1987, Norway issued an eight-page document called "Children's Rights in Sport" that has been transformative from a philosophical perspective. The document outlines the qualities of the exceptional sports experience that every child is entitled to, from safe environments to interpersonal connection to a strong voice in what their activities look like. It even states that children "must be granted opportunities in the planning and execution of their own sport activities." The document also describes what is not allowed, such as national championships before the age of thirteen, regional championships prior to eleven, and the publication of standings and scores for young children. It is a necessary guideline in a country with such a small population as they cannot afford to lose any athletes because the sport experience is a lousy one.

"It's impossible to say at eight or ten or twelve who is going to be talented in school or sport," said Inge Andersen to Farrey. Andersen is the former secretary general of the Norwegian Sports Confederation. "That takes another ten years. Our priority is the child becoming self-reflective about their bodies and minds." He continued, "We believe the motivation of children in sport is much more important than that of the parent or coach. We're a small country and can't afford to lose them because sport is not fun."

What a novel concept Norway is pursuing. In most countries, we treat children in sport as a basket of eggs; we throw them all against the high-performance wall and hope a few don't crack. We create boundaries to entry and commitments at very young ages that make sport unaffordable and unsustainable for many. In the process, we have created a sixteen-billion-dollar industry in American youth sports alone. The system is a meritocracy and is not designed to meet the needs of the child in sport but to meet the needs of the business of sport.[2] Yet countries like Norway, Finland, and Iceland are pursuing pathways designed to keep as many kids in sport for as long as possible in the best environment possible. And they do this by serving the needs of the athletes first.

In this chapter, we are going to discuss how to keep children and young adults in sports by making them all feel valued, even if they are not the MVP of the team. To do so, we will cover

- Why children play sports;
- How early sport specialization drives children out of sports;
- The need for patience in talent identification;
- How to "catch them being good";
- Winning the race to the right finish line; and
- A few activities to help you make everyone on your team feel valued.

Let's get started.

Why Children Play Sports

There have been quite a few studies around children's participation in sports, but one of the most interesting is a 2014 study by Amanda Visek from George Washington University.[3] In her survey of hundreds of athletes in the Washington DC area, many of them multi-sport and ranging in age from seven to eighteen, she asked them, "Why do you play sports?" As expected, their answer, nine times out of ten, was, "It's fun!" Then Visek took it a step further and asked the children to define fun. They came up with eighty-one characteristics of fun, which Visek labeled the "Fun Determinants." Here are the top six:

1. Trying your best
2. When the coach treats the athlete with respect
3. Getting playing time

4. Playing well together as a team
5. Getting along with your teammates
6. Exercising and being active

Further down the list of fun determinants we find a few items that may shock some coaches and parents:

48. Winning
66. Practicing with specialty trainers and coaches
67. Getting trophies and medals
73. Traveling to new places to play
81. Getting team pictures taken

I am quite sure that I have never coached a game where there were forty-seven things more important than winning from my perspective but apparently there are for many of our athletes. I am the first to admit I am a competitive guy, and outcomes matter to me, but certainly a big part of my evolution as a coach has been to focus more on the needs of "who is in front of me," as we spoke about previously. And to do that, we have to know what makes it fun. Luckily for us, Visek made it easy, and we don't have to remember eighty-one items.

The next step of her research was what she refers to as the Halloween analogy. "I asked the kids what they do after they trick or treat," said Visek, "and they said, 'We come home and sort our candy into piles of similar things.'" She handed the study participants eighty-one laminated cards with each of the fun determinants on them and asked them to sort them into piles, just like they would with their candy. She called these piles the "fun factors" and there were eleven of them, listed below in order of importance to the children:

1. Positive team dynamics
2. Trying hard

3. Positive coaching
4. Learning and improving
5. Game time support
6. Games
7. Practice
8. Team friendships
9. Mental bonuses
10. Team rituals
11. Swag (gear)

Look at those first three again: positive team dynamics, trying hard, and positive coaching. All three of those, the three most important fun factors, are heavily influenced by the coach. We intentionally build and sustain a positive team environment. We build the competitive cauldron and create challenging, effective practices that encourage athletes to work hard. And, without a doubt, we are 100 percent responsible for positive coaching, for it is up to us to respect and encourage the kids, listen to our players, encourage the team, and allow mistakes to happen. In other words, coaches, we make it fun, and we make it not fun. We must own this.

Now before you say, "I coach older, more competitive athletes; this does not apply to me," please realize that I do not think every athlete at every age and stage defines fun the same way. Without a doubt, an eight-year-old recreational athlete and an eighteen-year-old aspiring Olympian will define fun differently. I have never met a five-year-old who has said to me, "Coach, I am here to grind today!" But I have met many older athletes who love to show up and work their tails off. They might even call it fun. It is important to remember that enjoyment and fun never become irrelevant, regardless of who you are coaching. If you find a joyless team on the professional or collegiate level, you will find a team that is not playing to their potential. If you find a youth team not having any fun for a sustained period, you will find a team of children who will likely soon quit sports. And in my experience, two of the biggest determinants of lack of enjoyment for youth athletes are early sport specialization and outcome-focused, impatient adults. Let's explore both.

The Scourge of Early-Sport Specialization

This is a topic for an entire book, and, in fact, I have covered it before in multiple blog posts and in my 2015 handbook *Is It Wise to Specialize?* In 2019, *New York Times* best-selling author David Epstein explored the topic of specialization—in sports, academics, and life—much more thoroughly in his groundbreaking book *Range: Why Generalists Succeed in a Specialized World*. Both of these books detail how the path toward elite-level performance in dynamic sporting environments points to early sport sampling and later specialization, in spite of the attention given to early specializers such as Tiger Woods. For my purposes here, though, I want to focus on the 99.9 percent, the vast majority of athletes not on the high-performance pathway, many of whom end up burned out, injured, and out of sports by early adolescence if they specialize early.

From a purely physical standpoint, athletes who specialize in a single sport prior to the age of twelve are far more likely to get injured. In a 2015 Loyola University study of twelve thousand youth athletes, Dr Neeru Jayanthi, now working at Emory University, found that early specialization in a single sport is one of the strongest predictors of injury. Athletes in the study who specialized were 70 percent to 93 percent more likely to be injured than children who played multiple sports. Other studies have found that the likelihood of severe injuries, such as ACL tears and Tommy John reconstructive elbow surgeries, are far likelier in children who specialize at a young age. Yet many kids are forced to specialize at a very young age, either by a sport system that is more focused on the business of sport than the needs of the child in sport or by over-eager coaches and parents who force too much, too soon.[4]

Another malady of early specialization is the loss of ownership in an activity. As children are stripped of choices and given year-round schedules and training loads that mimic those of adults, they lose control of the experience. As sport scientist Joe Baker from York University says, the three critical ingredients of long-term sport participation are autonomy, enjoyment, and intrinsic motivation. "In our lab," said Baker, "we look at those things as that currency of skill acquisition. If you don't have those things, then you're not going to be around long enough to see the fruits of your practice." Specialization at too young an age can strip away the autonomy, suck out the enjoyment, and prevent an athlete from ever having enough intrinsic motivation to get out there and practice on her own and to do all the difficult things over time to truly become a high-level performer.

In a nutshell, early specialization should be avoided because it is not necessary for elite performance, and it is potentially harmful. Coaches are responsible for helping parents and fellow coaches understand that winning the race to the right finish line does not always mean getting a head start, as counterintuitive as this might seem. As the British sports scientist and high-performance coach Ian Yates shared with Epstein in *Range*, parents "want their kids doing what Olympians are doing right now, not what the Olympians were doing when they were twelve or thirteen." They want to skip the sports sampling period that helps athletes develop a wide range of athletic abilities and find a sport that fits best, going right to specialization. They want their children to experience sport training ten years before it is necessary and often, at times, when it is harmful. As Epstein concludes, "The sampling period is not incidental to the development of great performers—something to be excised in the interests of a head start—it is integral."[5]

Our Focus on Outcomes and Our Loss of Patience

In 2004, FC Midtjylland in Denmark set out to establish a youth soccer academy. As a new club, it did not have the pick of the litter of Danish soccer talent, which went to bigger, far more established clubs. And as the coaches put together their first youth team, they were short one player. One of those coaches, Rasmus Ankersen, shares the tale of that final player in his book *The Goldmine Effect*.

With the season about to start, the coaches still could not fill that elusive final spot on the roster. They settled on a player none of them wanted, the son of the club's materials manager, on the condition that he pay his own way to play. According to Ankersen, they selected the boy more to ensure that his father would not quit his job than the inkling that he had a future in the game. The boy's name was Simon Kjaer.

Six months after Simon Kjaer took the last roster spot at FC Midt-jylland, the club director collected the eight staff coaches in a room and handed them all a piece of paper. They were asked to list the five current players (out of sixteen on the roster) most likely to advance the furthest in the next five years. The results were then sealed in an envelope and locked away. Five years later, shortly after Kjaer was sold to Palermo for a tidy six-million-dollar transfer fee, those results were opened. Not a single one of the highly qualified coaches even had Kjaer on his list.

In 2010, that last boy picked was a starting center back in Denmark's first game of the World Cup in South Africa against the Netherlands. Since 2004, he has appeared seventy times for Denmark, playing in the 2012 European Championship and the 2018 World Cup, and he played club soccer for Palermo and Roma in Italy, Wolfsburg in Germany, Lille in France, and currently for Sevilla in Spain. Not too shabby for the kid no one wanted at age fifteen.[6]

We can learn a lot from this story and others like it. It is a myth that children develop in a linear fashion. It is messy, and it takes patience to allow athletes to develop on their own schedule. It takes time to ensure that the talent that whispers is allowed to emerge. And it rarely happens when we lose patience with the process and solely focus on the outcomes.

Athlete enjoyment is usually the first thing to diminish when the adults focus on outcomes. Less advanced children get diminished playing time. Fear of making mistakes increases, and space for exploration disappears when a bad giveaway or poor technique leads to a goal against and a bad result. Higher-level tactics are introduced at very young ages as structure breeds accuracy but rarely creativity. This nearly always results in a few more wins in the short term but at what cost?

Catch Them Being Good

When Tony DiCicco passed away at the age of sixty-eight in June of 2017, many of the greatest female soccer players of all time gathered in Connecticut to celebrate the life of a man who had helped elevate not only soccer but women's professional sports as well. Yet that is not why luminaries such as Julie Foudy, Mia Hamm, and Brandi Chastain gathered; they came to celebrate a man who had not only made them better athletes but also better human beings. They came to thank a coach who gave them a voice and ownership in their development and who made them believe in themselves on the world's biggest stage. They came to celebrate a coach who loved his job and brought passion and energy to his coaching, a philosophy that was encapsulated in a book he co-authored with legendary sports psychologist Colleen Hacker: *Catch Them Being Good*.

DiCicco was an All-American goalkeeper at Springfield College and had a five-year stint as a professional soccer player, but he made his biggest mark in the coaching world. He was an assistant coach for the 1991 World Cup Champion US Women's team, and upon becoming head coach, he led the team to the 1996 Olympic gold medal and the 1999 World Cup championship. Along the way, he developed a reputation for giving his players lots of ownership of the training intensity and schedule, as well as instilling in them a belief that they were capable of great things. He also was known for driving and challenging his players like the elite athletes they were but not singling them out and criticizing them publicly. In the words of Mia Hamm, "He coached us like men, but he treated us like women."

In a conversation I had with DiCicco shortly before his passing, he recounted many tales that demonstrated his belief that his players needed to own their development. He discussed how they created a leadership group on his national teams, four to five players beyond the team captains that could deal with team problems and bring any issues they saw to the coaching staff. "They could tell me if we needed to do more fitness, less fitness, if training sessions were good or if they weren't good," said DiCicco. "Maybe we're in an event somewhere overseas, and I would ask, 'Okay, what time is the curfew? You guys want to have it be midnight?' Carla Overbeck or Julie Foudy—national team captains—would probably say, 'No, this is important. Let's have eleven o'clock for this event.' But ultimately, we would say, 'Look, you can question whatever I'm doing, and I'll listen to your arguments, but at the end of the day, me and the coaching staff will make a decision. And once we make that decision, you have to support it.'"

By granting his players ownership, DiCicco and his staff were also able to get more buy-in to the competitive culture they were building. A big part of that culture was the importance of catching the players doing things well. "You try and bite your lip when you see a mistake, but you celebrate something that you see done well like, 'Julie, that was a great run. Because you made that run, you cleared that defender out of that space. That was a great run, a selfless run. Thank you.' When you coach that way, everybody on the field feels good. Conversely, if you're critical, everybody shrinks a little bit. There's going to be times where you have to use the classic coaching style of, 'This was not what I want.' That's fine. But we're never in your face; we're never screaming."

As we continued to talk, DiCicco chuckled. "Listen, I've crossed the line, and I've been negative, but for the most part, I try to build on the positives because it's real fun to coach that way. It's more fun to be coached that way, and I think it's more effective coaching to catch them being good." It also resonates with your players far beyond your time as their coach.

"Tony had a grace in the simple way," Brandi Chastain told *The New York Times* upon DiCicco's passing. "He didn't make things overly complicated. He would come in and say, 'You can do it, you've got this, go get it.' Those words were just enough to make us go, 'Yes, we can.'"[7] Whether you are coaching World Cup stars or youth players just beginning their sporting journey, catching your athletes being good is absolutely critical to give your athletes a sense of well-being and competence.

Winning the Race to the Right Finish Line

Kevin McLaughlin, USA Hockey's director of youth hockey development, was not looking forward to opening his email in January 2009. He knew it was going to be full of angry posts. He knew he and his colleagues at USA Hockey would be accused of destroying the game and taking the toughness out of the sport. He knew that the haters would be out in full force, trying to run the leaders of USA Hockey's youth development team out the door.

Yet McLaughlin, Ken Martel, and the rest of USA Hockey's leadership also knew that in order to survive, grow, and improve, youth hockey needed to change. They needed kids to play cross-ice hockey in order to get more touches, interactions, and enjoyment out of every game. They knew that body checking was not a necessary component of ten-year-old hockey as growing children were more susceptible to injury and less likely to develop skillfully if the game was overly physical. They also knew that there was no need for a twelve and under national champion to be crowned as this title served the egos of the adults watching far more than the needs of the children playing.

"We realized that where we were most broken was on our youngest age groups," said USA Hockey Technical Director Ken Martel when we spoke in early 2019. "We had our least experienced coaches working with our least experienced players and were following the typical youth sports model." That model looked something like this: if this is good for our eighteen-year-olds, then it must be good for our sixteen-year-olds. And if it's good for them, why not our fourteen-year-olds? This thought process was trickling down all the way to the youngest levels. "The next thing you know," said Martel, "you have got a similar playing structure and competitive model for your eight-year-olds as you have for your eighteen-year-olds, which is completely out of whack."

USA Hockey knew they needed a new model. Youth sports was on a race to the bottom, and hockey was about to pull out of that race. They knew they needed to win the race to the right finish line focused on enjoyment, development, and increased participation. They worried less about childhood achievement and more about developing lifelong hockey players. They knew that developing more players who were technically proficient would allow the cream to rise to the top, instead of the current model in many sports where we throw a bunch of eggs against a wall and hope one doesn't break.

Implementing the best research available, USA Hockey introduced the Athlete Development Model (ADM) in 2009, and today the sport is thriving. In an era when most major youth sports are losing numbers rapidly—since 2010, baseball participation is down 5 percent, basketball is down 8 percent, and soccer is down a whopping 23.5 percent—hockey is growing, setting participant numbers records year after year and now running programs in all fifty states.[8] Even more impressive, retention numbers for USA Hockey are way up. Prior to the ADM, retention rates in ice hockey were around 50 percent across all ages. By 2018 at the twelve and under category, 91 percent of youth hockey players returned the following season, and by fourteen and under, it was up to 96 percent. And if you are wondering whether this made US Hockey less competitive, here are the stats from 2017. There were four world championship events held, and USA Hockey won all four: Women's World Championship, U20 men, U18 Men, and U18 Women.

It seems they have not only identified the right finish line, but they are winning the race as well. It is a lesson we can all learn from.

Three Ways Coaches Can Make Athletes Feel Valued

Pull Them Aside after Practice

Nothing is more impactful than some words of encouragement or praise from your coach. Be intentional about finding a player or two to stay after each day and just tell them how you saw them living your team values and making a difference. If you reward that behavior, you will see more of it.

The Post-Practice Shout-Out

This works great with both boys and girls ages twelve and under and can work for older kids as well, depending upon the environment and culture you have built. I always have my team come together in a circle at the end of training, and I give them an opportunity to recognize one another: "Does anyone want to give one of your teammates a shout-out for epitomizing one of our values today?" When one raises his hand, I roll them a soccer ball, and he gets to give a shout-out. This gives your athletes the ability to catch their teammates being good, which, at times, can mean even more to a young athlete than the coach's praise. Keep it brief and focused on the team values. When they are done, they can toss the ball to another teammate who wants to give a shout-out. Pretty soon, everyone wants to get in on the action, and many players leave training or a game with their tanks full. Pro tip: try and be cognizant of players who might not get a shout-out ever and have one of the coaches fill his or her tank.

The Personal Note

Take a moment and write a note to a player and catch him being good. If your team has a locker room, take a moment to write the athlete a personal note and leave it for him in his locker. In my case, we do not have a locker room, so this note often takes the form of an email (and in the era of SafeSport, copy a parent when working with youth players). It's just a few lines and does not take much time, but it can have an extraordinary effect. Here is an example of a note to a player who was competing hard and chasing after her own dreams while encountering the peer pressure of teammates who were not as committed:

> I just wanted to say how impressed I am by your progress as a player. Watching you tonight is like watching a whole different player. Your movement, understanding, touch, it's all so much better. But most important, what I really appreciate about you is that tonight, when so many people were not working hard, you kept pushing yourself and competing. That is what will get you ahead. Don't ever lose that, no matter who is around you. It's your dream and no one else's. Have the courage to chase it!

I have written a lot of these notes in my coaching career. They don't take very long, and they can make a massive impact.

Summary

Children are dropping out of sport at an alarming rate, with over 70 percent leaving sports by the age of thirteen. Female athletes and children from lower-income households are dropping out at an even higher rate. For far too many kids, sport is not a place where they are made to feel good about themselves, partly because influential adults do not "catch them being good" often enough. We can change that.

In this chapter, we have covered

- The research around why children play sports to help you understand how important quality coaching and positive team dynamics are for our young athletes.

- How early sport specialization drives children out of sports and why it is not even necessary in the first place and the need to overcome this culture of the head start and keep more children in sport longer.
- The need for patience in talent identification.
- How winning the race to the right finish line ensures that youth sport fits the needs, values, and priorities of the children participating—not simply those of the adults running the leagues.

When Tony DiCicco passed away in 2017, we lost a hugely important voice in the world of sports. Not many coaches win a World Cup and then go back and start coaching children as DiCicco did. Why did he jump back to working with our youth? Because he realized that his influence in how to coach, how to run a proper organization, and how to "catch them being good" could rub off on the other coaches and parents on the sidelines. So can your influence. Make those moments count, and make all of your athletes feel invaluable, even when they do not have the ability to be the most valuable.

LESSON 8

"WOMEN TEND TO WEIGH THE ODDS; MEN TEND TO IGNORE THEM"

Understand the Difference between Coaching Boys and Coaching Girls

Everything I have learned in coaching on the women's side is through one disastrous moment after another.

—ANSON DORRANCE

My coach said I ran like a girl.
I said if he could run a little faster he could too.

—MIA HAMM

A nson Dorrance, head coach of the University of North Carolina women's soccer team, is widely regarded as one of the top women's coaches in the world, with over one thousand career wins and twenty-two national championships, as well as a World Cup title in 1991. His success on the women's side often overshadows his success as a men's coach as well. He won 172 games in a twelve-year stint as the UNC men's soccer coach, and of his seven NCAA National

Coach of the Year honors, his 1987 award was won for guiding the Tar Heel men to the NCAA semifinals. There is perhaps no other coach, especially in a team sport, with as much high-level coaching experience on both the men's and women's side as Dorrance. So when he describes his learning curve discovering the differences between coaching men and coaching women, it is worth listening. According to Dorrance, "Everything I have learned in coaching on the women's side is through one disastrous moment after another."

For a number of years, Dorrance did double duty as both men's and women's head coach at UNC. At this point, he was also considering going to law school, was recently married, and basically burning the candle at both ends. In preseason, rather than plan two separate practices, he would use the same session for both men and women, and that is where the trouble started.

Dorrance had one exercise he loved, which was basically a five vs. five tournament. Players had to man-mark each other and were not allowed to tackle anyone else except their own player. The point of the game was that the fate of each team rose and fell on the success of the individual man-marking assignments. Dorrance especially loved to match up players who were competing for the same starting position.

As Dorrance described it, the games were competitive, to say the least. "I'd have my two center forwards mark each other, and they knew what I was doing because, basically, they were matched up with a person they had to beat out in order to get on the field. The game ends up an absolute blood bath because this is a battle between you and the person you're fighting for the starting spot." When the games ended, Dorrance started to notice a difference. "The men that were just marking each other would be joking with each other," he chuckled, "showing each other the scars they had hacked out of each other's legs on the way back to the water fountain. During the game, there were heated arguments about how you whacked me or whatever else. But as soon as that was over, they embraced each other and were off to the water fountain, just basically showing their wounds."

When Dorrance tried to repeat such practices with his women's team, the post-game response was much different. His goal was to create the competitive cauldron I wrote about in lesson 6, but he soon realized this was initially not the way to go about it. "Now walking back to the water fountain, there were two camps. It was one camp of girls that were now mad as can be against the other girls that were marking them in the practice. This was a big learning curve for me when I was coaching men at first and then given a women's team. I had to adjust to this different culture where a lot of the competition was considered more personal on the women's side, and that was an evolution for me."

Dorrance soon realized how important the relationships were to his women's players. "Sometimes when you compete in a way that someone might think might be over the top," says Dorrance, "it might compromise that relationship. The challenge is to figure out a way for them to compete against each other like there's no tomorrow, and yet, when that part of the competition ends, they're still connected. It's not an easy juggling act because usually the ones that compete incredibly aggressively are excoriated by the ones that don't make this a part of their nature. The key to any successful competitive platform when you're training and developing women is for them to understand that we're going to embrace each other when this is over. So, whatever happens during this session isn't going to be carried off the field, but you've got to create a culture that embraces that."[1]

This chapter is about the differences that coaches can encounter when coaching boys and coaching girls, and it's one that hit close to home with me recently. Podcast listeners will know that from 2016-2019 I coached my daughter's middle school soccer team. In our second year together, the girls were finally allowed by US Soccer age guidelines to head a ball in a game. We worked on it in practice. We tried using lighter balls and modified service to get them confident using their head, but after nearly two years, only a few of the kids were confident enough to head a ball in a game if it had travelled any sort of distance or height.

In summer 2019, I switched to my son's team, a group of eleven- and twelve-year-old boys entering the season where they would be allowed to head a ball in a game. I was curious how they might behave when I asked them to work on heading. "Kick it higher!" one yelled. "Let's do diving headers!" said another. It was immediately clear that teaching them to head the ball correctly and then deploy it in a game was going to be a very different journey.

In tackling this topic, I realize I am wading into an area that immediately raises the ire of some people and puts others on the defensive. As Kristen Dieffenbach, an associate professor at West Virginia University and current president of the United States Center for Coaching Excellence, explained to me on our *Way of Champions Podcast* on this topic, "For a long time, when you said 'difference,' it was automatically the assumption of one is better than the other. I think we need to change that conversation around differences to one that doesn't mean there's an evaluation of one being better than the other. It's just an acknowledgment of difference."

In writing this chapter, please remember that I am making generalizations here, and all generalizations end on the individual level. Please also remember that the difference between coaching boys and coaching girls is just one of the many differences we could talk about, and within that difference we could also talk about biological versus gender differences. We could speak about coaching children in wealthy neighborhoods versus children in impoverished ones. We could speak about religious upbringing or whether they are urban or rural children. I have chosen to write about this one particular difference because it is one that a lot of coaches encounter, and it is also one area in which we are very likely to bring our own experiences and cultural upbringing into our coaching. A male is very likely to look at team dynamics, public versus private feedback, and other factors through a male lens and a female coach through her lens.

In 2019, the Women's Sports Foundation released a report called "Coaching through a Gender Lens," in which they set out to address coaching and administrative practices that contribute to the gender gap in sports. Their team of experts and consultants surveyed over one thousand female athletes and their families, as well as sixty-four programs that were outperforming their peers in terms of girls participation in sport. They also examined decades of research looking at the reasons why girls are two to three times as likely to drop out of sports as boys. What they found was that, on average, girls start playing sports later and drop out earlier than boys, and this was especially true in African-American and Hispanic communities. They also found that boys' sports took precedence over girls' in many families, which is exacerbated by the "pay to play" culture that is driving the increasingly expensive youth sports experience.

One of the biggest factors, they concluded, was the shortage of female coaches, for as of 2015, of the 6.5 million coaching in the United States, only 25 percent were women. The presence of female coaches provides positive role models and challenges the negative stereotypes around female participation in sports, and yet many young female athletes never have a female coach. When they do, research suggests that when asked to rate whether they "really like" or "really, really like" their coach, female coaches outperform male coaches 82 percent to 73 percent.

One of the biggest myths the report dispels is that girls do not like to compete. They do. In fact, running around and being active, as well as learning new skills, were the top reasons listed by nearly 50 percent of girls when asked why they like playing sports. There were two very important dynamics that beat out those two, though: "making and spending time with friends" (61 percent) and "feeling part of a team" (55 percent). The report concludes that "the top predictors found to influence girls liking or loving their sport are centered around social and mastery aspects of participation and include being with their friends, really liking the coach, not being afraid to try new skills, not being one of the least-skilled players on the team, having goals related to their participation in sports, and perceiving sports as very important in their lives."[2]

As Anson Dorrance discovered, female athletes will compete, but the environment is incredibly important to whether that competition is enjoyable or not. So, with that all said, let's wade into this critical topic. I will be covering four areas here, based upon certain phrases I have heard coaches use over the years about these differences:

- "Men compete to bond; women need to bond to compete."
- "Women weigh the odds; men ignore them."
- "Men are hard to coach but easy to manage. Women are easy to coach but hard to manage."
- "Praise and critique men in public and women in private."

There is no way I can do this topic complete justice in a book chapter, so in the notes I will provide for you a list of further reading on the topic outside of any sources quoted here.[3] But I also think that understanding some of these differences, and the reasons they may exist, is critically important for coaches of all ages. Let's dive in.

Men Compete to Bond; Women Need to Bond to Compete

In 2012, authors Po Bronson and Ashley Merryman set out to explore what science tells us about competing, the things that drive success in some people and make others hold back and fail. In their book *Top Dog: The Science of Winning and Losing*, they also confront the differences between how men and women view competition, group dynamics, and the chances of being successful, all of which are critically important to our discussion here. Especially the work of Harvard evolutionary biologist Joyce Benenson.

As a result of her research, Benenson believes that through evolution, men have evolved to spend most of their lives in groups while women tend to congregate in pairs. Various studies of pre-school-aged children have found that boys are twice as likely to play in groups while girls are twice as likely to play in pairs. One study of six-year-olds found that given complete freedom to play any way they wanted, boys spent 74 percent of their time in group activity while girls only spent 16 percent of their time in groups. The boys compete and fight to be the best while the girls take turns. And these differences seem to persist into adulthood.

When you think about group dynamics, you recognize that some commonalities emerge. There is usually a common interest, and while not necessarily a collection of equals, most people within groups can bring different abilities and resources to the collective. They each can fulfill a role. You can be the fastest, strongest, funniest, or nicest, but within the collective you serve a greater purpose while still being an individual. As Benenson says about groups of boys, "As long as you feel you have something unique to contribute ... [a boy] has a place there."[4]

Groups have some other common traits. They allow for newcomers, who can add something to the collective. They allow some to argue and others to mediate, and the people in conflict can turn their attention toward others in the group until the tension fades. Groups can encourage competition without a real cost for losing. In other words, even when you mess up or lose, you can still contribute and be an overall asset to the group. In the words of Bronson and Merryman, "Groups teach us how to compete, and then—win or lose—how to move on."

In research on pair-based relationships, there are quite a few differences that emerge from the findings on groups. There is no longer a collective purpose beyond the friendship itself. The emphasis is on finding commonalities and areas of agreement, even amongst strangers paired together. Pair-based relationships are also very egalitarian, and both parties are expected to contribute equally to the relationship.

According to researchers, since they have no larger purpose or mediators for disputes, pairs are inherently more fragile than groups. As a result, members are acutely aware of each other's feelings, and they do not want to be perceived as being better than one another in the relationship. As Bronson and Merryman write, "The inherent design of dyads discourages competition. To be willing to compete is to be willing to jeopardize a dyad. If that is your reference point for relationships, it isn't surprising that women need sure things when they compete. Because if competing means risking a relationship with a loved one, you'd better at least know that you'll come back to that empty home with the trophy in hand. Thus, the lesson of the dyad is that competition destroys relationships."[5]

One further aspect of this group versus pair dynamic comes when newcomers are introduced to the group. With boys, their group dynamic allows for a newcomer who can contribute something new. With girls, it can be seen as a threat to the pair-based relationships, for one member might have their friend stolen. As a result, girls might ostracize a newcomer, whereas boys are more likely to welcome one. In my experience coaching soccer, when inviting guest players to a college showcase-type event, boys would be very welcoming as soon as they saw that the guest player could contribute to the team. With my girls' teams, I often encountered an attitude of, "Why is she here, and whose place is she going to take?" It was a stark difference, and one that shocked me the first time it happened. I thought I was helping the team compete better and could not understand why my teams didn't want another good player. In actuality, I was tearing the team apart.

This group versus pair dynamic is incredibly important for coaches to understand once you extrapolate these characteristics onto a sporting team environment. In general, a boys team will compete no matter what, and through that competition, they will bond. My experience is that boys turn most things into a competition, even when they are not, such as when you give them a water break and an all-out sprint ensues to get there first. The collective will celebrate group success, even when it is clear that one or two members are responsible for it.

In female groups, the power of the dyad still reigns; no one person wants to exceed the average, or fall too far below the average, lest they upset the equality within the group. The culturalization of our young girls creates a situation where they often must bond first to truly compete later. We must create a fantastic team culture, one of love, respect, and trust with a clear shared purpose and the psychological safety to compete like crazy without fear of ostracization. Creating a culture where some of the best female players in the world have the freedom and confidence to dominate in training and games is one of the keys to Dorrance's success at North Carolina. For the rest of us, we have to create that same dynamic for our best athletes while also recognizing that players who fall too far below the average may want to quit, lest they upset the equilibrium in the opposite direction.

Dieffenbach sees a simple genius in Dorrance's work with college age athletes. "What he had to do in the beginning was understand where they were coming from culturally because he was an outsider to that culture," says Dieffenbach. "So, it wasn't that it was good or bad; it was just, 'Oh, this is how this culture works.' It would be the same if you moved to Spain, China, or to the UK. You're in a different culture." Dorrance recognized that he had to create a place where the women of UNC soccer could feel safe competing like crazy and still maintain the relationships once practice was over. Dieffenbach sees the inherent difficulty in that as a result of the way boys and girls are culturalized from a young age, as well as an evolution in sports due to Title IX an other factors.

"Sport has really evolved into a male-dominated, male-based expression," says Dieffenbach. "For the most part, most of our dominant male sports play to physiological characteristics like, 'We'll be greater, stronger, bigger, faster,' in the male body, due to genetics, hormones, and all that good stuff. So, you can't un-connect the developing of your identity with sport. We know that for men, it's really complicated. This is why boys are just as important in this conversation as girls because if you're not 'man enough,' you can't play sport. You'll be pushed out because you don't fit that stereotype of 'man enough.' So, boys really try to be man enough."

Girls in sport face the issue of being their physical selves, particularly in cultures where strong feminist characteristics are valued. In other words, how do you be a female when sport is traditionally male? "Anson is coaching at the college level," says Dieffenbach, "so you're talking about people who have spent pretty much their entire upbringing being socialized into what's acceptable behavior and what's not." For men, it is socially acceptable to be the king of the mountain and confrontational, but not so with women. Girls tend to be behind the back as opposed to direct confrontation. Dorrance tends to agree. "The first thing an intelligent, sensitive young woman is concerned about is her relationship with the groups she's joining. So sometimes a freshman comes in, and she wants to be everyone's friend and wants to bond with the team. This is a new team, and she's trying to search out for her place in the team. One of the harder things for her to do basically is to destroy everyone to win her starting spot. It's almost like she's got to go through a period of being a debutant into this environment and be embraced by it first before she's permitted to compete. So, it's an interesting thing for them to navigate, which is something we don't navigate as often on the men's side."

Dieffenbach sees this as part of culturalization. "Direct confrontation is not ladylike," she says. "It's not feminine. It's not approved. It's not what you're allowed to do. So, you get to that level of competition, and it's just not how that culture operates. It doesn't fit with what they know and how they know how to do it. So, they don't have the skills to handle it. Had they been doing that part of their training and their sport experience from a very young age, there's a good chance that more of them would have had the skills to handle it better."

But Dieffenbach sees hope if we start training our coaches better. "What we have seen over time is when women are allowed to compete, play, and perform from a very young age, those performance differences are much less than what they've ever been before."

Women Weigh the Odds; Men Ignore Them

When I hear the idea that women tend to weight the odds and men tend to ignore them, it always makes me think of the scene at the end of the movie *Dumb and Dumber* when Lloyd, played by Jim Carrey, asks out Mary Swanson, the frazzled wife of a kidnapped man. He asks her if there is any chance of a guy like him and a girl like her getting together. When she says, "Not good," Lloyd responds, "Not good like … one in a hundred?" "More like one in a million," she replies. Lloyd thinks about this for a moment and exclaims, "So you're telling me there's a chance! Yes!" In my experience, this is often how boys approach games they have little chance of winning, focused on everything they will gain if they pull this off instead of what could be lost with the likely failure. There is some interesting research to back this up.

In multiple studies of political races from the state to national levels, women on the ballot are elected just as often as men. The problem lies in the fact that women are less likely to run. In a study of state representatives who are considering a run for US Congress, Texas A&M professor Sarah Fulton found that "ambitious male state legislators will run for congress if they have *any* chance to win. Ambitious female legislators will run for Congress if they have a *good* chance to win." When the odds of winning are 20 percent or less, nearly all the candidates will be men, but when the odds of winning increase, due to things such as an incumbent retiring or a scandal, women will compete in an election. The better the odds, the more women will compete, and at higher odds of winning, women will run even more than men. Women seem to compete less, but that is because they will only compete when they have a decent chance of success. "You could vary the chance of winning, but it isn't going to alter the men's running all that much," says Fulton. "But for women, it's a really long, steep slope. They're extremely responsive to the chance of winning."[6]

Fulton's research also demonstrates that men and women compete differently. They judge risk differently, and they attach different meanings to success and failure, which is hugely influential for whether they will compete again later. They differ in whether they will play to win or play not to lose. Research by Stanford economics professor Muriel Niederle has demonstrated that men will enter a winner-take-all math tournament at three times the rate of women, overconfident in their abilities, focused upon what they might get for winning, and unable to resist the challenge to compete. Woman in the math tournament, even when they did well, were reluctant to enter another round.

Dieffenbach has seen this same dynamic in play when it comes to the difference between men and women seeking head coaching roles in sports. "I can't tell you the number of conversations I've had with young men who passionately want to coach basketball or football," she told me. "When I start talking, they've never played the game, but they're a huge fan, and they know all the plays. I have yet to ever encounter a female who wants to coach a sport who doesn't have pretty extensive experience playing, often to the point where as soon as I'm like, 'Yeah, you shouldn't be the assistant; you should be the head coach,' she replies 'Oh, no, no, no. I need more experience.'"

Whereas boys will compete in the race to get a drink, girls often need a critical element. According to Niederle's research, to get women to compete, they needed to be put in a social context where competing is relevant to their success.[7] Whether it is in business or in sports, if the social context is right, women will compete. This is why it is crucial as coaches to create the right type of environment where your female players feel comfortable competing and recognize that competition will not upset the group dynamic. "Typically, with a boys team," says Dieffenbach, "you can say, 'This is what you're going to do. This is how you're going to do it. This is what I want to see. Let's go.' With girls you need to be a little more inclusive: 'How should we approach this? This is going to be a challenge. Ladies, what do you think we need to do? How do we tackle this as a team and overcome this? How do we keep everybody's spirits up? How do we keep people trying?'"

Again, it is not that one way is the right way and the other is wrong, they are just different, and to successfully develop and get the most out of your players, you must recognize these differences. In my experience, mainly working with middle- and high-school-age boys and girls, if we were facing a difficult game that we were unlikely to win, I had to approach the games differently. With the girls, if we competed hard and if we got to half time and it was tied, then all of a sudden the mood would shift to, "Yeah, we can do this." I would often have a different team in the second half, as though someone took the governor off and we finally played with freedom and confidence. They had to be convinced through the competition that they could win the game, whereas the guys said, "Well, let's just go for it and hope it all works out in our favor." Sometimes the men would pull it off, and other times it would blow up spectacularly in our faces. But we had no problem going for it again next week.

Men Are Hard to Coach but Easy to Manage; Women Are Easy to Coach but Hard to Manage

This is another statement that reflects my own coaching experiences. When I write that men are hard to coach, it means that they always want to know why we are doing a particular activity or a specific tactical plan. They push back against the teaching more often than my female players have. On the other hand, managing the group dynamic has always been easier. On my boys and collegiate men's teams, when we added a player, as long as they added something to the group, they were welcomed. They got over both on and off field disputes quickly, and even if they did not like each other, they were likely to respect each other. My usual coaching cycle is about three years, meaning that after three years I am ready to move on from a team. With my men's teams, I was ready to move on because I was tired of disagreements over the technical and tactical aspects of the game. It was kind of like the clichés about men never asking for directions; they knew they needed them, but they would not ask and were often offended that they were given.

For the girls' and women's teams I have coached, I have always found them to be incredibly receptive to technical and tactical coaching. Whatever ideas or new concepts I introduced, they were open to them. I rarely ever got the typical male question of, "Why are we doing this?" By the end of a three-year cycle, though, I would be exhausted from managing the personalities and group dynamics. I found it hard to keep track of who was angry at who and how that affected how the group played. My male-centered approach was flabbergasted that we couldn't all just get along and play for a state championship. This was especially prevalent in places where my team members went to different high schools and competed against each other all fall, and then I had two weeks to get them ready for a college showcase event. When they left in August, they were best friends, and when they returned in November, they were sworn enemies. It was exhausting.

When I shared this with Dieffenbach, she smiled. "I like that one. I think when you start to get into middle school, it definitely is the case because the social complexities of adolescence are complex for both boys and girls. But, I think they become especially complex for young ladies. Boys will be more like, 'Hey man, I got a problem with you. Hit. You're fine; we're good. Let's move on.' You tend to see more drama on the girls' teams because they're not allowed to have that face-to-face confrontation. It's all going to be silent, behind backs, behind doors, written notes—nowadays text—all that kind of stuff."

As Dieffenbach reminded me, girls are encouraged, supported, reminded, and reinforced to be cooperative. Boys are pushed to be leaders and innovators. So, they're just reinforcing what they've been told, especially when you start getting into sport where they are top dogs.

Praise and Critique Men in Public and Women in Private

Recognizing how boys and girls generally prefer to receive feedback has been a critical element for my coaching development. This was a big eye-opener for Anson Dorrance as well: "One of the things that the men absolutely love is public praise. If a guy had a great game, I'd point to him in the locker room after the game and say, 'Jerry, you were great today. You carried us,' and every guy in the room is slapping Jerry on the back and telling him how great he was. Of course, Jerry's ego is soaring like a hawk."

Dorrance saw the effectiveness of this public praise and thought he would use this same motivational technique with his women's players. "I couldn't wait to honor one of my young women in this fashion," laughed Dorrance. "Sure enough, Mary carried the day, and I said, 'Hey, Mary, you were absolutely awesome today,' and you could hear a pin drop in the room because now every woman in the room hates Mary with a passion, hates you with a passion for not praising them. And what makes matters worse is Mary now hates you with a passion for humiliating her in front of her teammates."

What Dorrance eventually understood was that the best thing he could have done for Mary was to walk with her after the match and, in a voice only she could hear, say, "Mary, you were awesome today." Dorrance realized that praising her privately was far more effective. "All of a sudden the bond between you and Mary goes through the roof because you've highlighted her. You've made this personal because you haven't embarrassed her in front of her teammates," says Dorrance. "What a great lesson that I wish I had learned a lot earlier."

Dorrance's experience was echoed by Terry Steiner, who has

coached the US National Women's Wrestling team since 2002. Steiner had an incredible career wrestling under legendary coach Dan Gable at the University of Iowa. He was a three-time All-American and an NCAA champion, and he started coaching soon after graduating from Iowa. After stints at Oregon State and Wisconsin, he was offered the women's national team job. "The biggest difference I found was communication," said Steiner. "In my first three months on the job, I had more individual meetings with my team than I had in six years coaching men." The meetings ranged from technical and tactical advice to simple life advice. It was an eye-opening experience for Steiner, for his experience as a wrestler and a coach of men's teams had taught him to communicate in a very different way. "They needed that communication and that relationship. They needed to trust me," said Steiner.

Soon after his first world championships in late 2002, Steiner had another eye-opening experience. After a disappointing eleventh place finish, the team was having a particularly poor practice, and Steiner was fed up. "We're done!" he announced. There was no intensity and very little focus, so halfway through practice, he decided to shut it down. He told the team they had to be better than this and that they were wasting their time and his time. "I never gave them a chance to rebut anything," Steiner laughed. "I walked out of the room and showered, and when I went back to the office, I had so many calls that day from the team." Everyone was worried that he was mad specifically at them. "When I walk into a guys' team and tell them to pick up the intensity, they are all looking over their shoulder, assuming I am talking to someone else … In the women's room, every one of them is thinking you are talking directly to her."[8]

In her research, Joyce Benenson found that adolescent girls were bothered by the idea that one of their friends might get better grades or have a boyfriend when she didn't. She was also equally bothered by the possibility that she might do better on a test or have a boyfriend and her friends did not. It is kind of a no-win situation. In my own coaching experience, prior to middle school, there does not seem to be much difference between boys and girls when it comes to public acknowledgment. Both sets of kids seem to enjoy it. I like doing shout-outs with my teams after training, where they get to acknowledge each other for epitomizing our team values and acknowledge each other for contributions or exceptional play. Up through age twelve or thirteen, my girls' groups would always remind me if I forgot to do shout-outs. Once they were all in middle school, though, these came to a noticeable halt. They were not as concerned with giving a single player a shout-out, lest they did not receive one. When I inquired why they didn't like shout-outs anymore, one of them told me, "If I give a shout-out to one of my teammates, another one will get upset I didn't give her one. It's just not worth it. And we all kind of get upset when you acknowledge someone but not us. Just being honest with you, Coach," she said as she shrugged her shoulders.

Middle and high school boys, on the other hand, don't seem to mind the shout-out at all, especially if it has to do with skill-based praise. Acknowledge a player scoring a great goal or making a great play in front of teammates, and they will all pat him on the back and exchange fist bumps. But call him out for being nice or showing kindness to a teammate, and it usually turns into an embarrassing moment for him as his teammates exclaim as one, "Johnny, you are so nice!"

In a nutshell, says Dieffenbach, get to know who is in front of you. "When you approach the boys, you can be a little bit more motivationally intense and direct, but don't mistake boys for men and think, 'I'm going to scream at them and make them into men,'" she cautions. "You still look at them as individuals. Give them that one-on-one that they really are craving and that praise. When you look at the girls, think about that relationship a little bit more and make sure that it's balanced and you don't have perceived favorites. That really will destroy a girls' team really fast, but the biggest thing is to get to know your audience."

In the end, we really just need to look at some of the literature and get to know our audience. Understand their culture and what is happening in their lives. As Dieffenbach suggests, "Understand their landscape because it's not your landscape. You're old now. You're not one of them anymore."

Ultimately, regardless of whether you coach males or females, remember that you are coaching a person, and all people crave acknowledgment in their own way. I think Dorrance sums it up best. The job of a coach, he says, is to "let all of these kids know in different ways at every opportunity what makes them unique and special and why (you) value them and respect them. It should be in all of our coaching toolboxes to always remind ourselves—at every opportunity, in personal and private ways, with a note or in a voice only they can hear—to let them know that we think they're extraordinary."

Activities for Embracing the Differences between Coaching Males and Females

Be Observant
Now that you are aware of the potential differences, given the age and gender that you coach, look out for some of the differences described in this chapter. Being a great listener and observer of your environment is the first step in getting this right.

When in Doubt, Praise and Critique in Private
Saving your individual player feedback for private moments is a failsafe when you are unsure of how/where an athlete prefers to receive your words. You always have the possibility of offending or embarrassing someone in front of their teammates with public words but rarely with private ones.

Focus on Your Team Culture
We will talk more about team values and culture in lesson 13, but regardless of whether you coach males or females, a strong team bond

that creates an environment that allows teammates to compete relent-lessly but be a family afterwards will always be a competitive advantage.

Summary

The role of a coach is critical in determining whether both males and females stay in sports and in creating the type of environment that allows each gender to thrive. This is especially true with female athletes in a world in which many of them are still coached by males. We have to get to know them and understand their culture and the world they live in. As the Women's Sports Foundation report concluded, whether girls like their coach is strongly associated with future intent to keep playing, how highly they value playing, and their love for the sport. A mastery-based coaching approach—along with the need to build supportive relationships within the context of sport—was deemed crit-ical for driving girls' participation. They want to get better, and they want to feel great while doing it. They don't want to be treated as soft or fragile; they want to be treated like the warriors they are. Sports organizations must actively recruit female coaches and train both their male and female coaches to understand and embrace the differences between coaching boys and coaching girls. In order to do so, keep in mind a few of the basic principles we mentioned in this chapter:

- "Men compete to bond; women need to bond to compete." Be highly conscious of the environment you create for your athletes. Your male athletes are likely to bond simply by being thrown into the competitive cauldron. Your female athletes need to bond first and to feel safe and confident that by competing they won't jeopardize their relationships within the team.
- "Women weigh the odds; men ignore them." Your male athletes will likely go all in and completely ignore the odds of winning while, in general, female athletes need to see a reason-able chance for success before they will risk it all.

- "Men are hard to coach but easy to manage. Women are easy to coach but hard to manage." When coaching boys, they are very likely to push back against some of the things you are teaching, but as long as each team member feels valued by the group, the group dynamics will remain stable. Female athletes are more likely to accept a coach at his word, but the coach must remain intentional and conscious of the group dynamic and interactions between individuals.

- "Praise and critique men in public and women in private." And when in doubt, take all feedback for both men and women to an individual basis. But in general, after the age of twelve or thirteen, feel free to praise a male athlete in front of his teammates for a skill- or effort-based accomplishment. For your female athletes, praise the group publicly but save individual feedback for private conversations.

LESSON 9

"AS MANY AS POSSIBLE, AS LONG AS POSSIBLE, IN THE BEST ENVIRONMENT POSSIBLE"

Identify and Develop Talent, Not Simply Maturity

> *As many athletes as possible, as long as possible,*
> *in the best environment possible.*
> **—JOHAN FALLBY**

> *How would you coach if you just assumed that you were terrible at*
> *making talent identification decisions instead of*
> *assuming that you're good?*
> **—DR. JOE BAKER**

I n 2005, the coaches at one of the top English Premier League youth soccer academies held one of their semi-annual meetings to decide which players they would keep for the upcoming cycle and whom they would let go. As they were evaluating their players—many of whom would go on to star not only in the EPL but internationally as well—they were stuck on one particular fifteen-year-old boy. This was a critical year, for if they kept him, they would be making a three-year commitment to his development. He had been a very good player when he first entered their Academy, but recently he had hit his growth spurt. He was no longer scoring well in their physical testing nor playing with the confidence and athletic grace he had shown a few years earlier. In fact, the once speedy player was now only the seventh fastest kid on the team.

These incredibly qualified and highly respected coaches were torn; some wanted to keep him and offer him a scholarship to continue his training; others thought they should let him go. To break the tie, the coaches brought in their chief scout, a man named Rod Ruddick, to help them decide. Ruddick was the scout who had found the boy playing a small-sided game at age nine and had first invited him to join. Ruddick had a hunch that the player was going through a difficult time as he grew and that soon the athletic, attack-minded player he remembered would reemerge. He cast his tie-breaking vote to keep the player.[1]

Within two years, the player would make his first team senior debut for the club and become the youngest international player in his country's history. In 2013, that speedy winger proved that the staff at Southampton Football Club were right to keep him as he eventually became the most expensive signing in world soccer history when he was bought by Real Madrid for one hundred twenty million dollars. His name was Gareth Bale.

To date, Bale has won four UEFA Champions League titles, led Wales to the 2016 European Championship semifinals, and scored many legendary match-winning goals for club and country. So, what was it that Ruddick noticed that others may have missed? And what can we learn from the stories of elite professional athletes such as Gareth Bale, Michael Jordan, Steve Young, and others whom were overlooked at various stages of their youth sports careers, only to become truly world-class?

In this chapter, we will look closer at what exactly talent is. To do so, we will

- Discuss the relative age effect and how early maturity is often confused with ability;
- Redefine what is meant by the word *talent;*
- Learn about researcher Aine MacNamara's work on the Psychological Characteristics for Determining Excellence (PCDEs); and
- Look at how an early emphasis on winning yields talent selection, not talent identification.

Coaches must understand the differences between talent, ability, and physical maturity and how they are often confused with one another. One of our most important jobs is to be able to take the long view when developing athletes, as well as instill not only physical but also the psychological characteristics needed to succeed at progressively higher levels of play. Let's dive in.

The Relative Age Effect

If you have spent any time around a sports venue, you have probably heard someone say, "Man, that kid's got talent." Fans ooh and ahh as a young athlete weaves his way through defenders or dominates her opponents under the basket. We easily spot the biggest, strongest, fastest, and most skillful kids and immediately label them as "talented." I have done this countless times myself. But oftentimes, we are not looking at talent; we are looking at maturity.

In the 1980s, Canadian psychologist Roger Barnsley drew attention to the story of relative age in youth hockey players. (His work was later popularized in Malcolm Gladwell's book *Outliers.)* Barnsley noticed that an extraordinary number of elite youth and professional hockey players had birthdays in January, February, and March. In the

Ontario Junior Hockey League, nearly five times as many players were born in January than November. This held true for elite eleven- to thirteen-year-olds and again for players in the NHL. In his research, Barnsley eventually discovered that in any group of elite hockey players, 40 percent will have been born between January and March, 30 percent between April and June, 20 percent between July and September, and 10 percent between October and December. Is it the least bit surprising to know that the age eligibility cutoff for Canadian junior hockey is January 1? This is what is known as the "relative age effect," which is simply described as a bias found in both youth sport and academics where participation is higher amongst participants born within the first quartile after the arbitrary calendar cutoff and lower amongst those born late in the selection period. His studies have been replicated in numerous sports.[2]

For example, a recent analysis of the 2019 UEFA U17 Championships in soccer analyzed the birthdates of 344 participants who participated in two or more games at the championship. Fourteen of these players were born in 2003, and the rest were born in 2002. The calendar cutoff in European soccer is January 1, so researcher Laura Finnegan divided the year into four quarters. Once again, the relative age bias was demonstrated as 47 percent of the players were born in quarter one while only 6 percent were born in quarter four. The most well represented month was January, with fifty-seven players; December was least represented with only three players. Defending champion Netherlands had 62 percent of their players born in the first three months of the year.[3]

In youth sports, we nearly always organize children chronologically instead of developmentally. While this certainly makes it easy to organize and segregate teams, it puts our preadolescent children into situations where some may have a head start or be denied one because of birth month. Two kids may be seven years old, but there may be eleven months of additional development for the child born in January.

That difference can be huge at this age and affect them for the rest of their lives. Add to that the fact that a twelve-year-old boy, for example, can have a five- to six-year developmental age swing. That means he could have the body of a ten-year-old or a sixteen-year-old. We think we are selecting based upon ability, but it is far more likely that we are selecting maturity. Now, of course, not all January birthdays are early maturers nor are all December birthdays late maturers, but in general, a child born in January and eleven months older than one born in December is going to have physical, cognitive, and social advantages, especially when they are selected at increasingly younger ages.

When we segregate our youth athletes too soon—age seven to ten is pretty common across all team sports—the effects are amplified because we usually take those "top" athletes and give them the best facilities, the best coaching, better teammates to play with, and stronger opponents to play against. From a very young age, these "elite" kids are given a special advantage that other slightly younger and less physically mature kids are not. Over the course of a year, the differences in performance may be small. But when we project better coaching, stronger opposition in training and games, and additional positive reinforcement over ten years, we realize that we are creating athletes who have been trained better and who have more self-confidence than many of their peers, all because of the early "tryout" they went through when they were very young. This is a result of what sociologist Robert Merton calls the self-fulfilling prophecy, where "a false definition, in the beginning … evokes a new behavior, which makes the original false conception come true."

There are some interesting studies around the relative age effect when it comes to professional and Olympic athletes. Numerous studies have found that those "young" athletes who overcome the effects of relative age are often among the most successful professional athletes based upon average salary (in soccer), length of career (in handball), and draft position (in NHL hockey). Researcher Dr. Joe Baker has hypothesized that "relatively younger athletes who are able to continue in a system that may be biased towards their relatively older counterparts may end up developing superior skills … through competing against larger, more capable opponents during key stages of development."[4]

In a fascinating study on junior tennis players from 1994 through 2002, Piotr Unierzyski evaluated one thousand players age twelve to thirteen in fifty different countries, a pool that included future stars Roger Federer, Kim Clijsters, and others. His study found that of all these players, the ones who eventually made it into the Top 100 Professional Rankings were

- Three to four months younger than the mean age for their group;
- Slimmer and less powerful than their age group;
- Usually faster and more agile than average.;
- Practicing less tennis but doing more physical training than average;
- Practicing and playing fewer hours; and
- Backed by parents who were supportive but not overly involved.[5]

In a similar 2006 study on fifty-five Serbian U14 soccer players in professional youth teams, researchers found that when measuring skeletal age rates, the players demonstrated the following biological age:

- 43.8 percent early maturity
- 35.4 percent neutral maturity
- 20.8 percent late maturity

By 2012, sixteen of these players had signed top-level professional contracts and played on national teams and in a top-five professional soccer league, while thirty-two played at a sub-elite level. Seven could not be tracked. The breakdown of the players who reached the top level is fascinating:

- 11.8 percent of early maturing players reached the top level.
- 38.1 percent of average maturity reached the top level.
- 60.1 percent of late maturing players reached the elite level.[6]

In other words, you have a greater likelihood of becoming an elite-level performer if you are a late maturing child who gains a foothold in the system and develops the resilience and other character traits needed to stick with it until the physical differences start to disappear.

To conclude, children who are selected as gifted at a very young age, often only because of relative age, become smarter, stronger, faster, and more talented because they turn the higher expectations placed upon them and the systemic advantages into reality. At the same time, many potentially talented young athletes are funneled out of the developmental pipeline far too soon and then quit because they perceive their struggles to be a lack of competence instead of delayed physical maturity. Our system often eliminates huge numbers of potential high-level performers because of the month they were born. At the same time, those late maturers who survive are more likely to achieve elite performance status. That is why youth sports specialists such as Johan Fallby, a sports psychologist working with elite teams across many sports, describes the best system as one that allows for "as many as possible, as long as possible, in the best environment possible."[7] How can we do that? Perhaps first, we should redefine what we mean by talent.

Redefining Talent

I spoke at a conference called The Future of Coaching in Cambridge, United Kingdom, in January 2019. At the event, my friend Stuart Armstrong, head of coaching at Sport England, added a little nuance to the way I use the word *talent*. "I think we often confuse talent and ability," said Armstrong, who has spent many years in the talent development and identification space in sports such as golf, rugby, and field hockey. He even runs a website and a podcast called *The Talent Equation*, so you know that he has thought quite deeply on this subject. "We see a kid with skill and speed and strength, and we call it talent. But I think what we are looking at is ability, and those are two very different things."

Armstrong began his "Talent Equation" journey after hearing legendary rugby coach Sir Clive Woodward make the comment that "talent is not enough" when describing what it took to win a World Cup and succeed in sport at the highest levels. "I got what he was saying," chuckled Armstrong, " but I wanted to challenge that statement because I think what he was really saying was, 'Ability is not enough.'"

Armstrong was convinced that Woodward was talking about having athletes that were technically and tactically skilled but also mentally and emotionally capable so they could perform under the highest levels of pressure. Armstrong noticed that coaches and talent developers tend to look at the characteristics we can see in front of us—the physical, technical, and tactical elements—but fail to evaluate the drivers of those tangible characteristics, such as commitment, dedication, passion, drive, and resilience, as well as decision-making, creativity, and problem solving.

"Talent isn't just about ability," said Armstrong. "The reality is that we tend to look only at ability, and then we sort of hope that they have those mental skills, yet we know that those mental skills are what separates Kobe Bryant and LeBron James from those who do not become the best of the best. I believe that talent is ability multiplied by these internal factors and then massively influenced by the environment: parents, coaches, school, club." In other words, there is a talent equation: (Ability x Internal Factors) x Environmental Factors = Talent

In Armstrong's opinion, we need to look past what we see in front of us. Ability matters, but without the mental characteristics, good habits, and the right environment provided by parents, coaches, and the local sport culture, ability may never truly become talent. "The reality is, with talent development," says Armstrong, "we tend to look at the athlete with the abilities and then we hope that they might have some of the mental skills. We all know the athletes who are so capable, but they don't have the other side of it. When they have all these factors in balance, when they have all those capabilities, those are the golden eggs."[8]

In his 2009 book *The Talent Code*, author Daniel Coyle discusses some of those environmental factors that Armstrong notes. He uses the analogy of a windshield: what a young athlete sees in his windshield is going to heavily influence his choices in sport. A young Kenyan sees runners and not ice hockey players in his windshield, and a young Brazilian sees soccer and fustal. Writer Karen Crouse alludes to similar "windshields" when writing about Norwich, Vermont, a town of three thousand inhabitants that has sent an Olympian to every winter Olympics since 1984. While this is not the place to get into every environmental factor (as it is the subject of my book *Changing the Game*), it is important to realize that the environment and culture, when combined with ability and the right psychological traits, can be a multiplier. "Talent hotbeds possess more than a single primal cue," writes Coyle. "They contain complex collections of signals—people, images, and ideas—that keep ignition going for the weeks, months, and years that skill-growing requires. Talent hotbeds are to primal cues what Las Vegas is to neon signs, flashing with the kind of signals that keep motivation burning."[9]

So, what are these psychological characteristics that drive excellence?

PCDEs: The Psychological Characteristics of Developing Excellence

Coaches and sports programs often talk about developing character and how character drives excellence and success. I have argued here that character education only happens in sports when it is intentionally taught and incorporated into training environments. If we are going to teach character, then, are there some character traits or psychological characteristics more important for developing and sustaining excellence? The research says there are.

In 1998, researchers identified certain traits, such as long- and short-term goal setting, high commitment level, proper planning, imagery, and focus as important "success factors" that distinguished top-performing athletes from their less successful peers. More recently, researchers Dave Collins, Aine MacNamara, and Angela Button have identified what they call the PCDEs, or the psychological characteristics of developing excellence. These are "the attitudes, emotions, and desires young athletes need to realize their potential." The PCDEs they have identified as primary drivers include the following:

- Motivation
- Commitment
- Goal setting
- Quality practice
- Imagery
- Realistic performance evaluations
- Coping under pressure
- Social skills
- Competitiveness
- Commitment
- Vision of what it takes to succeed
- Importance of working on weaknesses
- Game awareness
- Self-belief [10]

Any coach looking at this list would recognize these as helpful traits that would allow an athlete to improve and put in the long hours necessary to get better. They are also developable skills. Coaches need to be stretching mental capacity, teaching athletes how to respond to setbacks, and how to perform under pressure. We need to be teaching our athletes not only technical and tactical skills but equipping them with these PCDEs as well. But when?

In the second phase of their work, MacNamara, Button, and Collins found evidence that suggests that not only were PCDEs important throughout development, but the manner by which they were deployed depended on the stage, domain, and characteristics of the individual performer. For example, early on, athletes might need the support of parents, coaches, and teachers to reinforce the PCDEs, but as they get older, they must become intrinsically motivated to develop them. "Since the goal of talent development (TD) is to provide the most appropriate learning environment to realize an individual's potential to excel," they write, "it is surprising that these crucial determinants of development are consistently overlooked."

Expert performance, then, is not simply a hardware issue. Elite performers are motivated to consistently take advantage of the development opportunities put before them, yet how often do we fail to evaluate these PCDEs? "By recognizing the multiple factors that influence development," they conclude, "the efficiency of (talent identification) models is increased by neither excluding 'potential' through inappropriate early identification measures, nor ignoring crucial talent development variables that contribute toward the fulfillment of potential."[11] In other words, we must start truly identifying talent, using a definition similar to Armstrong's Talent Equation, and stop merely selecting it by looking at ability and, more often than not, maturity.

Talent Selection vs. Talent Identification

When York University sports scientist Joe Baker gives talks to parents, he loves to put up a slide of an eighteen-month-old who was given a symbolic professional soccer contract. "I always put that up there because that's what talent identification looks like. We're terrible at identifying talent, and we should avoid it as long as possible. We need to get comfortable with the fact that when we do these early selections, most of the time they are wrong, and most of the time they are biased." The question for Baker is a simple one, and it is relevant to all of us who are involved in the talent identification and development space. "How would you coach," he asks, "if you just assumed that you were terrible at making these decisions instead of assuming that you're good?"

How would you coach if you assumed that you were terrible at talent selection, especially at the youngest ages? Would you put more coaching and development resources into your B, C, and D team players? Would you change the way you interact with your athletes on all the teams? Would you follow up with athletes that you're removing from the system or, better yet, find ways to keep them in the system? Would you create a system where you can hedge your bets instead of going all in on a few kids really early?

Evidence says that you should. One of my favorite authors and speakers on this topic, South African Sport Scientist Ross Tucker, concurs with Baker because they both understand that the system as we currently know it is not set up correctly. Tucker uses an analogy of two competing coffee shops. One owner reads the hypothetical science that says drinking coffee before eleven in the morning increases the risk of injury and death, so he decides not to open until eleven o'clock. His competitor ignores the science and puts him out of business. This is how we do it in sports as well, says Tucker. The business of sport encourages people to ignore the science around the detriments of early specialization and talent identification and instead collect as many kids as possible, as soon as possible, and force them to specialize. According to Tucker, there is almost no redeeming feature for early specialization and identification. "The only reason we do it," he laments, "is because we have created a culture that values the head start too much."

Tucker points to journalists and coaches who are quick to tell you about Tiger Woods, Venus and Serena Williams, and Andre Agassi, marking them as "precocious youngsters who were earmarked for success by their parents and communities. They will never tell you about the ones they got wrong. The problem is no one follows up on the wrong predictions so we have this great illustration of survivorship bias. We are brainwashed into thinking it is typical when in fact this is exceptional. We have created a race to the bottom."

This wouldn't be such a bad thing if we had a sports system that allowed people to float in and out of the selection system at different time points. If an athlete was not selected at age nine, that would be OK if he had a chance to get back in at age eleven. But we all know that's not the way the system works. Once you are out of the system, it's really hard to get back in. In order to be at a certain place performance wise at age eighteen, you have to be doing certain things at sixteen. And to have access to those training and coaching advantages at sixteen, you have to be performing at a certain level at fourteen. But in order to perform at that level at fourteen, you must enter the system at age twelve, which requires a specialist approach by age ten. The system is a mess.

In a nutshell, talent selection is the culling of players with the current ability to participate and be successful in events taking place in the near future. Our current "win at all costs" youth sports culture promotes talent selection. When a coach is pressured to win by parents or a club or when she feels the need to win to serve her own ego, that coach becomes a talent selector. You naturally select the biggest, strongest, and fastest young athletes and play them extensive minutes while limiting playing time for the kids who are not up to snuff.

Talent identification, on the other hand, is the prediction of future performance based upon an evaluation of current physical, technical, tactical, and psychological qualities, combined with the understanding of sport science and the humility to know that we are truly terribly at trying to predict future performance. Talent identification is an art. You must look not only upon the current output but also what has gone into that output and what is the potential ceiling of that person in front of you. You must promote all-around athleticism and sport sampling so that your athletes can find their best fit—not simply the only shoe they were ever allowed to try on. It is up to us to move away from a talent selection system that prioritizes maturity and early development over patience and toward an athlete-centered approach that prioritizes their needs, not the needs of adults. We need to become better talent identifiers and stop being talent selectors.

Activities to Promote Better Talent Development Environments

Delay All-Star Teams and Tryouts/Cuts as Long as Possible
Keep as many children in the system as possible by eliminating the race to the bottom in all-star selections and cutting children at very young ages because you are likely wrong in your selections if your goal is long-term talent identification.

Ensure Equal Access to Coaching and Resources
Do not place your top coaches only with small groups of lesser-ability athletes. Give as many athletes as possible access to great coaching and facilities as long as possible.

Promote the Regrowth of In-Town Leagues
We have lost the local league as a place for athletes to sample numerous sports on a seasonal basis and for our top-ability athletes to continue sampling. These have been replaced by high-cost, high-commitment programs for children as young as six years old, which is driving down participation numbers.

Make Character Education Part of Your Coaching

If character and the PCDEs drive performance and great habits are a predictor of future performance, then be sure you add a character lesson daily or weekly to your sessions. Read them a story, watch a film together, and reward the type of behavior that drives excellence.

Summary

"Let's be honest," says Dr. Richard Bailey, head of research for the International Council of Sports Science and Physical Education, "most elite sports programs are not designed to meet children's needs; they are designed entirely for adult ambitions." This is the sad state of affairs we coach in. But we can do better. And that starts with our young talent identification programs. If we want to improve them, we must

- Understand the relative age effect and how early maturity is often confused with ability. The resultant confusion can often lead to a self-fulfilling prophecy that certain children, based solely upon birth month, are sent into talent development programs at the expense of other, potentially greater sportsmen and women.
- Redefine what is meant by the word *talent* to incorporate not only ability but also environmental factors and internal characteristics, such as the PCDEs, which are psychological characteristics for determining excellence.
- Look at how an early emphasis on winning yields talent selection, not talent identification, and admit that all the evidence proves we are very poor at identifying future talent, especially when we try to do it before puberty.

"Even when we take athletes and we tell them they're talented and put them in a beneficial system and wait for another five years for them to emerge at the high-performance level," says Baker, "even when we provide them with all that great environment to develop in, our accuracy is still poor. Even considering the self-fulfilling prophecy element of this, we're still terrible, which means if we go back to it from a pure accuracy standpoint, we're probably way worse than we even think we are."

So, how do we combat this? As many as possible. As long as possible. In the best environment possible. Then let them grow and start making your selections while allowing others to exit the pathway but not disappear from sight entirely.

LESSON 10

——

"MOST SPORTS ARE PLAYED ON A FIVE-INCH FIELD"

Succeed in the Outer Game by Winning the Inner Game

It is not the mountain we conquer, but ourselves.
—SIR EDMUND HILLARY

Golf is a game that is played on a five-inch course –
the distance between your ears.
—BOBBY JONES

On Sunday, April 14, 1996, one of the greatest meltdowns in the history of sport was unfolding at Augusta National Golf Club. Greg Norman, who would finish his career with ninety titles and at one point held the number one world ranking for an incredible 331 weeks, headed into the final round of the Masters Tournament with a six-stroke lead over his closest challenger, Nick Faldo. To the outside world, Norman looked to be strolling to victory. But in between his ears, Norman was crumbling.

The morning of the final round, the forty-one-year-old Norman woke up with a stiff back and told his coach Butch Harmon, "This isn't going to be easy," with a gloomy disposition. Yet his problems were far more mental than physical. In his career he had held the lead going into the final round of golf's major championships (Masters, US Open, British Open, and PGA Championship) on eight occasions and had prevailed only once in the 1986 British Open. He had been beaten by Jack Nicklaus's famous charge to win the 1986 Masters; by a miracle bunker shot by Bob Tway to win the 1986 PGA; and in the 1987 Masters, Larry Mize sunk a 140-foot chip to beat him in a sudden-death playoff. He had been dogged throughout his career by questions of, "Why can't you win the big ones, Greg?" and those thoughts were swirling in his head as he headed to the first tee box. His playing partner, Faldo, had won the Masters on two occasions, and Norman later admitted that played into his nervousness as he convinced himself that Faldo knew what it took to win the event, and he did not. By the ninth hole, Norman's six-shot lead was down to two, and even Faldo could see the meltdown unfolding before his eyes. "I could feel the nervousness emanating from Greg," said Faldo. "He gripped and regripped the club, as though he could not steel himself to hit the ball."

The meltdown continued over the next few holes, a back nine, which Norman had played at eleven under par the previous three rounds. He bogeyed ten, lipped out a par putt at eleven, and hit his approach into the water at twelve for a double bogey. By the time Faldo knocked in a birdie at the eighteenth hole, Norman had finished with a final round score of seventy-eight and was five shots behind Faldo, a remarkable eleven shot turnaround that even left champion Faldo feeling sorry for his opponent. "Don't let the bastards get you down," he whispered to Norman after they embraced on the eighteenth green, knowing what lay ahead for his opponent.

Years later, Norman opened up about his mental game and the negative voices in his head, especially on that fateful day in 1996. He admitted he did not sleep at all the night before the final round and was plagued with thoughts of, "I don't think I can win this," all night and all day Sunday. As each subsequent shot went astray, Norman's self-doubt increased. "When you have garbage in your head," he later told an Australian TV Documentary, "you can't be that (focused) on the mission you want to achieve."[1]

For many years, professional athletes rarely talked about the inner game, the game played between their ears, but thankfully that is changing. Coaches are constantly looking for marginal gains in every area of physical, nutritional, technical, and tactical training, yet many coaches still ignore mental training. Seeing a sports psychologist is seen as a weakness by far too many in sport, often because we only employ the psychologist when things are going wrong and need to be "fixed." Even Norman briefly saw Fran Pirozzolo, a neuroscientist and sports psychologist earlier in his career, but deep down, he saw it as a sign of weakness. When asked years later about Norman, Pirozzolo described Norman as a classic case of learned helplessness, one who felt he had no control over the world around him. "You had a prewired mentality in Greg's case, or what's often called a 'fixed mindset,'" said Pirozzolo. "A fixed mindset person believes, 'I'm either good at this or not.' They say, 'If I fail, it's because there's something missing from my total package here.' Having that fixed attitude limits your ability to cope with the things that are happening to you."

Given that the best athletes in the world still experience fixed mindsets, self-doubt, negative self-talk, and poor mental preparation, I can guarantee your athletes do as well. People choke in big-pressure situations. Under stress, the brain releases cortisol and adrenaline, and athletes can lose fine motor skills and even the ability to think clearly. Vision can narrow, and a golfer like Norman can lose touch and distance control.

Sian Beilock, a sports psychologist at the University of Chicago and author of the book *Choke: What the Secrets of the Brain Reveal about Getting It Right When You Have To*, speaks about the performance-inhibiting thinking that athletes can face in high-pressure situations. They can turn their attention from task-relevant items, such as reading a putt or diving for a loose ball to irrelevant items, such as controlling the outcome or worrying about what the media will say if you blow it. Beilock became interested in the science of choking under pressure all the way back in high school when she realized that she did better on lacrosse faceoffs if she sang to herself. As she has continued her research at the University of Chicago, she has found that in highly trained athletes, overthinking can lead to failure (thus, the singing, which took the focus off the technical execution of a faceoff). For example, highly trained soccer players perform worse when dribbling through an obstacle course when asked to think about what part of their feet they are using. Baseball players hit worse when asked to think about swing trajectory or analyze noises during a specific time of their swing.

At other times, a deficit of attention can lead to failure at a task. "Sports aren't cognitively static," says Beilock. "Situations change, and you need to track things and make decisions. You can't just not think. There's a whole skill involved in knowing not just what not to think about but when to attend to things that need tending. You've got to be able to control what you're attending to."[2] The way we can control what we are attending to is by being present in the moment and training the inner game.

We need to start giving the inner game the same level of training and preparation that we do for the outer game. We must stop introducing mental training and sports psychologists only in times of distress and make it a regular part of your season, beginning the first day of preseason. While coaches can certainly notice things that may be signs of serious mental health issues—and, in those cases, you should immediately seek out a school counselor or a psychologist or encourage the families of your athletes to do so—you don't need to be a psychologist to introduce various aspects of mental training to your teams. In this chapter, I will introduce some ideas that will help you to help your athletes start winning the inner game. We will cover the following:

- Fixed versus growth mindsets and how to overcome the fixed mindset through proper praise
- Positive self-talk and how writing your own story is far better than listening to everyone else's story about you
- Mindfulness, awareness, and flow as keys to success
- Visualization
- Meditation

Coaching the inner game is not a very comfortable thing for many of us coaches to do. I get that. Some of you may be lucky enough to call upon a professional in your community to help out, but in my experience, winning the inner game is not a one-time thing. It is a process, not an event, so even if you bring in someone from the outside, the coaching staff has to support and continue the mental development of players. Here are some ideas on how to do that.

Help Your Athletes Establish a Growth Mindset

Have you ever heard one of your athletes say something like, "I lost my starting spot on the soccer team. I'm just not good at soccer," or "I failed my math test. I'm just not good at math"? If so, it is very likely that the single-greatest factor limiting their performance is a lousy mindset. Famed Stanford researcher Dr. Carol Dweck has found that when it comes to performance, there are two types of "mindsets," as she calls them: a fixed mindset and a growth mindset. In her internationally known book *Mindset*, Dweck discusses the difference between these two mindsets and provides parents and coaches with a path to instilling the proper mindset in their athletes, students, and, for that matter, performers in any type of achievement activity. Understanding the importance of mindset is crucial to helping your child perform his best in sports.

A person with a fixed mindset usually judges situations in terms of how they reflect upon her ability, which, in her mind, is permanent. In other words, if she does poorly on a test, she is not smart. If she plays poorly in a game, she is not a good player. As a result, fixed mindset individuals rarely seek out opportunities to learn or challenge themselves, for failure, to them, is vindication of their lack of self-belief. In their mind, risk and effort are likely to expose their weaknesses and lack of ability. They instead seek easy-achievement activities, fear failure, shun effort, and are constantly finding excuses not to perform their best.

A growth mindset individual, on the other hand, sees her abilities as capable of being cultivated. She recognizes that challenging herself is an exciting part of learning and that failure is a necessary component of success. Her attitude toward a poor result on a test is, "Next time, I just need to study harder." When confronted with a difficult task, she embraces the challenge. She is not afraid to fail, pick herself up, and try again. In Dweck's words, "A belief that your qualities are carved in stone (fixed mindset) leads to a host of thoughts and actions, and a belief that your qualities can be cultivated (growth mindset) leads to a host of different thoughts and actions, taking you down an entirely different road." A fixed mindset individual will not put forth effort, for he believes that if he were smart (or talented) he would not need to try hard. Effort is a bad thing. For a growth mindset individual, effort is the secret sauce that makes you talented.

Dweck has found that adults often instill a fixed mindset in their children by praising them in the wrong way. We live in a culture of effusive praise, where some people believe that the more praise we heap upon children, the better. Yet Dweck found that praising children for their ability ("You are so smart; you are so talented.") actually has the opposite effect. In a test of four hundred fifth graders, Dweck found that praising children for their intelligence ("You must be smart at this.") as opposed to their effort ("You must have worked really hard.") had a massive detrimental effect upon performance. Over a series of tests, children praised for effort tried harder, worked at a task longer, and enjoyed challenges more than those praised for intelligence. But beyond that, those praised for effort improved their test scores by 30 percent while those praised for intelligence saw their scores decline by 20 percent.

As a coach, until I read Dweck's work, I had different words for fixed and growth mindset players: uncoachable and coachable. What I did not realize was that a fixed mindset athlete was not uncoachable; he just heard me completely differently than a growth mindset player. When I offered critique or criticism, what a fixed mindset player heard from her inner voice was, "Coach does not think I am good because if I were good, I wouldn't need to try, and he wouldn't need to coach me." On the other hand, the growth-oriented player's inner dialogue said, "Coach is trying to make me better by teaching me new things."

For your athletes to reach their true athletic potential, they must have a growth mindset. They must come to realize that nothing relating to ability is fixed, and with effort and application, what you can be a month from now or a year from now is determined not by who you are but by what you do. You can help simply by learning to praise your athletes for their effort, not their ability. It's not about winning and losing; it is about winning and learning.[3]

Write Your Own Story

In 2017, I had the honor of working with an amazing group of young women on the Colby College women's lacrosse team. Their coach, Karen Henning, is an amazing coach who understands that there are advantages your team can gain from being mindful and building a strong culture, and I got to play a small role in helping that team come together. In 2017, we had an extraordinary season, finishing the regular season tied for first in the incredibly tough NESCAC conference and winning the NESCAC tournament for the first time since 2008. Along the way, we twice defeated Middlebury College, a multiple-time national champion, including in the NESCAC tournament semifinals on Middlebury's home field. We were set to receive a very high seed for the NCAA tournament and looked forward to a few more home games, where we were really tough to beat. Then disaster struck.

Due to a lack of hotel availability because of a college baseball tournament and a local gymnastics meet, the NCAA denied our bid to host, and we lost our high seeding. We were sent back on the road to Middlebury for a third match-up with an incredibly tough opponent. We were devastated as we could not have gotten a tougher opponent or place to play after a season of hard work. We started to lose track of our story and our self-talk, and it was replaced with many outside voices. Those voices told us how we got screwed. They told us that life was unfair and it was impossible to go back and beat Middlebury again. They railed against the NCAA and the local hotels. All in all, we stopped focusing on what we controlled and turned the focus on the uncontrollables. We were focused on all the reasons we should lose, instead of what we could do to compete and win. We were in trouble. We had to change the narrative. I wrote the team this email:

> This week you will hear lots of stories, lots of other people's stories. Friends and family may tell you it's unfair that you have to go there to play. We have finals. People might talk about long bus rides or better draws for other teams. Media might talk about what you face or ask, who is this upstart Colby? Who cares? These are other people's stories. Other people's stories will never help you, never serve you, and never make you better. But we are a group of powerful, tenacious women. We are champions. Champions write their own story. They feel it. They live it and tune out the rest. That is what we will do.

At practice that Tuesday, I asked the coaches to bring paper and pens to the locker room. We took the first fifteen minutes of practice and had each player write her own story. How does she want it to read? How does she want it to feel? What is your *why* for this weekend? We wanted to build our own story and let that be our narrative. I gave them the following prompt for their writing: "We are going back to

Middlebury. We are the NESCAC champions, and now we have been given the privilege of competing for an NCAA Championship. This is what is going to happen …"

I asked the players to finish that story in one to two paragraphs. What are you doing this week to prepare? To focus? What do you need to be held accountable for? What does it mean to you to be here playing for a national title? Write your *what*.

Then I asked them to write their *why*. This was the most important part. Why am I willing to give everything for my team? Why does it mean so much to be competing with my teammates, whom I love so much? Why am I willing to fight for every ball, to hustle on every play, to cheer my heart out when I am not in? When you know your *why*, the *what* starts to take care of itself. Here's what I wrote to them.

Throughout the week, we should not only live our story, but we must also share it with teammates. We need to get in our circle and read our stories to our teammates, a few each day. We will share all week what it means to us to have the privilege of competing with such great warriors and people. We will share our stories and then go live them out. Do this, and our spirit will rise to a whole new level. No one will define us. We define ourselves.

We went back to Middlebury and played an extraordinary game against an amazing team. We competed like crazy. We tuned out all the distractions. And we lost ten to nine on a last-minute goal. Life is not a fairytale, and sometimes you don't win when you do everything right. Most important, though, we did not lose before the whistle even blew. We wrote our own story and constructed our own narrative. We walked off the field with our heads held high, feeling lousy about the result but great about our Colby family and the season we just had.

Far too many teams and athletes have already lost the game

before they step onto the field, due to negative self-talk and a poorly constructed narrative. It may be the voices of their parents or coaches telling them they are not good enough or they always choke in big situations. This internal dialogue frames how they react to life. Their self-talk is a reflection of the messages they hear most often, and it can be trained to be positive instead of negative.

"Positive self-talk," writes psychologist Gregory Jantz, "is not self-deception. Positive self-talk is about recognizing the truth in situations and in yourself. One of the fundamental truths is that you will make mistakes. To expect perfection in yourself or anyone else is unrealistic. To expect no difficulties in life, whether through your own actions or sheer circumstances, is also unrealistic. When negative events or mistakes happen, positive self-talk seeks to bring the positive out of the negative to help you do better, go further, or just keep moving forward."

Jantz recommends the following exercise to his patients, and I think it works great with athletes as well:

- Write down some of the negative messages you tell yourself that affect your performance. Be specific and include names of people who contribute to that message.
- Take a moment and intentionally find a positive truth that counteracts each of those negative messages. These may not come quickly, but take the time needed to counteract each one. Teach yourself to make that your mantra when the negative thought pops into your head.

As Jantz writes, "You may have a negative message that replays in your head every time you make a mistake. As a child you have been told, 'You'll never amount to anything' or 'You can't do anything right.' When you make a mistake—and you will because we all do—you can choose to overwrite that message with a positive one, such as 'I choose to accept and grow from my mistake' or 'As I learn from my mistakes,

I am becoming a better person.' During this exercise, mistakes become opportunities to replace negative views of who you are with positive options for personal enhancement."[4] In other words, help ensure that the message your athletes hear the most is one that is affirming, positive, and hopeful.

Mindfulness, Awareness, and Finding Flow

The ability to be completely present, unencumbered by things that have happened in the past and with no attention placed upon what might happen in the future, is a key to achieving athletic success. Many of the top professional teams are incorporating this practice, known as mindfulness, into their everyday activities. The Golden State Warriors have mindfulness as one of their four core values. Winning the inner game is not something that people do to get all "touchy feely." It is a competitive advantage. So, what exactly is mindfulness, and how can it help?

Amy Saltzman, author of *A Still Quiet Place for Athletes: Mindfulness Skills for Achieving Peak Performance and Finding Flow in Sports and Life*, defines mindfulness as "paying attention here and now, with kindness and curiosity, so that we can choose our behavior." It is not dwelling upon the past or fretting about the future; it is paying attention to this exact moment. Numerous studies across a variety of sports have demonstrated that mindfulness practice can reduce stress, negative thoughts, depression, perfectionism, fatigue, substance abuse, injury, and burnout. Mindfulness can increase performance-enhancing qualities such as flow, relaxation, confidence, concentration, resilience, coachability, sleep, recovery, enjoyment, and general life satisfaction. If I offered coaches a practice session that did all those things, they would jump at it. But talk about those few inches between the ears and, despite all the benefits, the reaction is usually, "That's not for me."[5]

Athletes perform their best when they are in a flow state. In the 1970s, famed University of Chicago psychologist Mihaly Csikszent-mihalyi coined the term *flow* to describe a previously unacknowledged mental state of performance and satisfaction. In flow, people have clear goals and a perfect balance between what they have to do and what they are capable of doing. They are challenged, which serves to focus attention and prevent boredom. Yet they are not challenged in an excessive way, which would create anxiety.

In flow, a person's body and mind are stretched in a way that increases focus and makes effort a satisfying reward. They are so deeply involved in the moment and in control of their experience, that time and place melt away, leaving them in the zone of high performance. They have a clarity of purpose and receive and process feedback with seeming effortlessness. This brings a sense of control and confidence and a loss of self-consciousness; time ostensibly stops or speeds up because the focus on the task is so complete.[6]

These days I find flow skiing, mountain biking, fly fishing, and even writing this book. I watch my son painting or my daughter reading, and I see the hours float by effortlessly. You likely have experienced it as well. Flow is a high-performing state, and one all athletes want to achieve. "The real key to high-performance and tapping into flow," writes famed mindfulness coach George Mumford, "is the ability to direct and channel (your) strengths and skills fully in the present moment—and that starts in your mind. The flip side is also true. No matter how strong or skillful you might be, your mind can also impede talent from being expressed, and it often does so in insidious ways if you don't take care of it."[7] We can train ourselves and our athletes to be more mindful, present, and aware, and through that practice, we help them find flow more often.

Activities That Help Train the Inner Game

Visualization
Australian psychologist Alan Richardson was curious whether visualizing an act being performed could have similar effects to actually

performing that same act, so he set up an experiment. His subjects shot one hundred basketball foul shots and recorded their base numbers. He then randomly divided the subjects into three separate groups. Group A practiced foul shots for twenty minutes five days a week for four weeks. Group B was told to do no basketball-related activities for four weeks—not even to think about basketball. Group C was asked to come in five days a week for twenty minutes each, but instead of practicing foul shots, they were guided by a professional in visualizing shooting foul shots without touching a ball. They were encouraged to "feel" the ball in their hands, "hear" it bounce, and "see" it go through the hoop.

Four weeks later, Richardson had the subjects shoot one hundred foul shots again. Group A, the group that practiced free-throw shooting, had improved in their ability by 24 percent. Group B, the no practice group, made no significant improvement. But Group C, the visualization group, improved by 23 percent, nearly as much as the group physically practicing every day. This is not a call to scrap practice and visualize as, clearly, physical practice is critical. But visualization practice can be a great supplement to physical practice and help your athletes overcome some of the stress and anxiety they may feel when the game is on the line.

Many top athletes now incorporate visualization training into their daily routines. Wayne Rooney, the former Manchester United star, recounted how he would go to the equipment manager the night before games and ask him what they would be wearing the next day. Then he would visualize himself wearing that exact uniform. "I lie in bed the night before the game and visualize myself scoring goals or doing well," Rooney told ESPN reporter David Winner. "You're trying to put yourself in that moment and trying to prepare yourself, to have a 'memory' before the game. I don't know if you'd call it visualizing or dreaming, but I've always done it, my whole life."

Kids can do this, too. When asked by Winner whether he was specifically taught to visualize, Rooney said no. "When I was younger,

I used to visualize myself scoring wonder goals, stuff like that. From thirty yards out, dribbling through teams. You used to visualize yourself doing all that, and obviously when you get older and you're playing professionally, you realize it's important for your preparation—and you need to visualize realistic things that are going to happen in a game."[8]

We use visualization activities with our teams often, and you do not need to be a PhD to do so. Simply get your athletes to relax, take a few deep breaths, and then close their eyes. Have them start imagining the competition environment, what it feels like and smells like. What does the crowd look like? Then look at it from a third-person perspective: where are you on the field or what lane in the pool? Then experience it first-person, making a great tackle, hitting the shot, or running down the sideline.

Really encourage your athletes to feel it, touch it, and experience it like it was real, like a dream that you woke up from and could not believe you were dreaming. Then come back to present, let the image fade, and have them open their eyes. That's it. Just take a few minutes and try this. It works really well for many athletes. And if you doubt this, just take a few minutes now and close your eyes. Think of a lemon. Feel it in your hands. Smell it. Peel it. Now bite into it and taste the tartness. Are you salivating yet? Did you squirm? I did just writing this!

Meditation

Meditation is engaging in a mental exercise, such as concentrating on one's breathing or repeating a mantra, for the purpose of reaching a heightened level of spiritual awareness. It is key to achieving mindfulness and total focus on the present moment. As it has grown in popularity recently, mindfulness meditation has been the subject of numerous studies to see if it has actual benefits, and the results are impressive. Studies have proven that daily meditation can reduce stress, control anxiety, and promote emotional health. It can enhance self-awareness and lengthen one's attention span, decrease pain, and improve sleep.[9] Meditation can physically change the structure of the brain for the better and change the way it reacts to certain stimuli. And best of all, it takes mere minutes and can be done anywhere.

Many people do not meditate because they think they are doing it wrong or are not good at it. When you start, you will soon notice how easily distracted you are. It's like looking at a highway full of cars; as you try to stare at one car, other more flashy cars distract you over and over. These are the ideas that flash in your head as you worry about different issues in your life. It does not mean you are doing it wrong. You just need more practice.

I recommend an app for my players called Headspace. Headspace was co-founded by Andy Puddicomb, a former Tibetan Buddhist monk whose goal was to demystify meditation and make it more accessible and attractive to everyday people. You can try it for free, and it is highly engaging and easy to use. Meditations range from three to thirty minutes and cover a variety of topics (sleep, dealing with stress, athletic performance). You can learn more at www.headspace.com.

Self-Talk Exercise

Try psychologist Gregory Jantz's simple self-talk activity:

- Write down some of the negative messages you tell yourself that affect your performance. Be specific and include names of people who contribute to that message.
- Take a moment and intentionally find a positive truth that counteracts each of those negative messages. These may not come quickly, but take the time needed to counteract each one. Teach yourself to make that your mantra when the negative thought pops into your head.

Summary

"What people don't realize," says Wayne Rooney, "is that [soccer is] obviously a physical game, but after the game, mentally, you're tired as well. Your mind has been through so much. There are so many decisions you have to make. And then you're trying to calculate other people's decisions as well. It's probably more mentally tiring than physically, to be honest." Most athletes would agree with Rooney. Everyone has ability at the top level. Mental state and inner game are what separate the elite from the near elites. And if the inner game is truly a difference maker, then we must incorporate it into our training and not just pay it lip service. To do so, you can

- Understand the difference between fixed vs. growth mindsets and how to overcome the fixed mindset through proper praise.
- Teach your athletes about positive self-talk and how writing your own story is far better than listening to everyone else's story about you, just like Colby College women's lacrosse did.
- Help your athletes become more mindful and aware so they more easily achieve flow.
- Add simple visualization exercises before training and games.
- Try Headspace or another tool to encourage your athletes to begin a healthy meditation practice.

"Neither mastery nor satisfaction can be found in the playing of any game without giving some attention to the relatively neglected skills of the inner game," wrote Tim Gallwey in *The Inner Game of Tennis*. "This is the game that takes place in the mind of the player, and it is played against such obstacles as lapses in concentration, nervousness, self-doubt, and self-condemnation. In short, it is played to overcome all habits of mind which inhibit excellence in performance." What he meant was that sports are played between the ears, as well as on the court or in the pool. Coaches need to start giving the inner game the same level of training and preparation that we do for the outer game. We need to make mindfulness, visualization, meditation, and positive self-talk a regular part of our seasons, beginning the first day of preseason. It is a competitive advantage. And it helps to make every moment matter a little bit more.

LESSON 11

"SOME PARENTS ARE CRAZY, BUT MOST ARE JUST STRESSED"

Effectively Engage Your Athletes' Parents

Some parents are crazy, but most are just stressed, and we have to stop using the bad parents as an excuse not to engage with all the good ones.

—SKYE EDDY BRUCE

One of the scariest things for me is to sit on the sidelines of youth soccer or youth lacrosse or poolside, just listening to the things parents say to their kids. And I am sure if I videotaped them, and played it back to them, they would be appalled.

—DR. JIM TAYLOR

By all accounts, things were going pretty well for Springville High School girls basketball and Head Coach Nate Sanderson. The small, 1A school from eastern Iowa had made the state championship game two years in a row, losing the final in 2015 before winning in 2016. Their success was driven by a great culture of positivity and support and the bond that all great teams share. But as the 2017 season approached,

Sanderson and his staff wondered if they were leaving something on the table in terms of culture. The culture within the team was great, but they had excluded some very important people from that culture: the parents.

"For the past fourteen years I have begun every basketball season by conducting a parent meeting," Sanderson wrote in a blog for *Breakthrough Basketball* and reiterated when we interviewed him on the *Way of Champions Podcast*. "Every one of those meetings had one goal in mind: to insulate myself from parent complaints. I've used all the standard approaches to communicate our policies and expectations verbally and in writing for players and parents prior to the season. The purpose of every single item in our thirty-three-page parent manual is to communicate as much information up-front as possible so that we will not have to deal with the parents once the season begins."[1]

Yet Sanderson and his staff wondered if there was a better way. He started thinking a lot about the phrase "dealing with parents" and all the negative connotations and emotions "dealing" with stuff brings.

"We usually deal with things that are unpleasant. We deal with problems. We deal with difficult people," wrote Sanderson. "I would never walk into a practice thinking, 'Today I have to deal with these players again.' Rather, we strive to appreciate, love, and encourage our players every day. That's our focus going into every practice. What if we approached the parents the same way?"

As a result, the Springville girls basketball coaches decided to do something crazy. They decided to ask the parents what they thought. They decided to invite them to join the culture and to learn how they could support their daughters in their quest for another state title. "The more I thought about the sports parent experience, the more I realized, I have no idea what the parents want their experience to be like," said Sanderson. "So, we created an exercise to find out."

Each parent was asked to provide written answers to the following five questions. These answers would then be shared publicly, just like the answers the girls on the team provided as they established their team goals and shared values. The questions were as follows:

- Write down at least one reasonable, measurable goal you have for our team this season.
- What do you want your daughter's experience to be like if she *can't* accomplish any of the goals you wrote for her or for the team?
- What do you want your experience to be like as a parent?
- What can you do to help create that experience for other parents?
- What can the coaches do to help facilitate that experience?

This process was a transformational one for the team. The parents were open and honest about what they wanted from the season. The coaches were open to any feedback that could be perceived as critical and sought to improve. And the players were able to read what their moms and dads wanted for them and actually hold their parents accountable for their behavior and for upholding the culture.

This exercise is a real eye-opener because it reinforces the fact that for the vast majority of parents, their true goals and desires for their children in sport, once you strip away some of the extrinsic, outcome-based things, are very reasonable. For example, some of the Springville parents, in response to question two ("What do you want your daughter's experience to be like if she *can't* accomplish any of the goals you wrote for her or for the team?"), wrote things such as:

- I want my daughter to grow inside. I want her to care, really care, about others. I want her to be less self-absorbed and more others-focused. A true team player … with heart. One who always does her best and *never* gives up.
- I want her to be accepted and feel she belongs.
- I want her to continue to give 100 percent and understand that when you don't succeed right away, you just don't give up.

In response to questions three and four ("What do you want your experience to be like as a parent?" and "What can you do to help create that experience for other parents?"), parents wrote

- I would like to feel part of the group, accepted and liked by coaches, parents, and teammates like family.
- To enjoy the game without negativity from the coaches/players/fans when things aren't going as planned.
- To have fun watching the girls play.
- To be positive and cheer for the team, not just my daughter.[2]

Finally, in response to question five ("What can the coaches do to help facilitate this experience?"), the number one answer, by far, was, "Communicate! Just keep us in the loop."

Does this sound like a bunch of unreasonable people? Does this sound like a group of people we have to "deal with?" No way.

What Sanderson and his staff found is that when you engage parents, instead of dealing with them or shutting them out altogether, you open the door to some magical moments. Although Springville returned most of their team from their 2016 championship season, they went through a mid-season slump. As the team struggled to gel, Sanderson waited for the team culture to come together, and in his words, "have our 'come to Jesus moment.'" But while the team culture was still struggling, the parent culture held it all together. The usual sniping or complaining about who is playing or who is not was replaced by a united front. At the tipping point for their season, Sanderson saw the parents become the glue that helped hold the team together.

"When you think about a player, their inner dialogue, especially when they make a mistake or things are not going well, is the product of the voices they hear most frequently and intensely in their life," says Sanderson. "That is usually a parent. So what do you want them to hear? Are we doing our part to plant that inner voice in their minds?

That is an awesome way to say to parents, 'You can make our team better by being intentional about how you communicate with your daughter after she makes a mistake or doesn't get playing time or isn't a starter."

So, what was the result of all that hard work to engage the parents? Just another state championship for Springville girls basketball.

For some coaches, engaging and educating the parents of your athletes may seem like the last thing you have time for. But if you read on with an open mind, hopefully by the end of the chapter I will have convinced you that, in fact, not only do you *have* time to work closely with your team parents, you don't have enough time *not* to engage them.

In this chapter, we will cover the following topics:

- Why parent engagement matters
- Organizations that have successfully implemented robust parent engagement programs
- Some tools and activities you can use to help get your coaches, parents, and athletes all moving in the same direction

I do not think any coach is insulated from parental actions, unless you coach in an orphanage. Parents are potential allies, and engaging them can be the key to your success or, if you choose not to, a contributor to your downfall. Even at the highest levels, parents matter. In his book *Above the Line*, recently retired coach Urban Meyer tells the story of Ohio State Football's 2014 NCAA Championship season. I was stunned by how often he spoke to the parents of his eighteen- to twenty-three-year-olds. Many of the times he was trying to get a player to step up and play to his potential or stay out of trouble, he met with the player *and* a parent, grandparent, or other important adult figure in his life. If Urban Meyer knows that the best way to help an athlete reach his potential is to get all the influential adults in his life rowing in the same direction, why would we think this does not apply to children?[3] It does. Let's stop dealing with parents and engage them instead.

Why Does Parent Engagement Matter?

Dr. Jim Taylor is an internationally known sports psychologist who has spent over three decades working with elite junior Olympic and professional athletes. He is also the author of books such as *Positive Pushing* and *Train Your Mind for Athletic Success*. In 2018, he released *Raising Young Athletes: Parenting Your Children to Victory in Sports and Life*, which has some great insight into the coach-parent-athlete dynamic. One of the biggest takeaways:

"Children become the messages they hear the most.*"*

"Some of the messages kids get from youth sports are not healthy," says Dr. Taylor. "One of the scariest things for me is to sit on the sidelines of youth soccer or youth lacrosse or poolside and just listen to the things parents say to their kids. And I am sure if I videotaped them and played it back to them, they would be appalled."

I don't know many people who would disagree with Taylor's assessment. These are the messages our children are hearing on far too many sidelines. Add them to the messages they hear on the car ride home, over dinner, or during a forced practice session because they played poorly, and you get the picture. Our athletes' parents are the voice they hear the most. It is the voice building them up, supporting your great work as a coach, telling them to "go ask coach" instead of saying, "Coach is stupid," and so much more. Every bit of good work you do can be undone in five minutes on the car ride home.

So, why not coach the parents, too? Why not teach them what to look for and what to say? Why not answer their questions and provide them with helpful information and tips on how to have those difficult conversations? Why not build trust and rapport with them so that when their athlete is struggling, they come to you for help?

Not every parent will be easy to work with. There will be times when you will have to agree to disagree. There will be times when you must bring in your athletic director, coaching director, or a neutral third party because you and a parent are miles apart. As Taylor said to me recently, half joking, half not joking, "All parents love their children and are well-intentioned. Some are misguided, and a few are mentally ill. In thirty years of practice, I have come across very few of the latter group, but a lot of the middle group, and certainly all of the first group of being well-intentioned." If we show parents positive approaches to raising young athletes, they will usually do their best to adhere to those guidelines.

In my experience, as both a coach and a parent, there is a lot of pressure and stress that parents deal with today to ensure their child does not fall behind in sports or school or extracurricular activities. As Operation Varsity Blues, the 2019 college admissions scandal, has shown us, the pressure to help our children achieve will make even reasonable people do unreasonable things. The reason: FOMO (the fear of missing out).

I remember the day I coached my son TJ's first soccer game. He was only five, and I was so proud, so excited. I couldn't wait for him to play the game I loved. There was one problem: he didn't want to play.

When the game was about to start, he said, "Dad, I don't want to play today." I was OK with it and the game went on. That week, he went to practice and had lots of fun, so I thought all was right in the world. The next weekend, I was equally as excited for TJ to play his first game. Sadly, he was not.

As I set lineup, he again said, "Dad, I don't want to play." I don't think he liked the screaming parents and coaches from the previous game or all the hustle and bustle that is five-year-old soccer. This time I was angry. I was embarrassed. I was this A-licensed, "all-star coach," and my own son refused to play. TJ, on the other hand, found a cricket to play with over by the fence. He was content. I was a mess.

What is wrong with my son? Why won't he play? What if he doesn't like soccer? Isn't he going to fall behind? The negative thoughts cascaded through my brain.

On the car ride home, I felt the need to address this issue (likely to make myself feel better as he was fine). "So, TJ ..." was all I could say before my wife, who was in the passenger's seat, karate chopped me across the chest.

"What was that for?" I asked her incredulously.

"Really, didn't you just write a whole book about this?" she said with a stern look.

Indeed I had. But I was scared. I was afraid TJ was missing out on a game I loved. I suffered from the fear of missing out.

I know I was not alone in feeling this way. I hear from parents all the time who feel stressed and anxious about their child's sports experience. Are my kids falling behind? If they don't do extra training now, will they make the travel team? Will they make the high school team? Will they have a chance to play in college? These are very legitimate concerns for the modern-day sports parent.

FOMO causes parents to focus only on the present, not the long term. FOMO leads us to suck the enjoyment out of the sport in pursuit of dreams of stardom and scholarships. FOMO makes us feel that we are letting our kids down by not providing them with every single opportunity, regardless of costs, time commitments, and the stress endured by our family.

Coaches, we are the solution to FOMO. And we can only be the solution when we build trust and connections with our athletes *and* their parents. We must give them permission to take a deep breath, trust the process, and trust that you know what you are doing and that you have their child's best interests in mind. You do this *not* by shutting them out but by letting them in.

Organizations That Are Making a Difference

When youth sports organizations and schools engage, empower, and educate their parents, good things happen. I know this because since 2013, my organization Changing the Game Project has been helping to rebuild the trust eroded between coaches and parents. To date, we have presented to hundreds of thousands of parents and coaches across all sports in North America, Asia, Australia, and Europe. Our speaking team does well over one hundred live presentations per year, plus we have nearly one million words of blog posts, hundreds of hours of podcasts, dozens of hours of online courses for parent and coach education, and tons of book recommendations and other material. We are neck deep in this space, and we are seeing some wonderful results happening. Sometimes it's just one team, and sometimes it's a whole club or school. The resources are out there for anyone who wants to start shifting the culture of their organization. And we are not alone in this movement.

Skye Eddy Bruce was not your typical soccer mom. She was a multi-sport athlete in high school and an All-American soccer player at George Mason University, leading her team to the 1993 NCAA Finals against Anson Dorrance and North Carolina. She then played professionally, coached in college, and started a successful real estate agency. But when her daughter started playing club soccer in Richmond, Virginia, she was not happy.

"She went to her first tryout and was selected at eight years old," said Bruce, "and it was her first time with a 'professional coach.' But after her first few days of training, she wasn't really inspired, and over time I started to see her love of the game dwindle. As a coach, I went to go see what was going on at practice, and I wasn't happy with it. The environment was not good, and most of the coaches were not qualified to work with kids this age."

After observing this for a few weeks, Bruce quietly reached out to a few other parents to see what they thought. They were totally fine with it. Others were a bit nervous to even speak up about it. But no one knew what "good" really looked like. And that's when Bruce decided she had to do something about it. In 2015, the Soccer Parenting Association was born.

"Until we completely change the dynamic, educate and support parents, teach them what to look for and what good looks like, nothing will change. This is not parents versus coaches. Parent engagement is clubs, coaches, and parents working together to support and inspire players and improve the culture. The Soccer Parenting Association is starting to become the PTA of youth soccer.

"Engagement has many layers and includes parent education, coach education, and so much more. It is about having a system for giving feedback to players and coaches and lodging complaints if there are clear violations of club policy. These conversations can be awkward for parents," says Bruce, "and this gives parents and coaches a framework for having these important conversations. Ultimately, it is about establishing trust."

Another great organization doing amazing work in this space is the Positive Coaching Alliance, founded by Jim Thompson while he was teaching at Stanford Business School in 1998. Today, they have almost two dozen chapters

Resources for Improving the Parent/ Coach Partnership

Changing the Game Project: **ChangingTheGameProject.com.** A great place to start is to grab a quick index of our blog posts, all organized by topics and hyperlinked. It is available for free here: changingthegameproject. com/resourcebooklet.

Soccer Parenting Association: **SoccerParenting.com.** This organization has a ton of both free resources and paid partnerships that allow any club or school to provide their coaches and parents with a lifetime of great information.

Positive Coaching Alliance: **positivecoach.org.** I proudly sit on the National Advisory Board for the PCA, and they do amazing work across the United States with their Double Goal Parenting and Coaching workshops.

Proactive Coaching: **proactivecoach.info.** Bruce Brown, Rob Miller, and their team have been doing parent and coach education in sports for decades and do terrific work. They have a massive library of coaching and parent education booklets and videos.

National Alliance of Youth Sports: **nays.org.** Another organization that has been at the forefront of improving the environment of youth sports for decades.

ISport360: **isport360.com.** ISport360 is a great tool for promoting open dialogue and feedback among parents and coaches.

across the United States and maintain partnerships with most major youth sports organizations and many professional teams; they do more workshops than any organization I know of. For over two decades, the PCA has gleaned the knowledge and expertise of the world's leading coaches, athletes, psychologists, and others and has been providing tools and workshops for coaches, parents, and athletes. I am honored to sit on the National Advisory Board for the PCA, along with far more famous luminaries, such as Phil Jackson, Steve Kerr, Summer Sanders, Julie Foudy, Steve Young, and others.

Finally, I would be remiss if I did not mention Proactive Coaching and its leadership team of Bruce Brown and Rob Miller. Seeing Brown speak inspired me as a coach and a father and changed the trajectory of my own coaching. When I decided to write my first book, *Changing the Game*, Bruce Brown was the first person I called and interviewed. Their workshops and talks are inspiring for coaches, parents, and athletes, and their speaking team is in front of hundreds of thousands of parents, coaches, and athletes every year.

Activities to Help You Engage Your Parents

If you have been adhering to the guidelines in this book, if you are clear on your coaching why and you are putting your players first, chances are you are halfway there in terms of parent engagement. While there are a huge variety of different tools you can use to engage your parents, here are a few of my favorite best practices.

Preseason Goal-Setting Exercise

I was well into my coaching career before I truly recognized the importance of goal setting, as well as the importance of the role of parents in the process. When I did, I began to require each of my players and their parents to fill out similar questionnaires in the preseason. I asked the players to complete five simple statements:

- Three ways I am an asset to my team are …
- My role on the team is …
- Three things I want to improve on are …
- Three individual goals for this season are …
- Three team goals for this season are …

At the same time, I provided the parents with a similar list of tasks to complete:

- List three things your son/daughter already does well as a player.
- What is your child's role on this team?
- List three things you would like to see your child improve upon.
- List three individual goals you have for your son/daughter.
- List three goals you have for the team this season.

I ask the players and parents to fill these out on their own and then to sit down and compare notes. What I discovered was that the players and parents who shared the same goals and ambitions often had a great relationship. As for the families where there was no compatibility or middle ground between players and parents, I often saw strife and poor performance from the players and anger, frustration, and a feeling of "I'm wasting my money" from the parents. The biggest divide for parents and players was usually regarding the player's role on the team and the parents' goals for their child. The players often were very realistic about their expected contribution based upon their current abilities and those of their teammates. Many parents were not. The child's goals often aligned with their effort, commitment, and ability. The parents' goals aligned with the athlete they wished they had instead of the one they did.[4]

Set Appropriate Boundaries

Without a doubt, as a coach you must set appropriate boundaries that define how and when you will interact with parents, the topics you will discuss, and the ones you will not. This is very important and not something to be dealt with in highly emotional situations, such as post game, post tryouts, etc. Having guidelines that are clear, consistently enforced, written down, and provided to parents is a huge first step in defining and developing the coach-parent relationship.

Every team, coach, and club will likely have their own specific boundaries, but here are some I have found useful:

The twenty-four-hour rule: If you are emotional after an athletic event, parents and coaches must wait twenty-four hours before having a conversation, firing off an email, or, worst of all, posting something on social media you will later regret. Giving yourself and the parents a day or two before dealing with a difficult situation—such as playing time, role on the team, something you may or may not have said, etc.—is the best way to ensure your meeting or conversation will be constructive.

Office hours and other appropriate times to connect: Do not make yourself available twenty-four/seven. You deserve down time and family time, too. But be available and timely in your responses when you are on coaching time.

Outline of philosophy, commitment, and playing time expectations: Lay this out up front so there is no confusion. Then stick to it. I once read on a club volleyball website that on their travel teams, which may fly across the United States beginning at twelve years old, not a single minute of playing time was guaranteed. Yup, fly five hours each way, lay out thousands of dollars, and don't get in. Now, while I unequivocally disagree with this short-sighted and sport-destroying policy, at least they put it front and center on their website. If you still signed your kid up, well, then you got what you paid for.

Things that I will discuss with a parent: Lay out the appropriate topics for discussion, such as the following:

- Playing time
- Your child's performance

- Things to work on at home
- A personal improvement plan for the child
- Issues that may be affecting your child's performance, which may include behavior from other team members but nothing sport specific (i.e., bullying)

Things that I will not discuss with a parent: Lay out all the inappropriate items, such as but not limited to the following:

- Anything related to the performance of another child on the team
- Tactics
- Practice planning and session topics
- Substitutions, playing styles

Nate Sanderson's Five Questions Exercise

I think the five question activity described at the opening of this chapter is an excellent way to engage your parents, help them understand the team culture, and encourage them to be a positive contributor to it. Again, those questions are as follows:

- Write down at least one reasonable, measurable goal you have for our team this season.
- What do you want your son's/daughter's experience to be like if they *can't* accomplish any of the goals you wrote for them or for the team?
- What do you want your experience to be like as a parent?
- What can you do to help create that experience for other parents?
- What can the coaches do to help facilitate that experience?

Invite Parents for the Pre-Game Talk

I love to do this, especially with children who are twelve and under and have been working on something new in practice. Say, for instance, you have been working on the pick and roll with your basketball team. Prior to the game, call in the parents, tell them what you have been working on, and help them know what you want them to cheer for.

Invite Parents for the Post-Game Talk

I learned this one from world-famous sports psychologist Bill Beswick. After coaching the England Men's Basketball team, plus consulting at multiple Olympics and World Cups as a sports psychologist, Beswick coached his local eight and under rugby team. After every game—and a season in which they lost all of them—Beswick invited the parents to the post-game talk as he addressed the team. In his mind, while lots of things may not have gone well, some things did, and he wanted to highlight that to the parents. He wanted to frame what the post-game conversation should be like to keep their children engaged and enjoying the sport. Was it successful? "Well," said Beswick, "even though we lost all our games, every single kid came back and played the next season. And a couple of them from that winless team went on to represent the men's senior team. I would define that as successful."

Learn Their First Names

This one requires no explanation. Clearly, get to know your kids' names first but, sooner rather than later, get to know the parents as well. When we treat each other as fellow human beings, we tend to give each other the benefit of the doubt.

Summary

Engage, empower, and educate your team parents. They are the voices their children hear the most. Coaches who do their part to ensure that those voices are reinforcing the culture and the plan have the best chance of getting everyone pulling in the same direction. To do so, do the following:

- Gain a deeper understanding of why parent education and engagement matters. Coaches who stop dealing with parents and start engaging them will have a parent group that is more likely to support the culture instead of tear it down.
- Connect and partner with organizations such as Changing the Game Project, Soccer Parenting Association, Positive Coaching Alliance, ISport360, and others that provide both free and paid resources to help with parent engagement.
- Do some goal setting, set appropriate boundaries, communicate often, and help get the parents on board with what you are doing and why you are doing it.

If you decide to keep dealing with parents instead of engaging them, do so at your own peril. But if you are a coach that truly believes every moment matters, then spend a few of those moments with the parents, and you will build a stronger, more unified team.

PART III

———

HOW DOES IT FEEL TO BE COACHED BY ME?

I've learned that people will forget what you said, people will forget what you did, but people will never forget how you made them feel.

—MAYA ANGELOU

In order to be a coach of Barcelona, it is more important knowing how to lead a group of players than knowing how to correct a mistake made on the field. You have to have influence over the group, to be able to seduce, convince, and understand them.

—JOHAN CRUYFF

Making the transition from player to coach is never an easy thing. Just ask Jenny Levy. She was a two-time All-American and national champion lacrosse player at the University of Virginia and one of the best Atlantic Coast Conference players of all time. By her account, the game came easily to her throughout her collegiate career as she seemed to easily slip into a flow state while playing. The game would slow down, and she would perform at a very high level.

Then, at the ripe old age of twenty-four, she was named the first head coach of women's lacrosse at the University of North Carolina, Chapel Hill. In an instant, it was now her job to help other players to play like she did.

"I made a huge mistake early on thinking that every player thought and acted like me," Levy told me back in 2017. "But I soon realized that there was a huge difference between how I thought and acted and how my team acted." Even so, she had immediate success by all definitions. The first season of the program was 1996, and by 1997-98, UNC Women's Lacrosse was an NCAA Final Four team.

"That was just based on grit, hard work, and fear," lamented Levy. "I told my team, as my alumni like to remind me, 'We won't be the most skilled, we won't be the most talented, but we will be the fittest.' But this was just a physical, transactional type of program. And it gave us success, but what it didn't give us, and me, more important, was satisfaction."

We live in a society that values winning. And there is nothing wrong with winning. But when the outcomes completely overshadow the process, the culture, and the satisfaction of creating an environment that serves your athletes far beyond the sports field, you lose something. Actually, you lose a lot and so do your athletes.

Even though her teams continued to win more games than they lost and went deep into the NCAA tournament year after year, she knew something was missing. "The relationships I had with my players and the ability to connect and really inspire was lacking. The foundation was not strong. You cannot just build a program out of 'win at all costs' and just physical hard work. There has to be something bigger in it for the players. After the 2002 season, it was evident to me that we were nowhere near building a true championship program, and at that point, I had to evaluate what was important to me and what direction I was going to go."

Luckily for Jenny Levy, she worked at UNC, a bastion of coaching excellence. Two of those UNC coaches she got to observe every day had a profound effect upon her program, as did a third, outside consultant. The first coach was Anson Dorrance from UNC women's soccer.

"I watched Anson's practices, and it wasn't the winning that captured me. It was the atmosphere, the culture, the joy, the energy of his players, the authenticity of his players," said Levy. "It had a lot of influence on my thinking about what I wanted my program to *feel* like. It wasn't anything to do with wins and losses, even though I am judged by that. I wanted a *feel* to my program that was fun, hard-working, gritty, tough and humble, and yet successful. If you have that, you are going to be successful."

Levy continued to tweak her training and recruiting, and on the field, she and her staff continued building a culture of excellence and competitiveness in the program. The wins kept coming, yet they could still not get over the hump and win a national title. After another NCAA tournament loss in 2007, this time in the quarterfinals, she reached out to Dr. Jerry Lynch, who had been working with Head Coach Cindy Timchal and the University of Maryland Women's lacrosse program, where Levy's sister had played as they won eight NCAA titles between 1992 and 2001. It was another critical step in the development of the program.

"Working with Jerry gave me the opportunity to coach the way I wanted to coach. It gave me the opportunity to be me," Levy told me. "There were so many coaches who were yellers and screamers and disciplinarians, but it's not my personality to be like that. The modus operandi on me was that I wasn't tough enough. We worked the team hard and we had all this talent, but we could not win. I started working with Jerry, and it gave me permission to figure out my vision, my core values, my non negotiables, and create language and give me words that really resonated with me. This allowed me to sell to my team where we were headed, what our vision was, what it felt like to be a UNC player, what it looked like, and what was important to us. It started us down a great path."

The final piece of the puzzle came together in 2012 after losing an NCAA quarterfinal heartbreaker to Syracuse on a last-minute goal. Levy was heartbroken and began to wonder if she was good enough to lead the program to a national title. So, she took advantage of her UNC coaching family and knocked on the door of legendary men's basketball coach Roy Williams.

"I called Roy after we lost and asked if I could meet with him because I had a question for him: 'You spent all those years at Kansas and had so much success, yet you never won a title, and there is all this criticism. And then you came to Carolina and won in 2005 and 2009. What changed?'"

"'Jenny,' said Williams, 'you have to be OK doing what you think is best for the program, *and it may mean you may never win*.'"

"I looked at him like he had twenty heads," said Levy, "and thought, *Are you out of your mind? That's easy for you to say now that you have won a national championship!*"

"'You can't worry about winning,' continued Williams. 'Follow the path that you believe is correct, stay the course, believe in what you are doing, change where you need to as the game evolves, but your philosophy and core values don't change, and you have to really dig in and believe in these things. And you have to be OK with never winning.'"

"I almost died when he told me that," chuckled Levy. "But even though it really irritated me at the time, it turned out to be a wise comment. The next year we had this amazing energy and spirit, and we gritted out an amazing five-overtime win over Maryland in the championship game and had our first national championship."

Heading into the 2020 season, Levy's Tar Heel program has won almost three hundred fifty games over twenty-four seasons, including thirty-two NCAA tournament wins. They have won two NCAA titles and been to the NCAA Final Four in eight of the last eleven years. In 2017, Levy was named head coach for the United States National Women's Lacrosse Team. Her secret: it has to feel right.

"I cannot coach like Anson Dorrance or Roy Williams," Levy said. "I have to coach like me—especially if you are a female coach, where confidence is key and lack of confidence is pretty common. You gotta know what you believe in and what your values are, and you have to be true to yourself first. You have to know yourself really well."

I then asked Levy, "What is the key to 'The Carolina Way'?" Here is what she told me: "You might not remember what people say to you, but you remember how they made you feel. It doesn't mean it's always comfortable. Our culture is about making people feel good about themselves and making them comfortable with being uncomfortable."

Then she said something that really stuck with me: "At the end of the day in our society," said Levy, "winning gets rewarded, not great culture, and those teams with great culture that don't win do not get rewarded, so team culture gets overlooked. At UNC, what we say we value and what has been proven to be successful—whether it is a business like Southwest Airlines or Nordstrom or a sports team like Steve Kerr and the Golden State Warriors or Pete Carroll and the Seattle Seahawks—is having an extraordinary culture. Yet, what gets really highlighted in our society is winning, not culture, although culture is what creates the opportunity to win."

This section of the book is all about creating a culture and environment that leads to sustainable excellence.

When you intentionally develop these key cultural elements, you develop a way of doing things around your program, much like "The Carolina Way." In other words, it feels a certain way to be part of your program. It feels a certain way to watch you practice and play. It feels a certain way to be an alum and stay connected to this family. It is an honor and a privilege to join your group and be more like you because what you have going here feels incredible.

"I never thought I was going to coach," laughed Levy as we finished up our interview. "My first job out of college, I was a roller-skating waitress in Boulder, Colorado. I didn't know it at the time, but coaching was the perfect job for me."

Yes, it was, Coach. And thankfully for all of us, you found coaching, and coaching found you.

LESSON 12

———

"DON'T TAKE YOUR CULTURE FOR GRANTED"

Establish Your Team's DNA

*Talent will always get you in the dressing room, but how you behave
within the culture will determine how long you remain there.*

—TXIKI BEGIRISTAIN

Great cultures are outcome aware, but purpose and process driven.

—ERIN SMITH

On a typical mid–October day in 2015, the sun was shining,
and the aspen leaves were a sparkling of reds and oranges on
the mountain sides of Vail, Colorado. I was working with
forty amazing coaches from the Vail Ski and Snowboard Club as part of
their annual two-week coaching education program prior to the start of
another season of ski racing, snowboarding, and freestyle competition.
The coaches were taking a deep dive into leadership, team building,
periodization, technical skills, and sport science. It is no wonder that
skiers such as Lindsey Vonn and Mikaela Shiffrin have come through

205

VSSC on their way to becoming some of the best skiers of all time; this is truly an organization that values its coaches and knows that they make or break the experience for the athletes. I had finished speaking and was eagerly awaiting the next speaker. His name was Christian Mitter, and he was the head coach for the Norwegian Men's Alpine Ski Team—at the time, the best alpine ski team in the world.

I was curious what his topic was going to be that day as I could think of no sport more individual than alpine skiing. Basically, you ski as fast as you can through a course and try not to crash. The fastest skiers are always on the edge of total catastrophe, and only on that edge can you ever be victorious. Then Mitter put up the first slide of his talk, and I was shocked. The coach of some of the greatest individual athletes in the world was about to give a talk called "Team Culture Comes First."

"I realize that many people think skiing is an individual sport," said Mitter, "and it may be all about the individual while on the course. But everything that happens before that is about the team and about the culture. When you get that right, everything else follows." Mitter went on to explain how unique skiing is compared to many of the other sports we coach. If we are running a ninety-minute soccer or hockey practice, most of the time, a well-run session is spent moving and performing game-like activities. But skiing is very different. A typical ski practice might consist of only six to eight training runs of ninety to one hundred twenty seconds in a six-hour practice. The rest of the time is spent speaking with coaches, skiing down to the lift, riding a lift, and skiing back to the course to do it again. The smallest portion of your practice is spent actually engaging in your race-like practice. All that other time, according to Mitter, is what separates the very best from all the rest. And this is where team culture comes in.

In part I, we discussed the importance of establishing a team purpose. In this chapter, you'll take the next step of establishing a team culture based on that purpose. By establishing our culture, we bring to life what Todd Beane of TOVO Academy refers to as our DNA, our "do not alter." Our DNA, as Beane says, are the things "that every coach, athlete, parent, and board member knows that we stand for, the things that define who we are when we win, when we lose, on and off the field."[1] Our DNA is the way we do things here that makes us different from others we compete against. It's what galvanizes our purpose into a way of life. All coaches interviewed in this book have worked tirelessly to establish a DNA for their program, and you must, too. Your DNA will promote continued excellence when things are going well and sustain you when the losses pile up. It will become your guiding light and the foundation of what it feels like to be a part of your program. To help you establish your DNA, this chapter will cover how to:

- Establish the foundation of your DNA with core values;
- Create a Shared Purpose Statement;
- Relentlessly communicate your values;
- Promote your cultural architects and eliminate your cultural assassins;
- Reward the things you value most;
- Craft activities for establishing your values and shared purpose; and
- Take a quick DNA test for your team or club.

Let's go!

Core Values: The Foundation of Your DNA

I often start my coaching talks asking the audience if they can name the most successful team of the professional sporting era. "Barcelona!" "The New England Patriots!" "The New York Yankees!" are all common responses. And they are all wrong. The answer is the New Zealand All Blacks, and the sport is rugby.

In over one hundred years of play, the All Blacks have won 84 percent of their games. Since rugby became a professional sport in

1996, the All Blacks boast an 80 percent winning percentage and have been ranked number one in world rankings longer than every other nation combined. They possess a winning record against every single nation they have ever played, and under the tutelage of their last two coaches, Graham Henry and Steve Hansen, the All Blacks have won the last two World Cups and are poised to win a third straight in 2019.

How do they do it? According to James Kerr, author of *Legacy: What the All Blacks Can Teach Us about the Business of Life*, it all comes from their core values. These values are the guiding principles for the All Blacks. They tell them when they are on the right path and when they are wavering. Their values help them know whether they are moving forward, even if the scoreboard says they are not. They are clear, concise, and believable statements of intent that are lived and breathed every single day. For example, the All Blacks call one of these values "Sweep the Shed."

This value means that the goal of every All Blacks player is to leave the national team shirt in a better place than when he got it. His goal is to contribute to the legacy by doing his part to grow the game and keep the team progressing every single day. He must also ensure that he gets better every day. The players realize that in order to continuously improve, you must remain humble and never be too big to do all the small things that need to be done. You must eat right. You must sleep well. You must take care of yourself on and off the field. You must train hard. You must sacrifice your own goals for the greater good and a higher purpose. You must, as the All Blacks say, "Sweep the shed."

Every match is played in front of sixty-thousand-plus fans, as well as millions more on TV. After the match, once the camera crews have left and the coaches are done speaking, once the eyes of the world have turned elsewhere, there is still a locker room to be cleaned.

It gets cleaned by the players. That's right. After each and every game, the All Blacks, led by their team captains and most senior players, take turns sweeping the locker room of every last piece of grass, tape, and mud. They leave the locker room in a better place than they got it.

They leave the shirt in a better place than they got it. They are humble. And through the simple act of sweeping a locker room, they remind themselves of this every time they play. In the words of Kerr, "Sweeping the sheds. Doing it properly. So no one else has to. Because no one looks after the All Blacks. The All Blacks look after themselves."

When a player first makes the All Blacks, he is given a beautiful, black-bound leather book. The first page shows an image of the jersey of the original 1905 team. The next page is a picture of the 1924 "Invincibles" team. The next few pages are images of other legendary teams, up to the present day, all reminders of what you are representing when you put on the shirt. Next, the book outlines the guiding principles and values of the All Blacks and tells the stories of some legendary players. Those values include the following:

- Sweep the sheds
- Create a learning environment
- Play with a higher purpose
- Know yourself
- Keep a blue head
- Embrace expectations
- Sacrifice

The rest of the book is left blank. It is left blank so that the player can journal about his experiences and reflect on his development. It is left blank so he can make his own mark. It is left blank so that he can create his own legacy.[2] The values drive the behavior. The behavior builds the legacy. This is why core values matter. This is why they are the foundation of your DNA.

To start, your values should be believable, clear, and concise. You cannot have too many, or they become a list of "nice to haves" instead of "non-negotiables" that everyone can remember and uphold. They must also be believable as it is counterproductive to value things you cannot possibly do. Most important, they must be values that everyone is willing to hold everyone else accountable for. You cannot value effort if you allow your best player to give 80 percent at training, even if she is still better than everyone else. You cannot value respect if you continually yell at officials or show up late and unprepared and allow your players to do the same. Many teams go through the process of establishing some core values and commitments but then fail to hold each other accountable for them. Those are no longer core values. I will give you some activities at the end of the chapter to help you establish your core values, but for now, I want to help you bring them to life. One of the ways to do that is creating a shared purpose slogan.

Creating Your Shared Purpose Slogan

In lesson 3, you began the process of creating a team purpose. How might you encapsulate that purpose into a team slogan? One thing that many great teams do is to take their core values and organize them into a shared purpose slogan, something that can go on a wall or on the back of a shirt. This slogan becomes a constant reminder of what the group stands for collectively. In *The Culture Code*, Dan Coyle recounts walking into the practice facility of the San Antonio Spurs of the NBA. Again, under Head Coach Gregg Popovich, the Spurs have been consistently excellent. The franchise has only missed the playoffs four times in its history. So how do they do it? They "Pound the Rock."

When you walk into the Spurs facility, you see a sculpture of a giant rock and hammer. Then you see the following quote, written in the five native languages of Spurs players, adorning the walls:

When nothing seems to help, I go look at a stonecutter hammering away at his rock perhaps a hundred times without as much as a crack showing in it. Yet at the hundred and first blow it will split in two, and I know it was not that blow that did it, but all that had gone before.

—JACOB RIIS

Practice after practice, day after day, season after season, the Spurs pound the rock. They get 1 percent better every day. They know that the first one hundred attempts may not yield the outcome they hope for, but only through one hundred unsuccessful blows will come the one that cracks the rock, the one breakthrough victory, the next world title. Ask any Spurs player what it is all about being a member of that team or listen to press interviews about what they are doing to get better, and they will all tell you one thing: pound the rock.

A huge reason for the Spurs' success is their shared commitment to do all the little things it takes to be great. They embrace the process, look at adversity as nothing more than an unsuccessful blow, and constantly seek excellence. That excellence is encapsulated in those three simple words. They are clear, concise, believable, easy to communicate, and something that everyone is willing to be held accountable for. Pound. The. Rock.

Communicate Your Values

Recent research in the business world demonstrates how important— and how difficult—it is to create a shared purpose and core values and communicate them effectively. A research paper from the MIT Sloan Business School's Strategic Agility Project analyzed a company in which 97 percent of its leadership said in a survey that they had a clear grasp of the company's strategic goals. This excited the company CEO, who was confident that its five strategic priorities were well known as they had not changed in years; and, in her mind, they were well communicated. Yet when the researchers asked the company leadership to list the five priorities, only 25 percent of the managers could list three of the five. One-third of the leadership, the very people charged with implementing company strategy, could not list a single one. These same researchers analyzed 124 additional organizations and once again found that only 28 percent of the top managers could list three of the five organizational priorities.[3] The takeaway is this: whatever your team or organization values must be communicated relentlessly. You cannot over-communicate those values. Stop assuming people know and assume that they don't know.

I share this because for many years as a coach I simply assumed all my athletes knew exactly what I wanted from them and exactly how we were supposed to do things on our team. I assumed that because I knew it and spoke about it, so I felt sure that they had learned it. And I was wrong. Today, I am much more intentional about establishing team core values and shared purpose, and I am relentless about communicating them. As Nancy Stevens, the three-time NCAA champion field hockey coach at the University of Connecticut reminded me, we can never forget that our team always has a culture. We have to be intentional about it because, as Stevens says, "If you are not really proactive in working to create the culture that you want your team to have, the culture may develop in a way you really don't want it to."

I want to share with you some of the ways we intentionally communicate our core values with the teams that I work with. Here is an excerpt from a letter I wrote to one of the college lacrosse teams I work with as we prepared to start preseason. We read a book together called *The Hard Hat* by Jon Gordon, and from that book, we selected our team values for the season.

Coach sent me your three favorite values from *The Hard Hat*, and I love what you have selected for your values this season:

- Well done is better than well said.
- Be hungry and humble.
- Never take a play off.

Our work together will be to build upon these values you have selected. It will not be about Xs and Os or mental skills. You have a great coaching staff for that. We will be working on spirit, the togetherness and bond that will make this group a championship-caliber team. All the teams you play will have physical talent; many will have some mental skills; but if we put in the work, no one we play will have the culture and spirit that our group will. We will have spiritual talent. And make no mistake about it, culture and spirit create a team of warriors that never take a play off and let their actions do all the talking necessary.

A few weeks later, we were a couple of games into the season, and, on the scoreboard at least, we had a tough start. But we were competing hard; we were hungry and humble; and we were embracing the process. After a gut-wrenching overtime loss to a team that had been to five straight NCAA finals, I sent them another letter. Here is an excerpt:

Yesterday on our Skype, we talked about playing with confidence, not being in awe, and seizing the moment. That is what I saw. We talked about being aggressive and winning the ground-ball battle. Seventeen to eight tells me we were. Outshooting the team that has been to five straight NCAA title games by twenty-four to fifteen tells me we were on our toes all game. We talked about winning draws and putting ourselves in good positions, and we did. We controlled everything we could control. If anybody asked a neutral there today what our values were, they saw them in action. They saw people getting it done. They saw hungry players. They saw a never-say-die attitude. Regardless of the score, these things can never change.

And this is part of the process. This is the Way of Champions. We come up short, and we learn. We win, and we learn. We continue to build an unbreakable spirit and bond. Every game, every week, our bond must continue to grow, and our love for each other must continue to get stronger. It is that spirit that we must bring to every game, to play in the now and to burn inside us, knowing that we can stand toe to toe with the best teams in the country and give them everything they can handle.

Your values and shared purpose are important when you are winning, but they are even more important when you are losing. They tell you that you are on the right track. They keep you focused on the process and the controllables. And they give you a better way to determine if you are progressing than simply looking at the scoreboard. Our group knew that we were close, but after a few close losses, we had a losing record, and it's easy for doubt and negativity to creep in. My job, and the job of the coaching staff, was to keep the team focused on those three values and to measure our progress according to upholding those values, not simply the scoreboard.

From that day forward, we won thirteen straight games, eventually winning the program's first conference championship in ten years. And although we lost a heartbreaking game in the NCAA tournament, I wrapped up the season by again reminding the team of how we do things here:

At some point, when the sting fades, you will be able to look back on our magical season with great pride and satisfaction. Conference champions! Thirteen-game winning streak against the toughest schedule in the country. Tied for first in the regular season. Knowing that you can step on the field with anyone, anyplace, anytime to compete and win. You have raised the bar. There is a new standard that our players must uphold. Those who are leaving were integral in creating it. Those who are returning have the privilege and responsibility to uphold it, to teach our new players about it, and to live it every day. That is how we accumulate the gains from this season and prepare for the future.

Thank you all for living the Way of the Champion, for never giving up, for being hungry and humble every single day, and for inspiring me by showing that well done is much better than well said. And most important, for demonstrating that kicking ass day after day, week after week, month after month is the only way to live.

If you are saying to yourself, "That is great, but I work with young kids," I hear you. If you are saying, "This is great, but I don't have time to establish values," I challenge you that you do have time. I challenge you that you do not have time *not* to establish values. Quality of training is more important than quantity, and establishing a strong culture helps your team to become more focused, more energized, and more accountable. In other words, you become better at practice. You must establish an identity and way of doing things in your own little kingdom. And at the end of this chapter, I will give you two simple ways to do that. One exercise takes about twenty minutes and the other about ninety minutes, but I promise you will get those minutes back through the quality and efficiency of your sessions after you do these exercises. But before I share those with you, I want to discuss two types of people that will either supercharge your culture or tear it apart: cultural architects and cultural assassins.

Promote Your Cultural Architects and Eliminate Your Cultural Assassins

When Pep Guardiola took over as manager at FC Barcelona, a few eyebrows were raised. He had been an extraordinary player for the club and for Spain, but he had never coached at the highest level before. Many pundits wondered why he was being given the reins of one of the biggest clubs in the world. But Guardiola was steeped in the culture of Barcelona, and he knew how he wanted to play. He also knew that he needed every player on the squad to buy into his team-first philosophy.

At his first press conference, the brand new manager was asked about the role of his three star players: Portugal superstar Deco, former World Player of the Year Ronaldinho, and African Player of the Year Samuel Eto'o. Guardiola's response shocked the world:

> These three are not in my mind for the future. In fact, we will go on without them. My view is that it is all about performance and what players can give to my squad. What I will not tolerate is a lack of effort to rebuild the success of the team. I want the talented, inspired players to understand that, individually, they are worth much less than when they invoke team values.[4]

Within a year, all three players had been sold, and Guardiola was able to give playing time to young players from the club's famed youth academy La Masia. Those young players were named Lionel Messi, Xavi, Anders Iniesta, Carlos Puyol, Gerard Pique, and Victor Valdes. They understood the ethos, playing style, and culture of FC Barcelona and led the club to unprecedented success over the next decade.

The reason Eto'o, Ronaldinho, and Deco were sold was not that they were no longer good players. As author Damian Hughes writes about in *The Barcelona Way: Unlocking the DNA of a Winning Culture*, Guardiola was worried that their off-field behavior could negatively affect his up and coming young stars and that their refusal to buy in to the team-first philosophy would prevent his team from playing a high-tempo, possession-based, pressing style of play. Their lifestyle and choices made them cultural assassins, no longer cultural architects.

"Cultural architects," writes Norwegian psychologist Willi Railo, "are people who are able to change the mindset of others. They are able to break barriers; they have visions. They are self-confident and are able to transfer self-confidence to other players." They are the teammates who build trust, promote good communication, and bring others into the fold. Railo recommends that teams have three to five such players in order to influence those around them and extend the team's shared culture.[5]

Cultural architects are prevalent on some of the world's most successful teams. Sir Alex Ferguson of Manchester United has spoken often on how Eric Cantona changed the culture of the dressing room as he influenced players to stay after training and continue practicing. Jon Torine, a Super Bowl-winning strength and conditioning coach with the Indianapolis Colts, told me about the influence of Hall of Fame quarterback Peyton Manning. "The work ethic of this man was indescribable," gushed Torine. "He would go to Scotland on a golf trip in the offseason, and we would have to make up workouts for him to do in the middle of the golf course. He would write them down and report back. The great ones all have this singular 'I want to be great at this thing' focus, and it is infectious." [6]

Cultural architects are athletes who ask themselves, "What can I give?" to the team. They come from a place of service and believe things such as:

- I can give my best effort in practice and games.
- I can give my team a positive attitude, no matter what the circumstances.
- I can give my team a boost, no matter how many minutes I play.
- I can give my team a better chance to win, no matter what position I play.
- I can do the dirty work so my teammate can score the goal and get the glory.
- I can sacrifice my personal ambitions for the betterment of the group.
- I can lead by example.
- I can be an example of our core values in action.

Steve Kerr told us a great story about one of the cultural architects for the Golden State Warriors, Andre Iguodala. Iguodala was an NBA all-star and an Olympian when Kerr took over the team, and Kerr believed they would be a much better team with him coming off the bench than starting. Imagine that, being recognized as one of the twenty best players in the league yet being asked not to start on your own team. Yet Kerr knew that if he anchored the bench unit and gave the team a huge lift whenever he came into games, it could make the Warriors a much better team. "Andre is a brilliant basketball player and basketball mind. He knows the game as well as anybody," Kerr told us. "So he understood where I was coming from. It didn't make it easy because he was used to starting, but I asked him to give it a shot. And he agreed. And the way that season went was one of the most gratifying things that I've ever felt in sports. Andre Iguodala became our sixth man, helped us win sixty-eight games and became finals MVP when we've got to go small. We've got to start Andre in the second part of the finals, and he gets the MVP in the finals and wins a championship. I mean, you couldn't have written it any better." Andre Iguodala embraced his role as a cultural architect and embraced the ethos of asking, "What can I give?" to his team. Last year he released his autobiography. The title? *The Sixth Man.*

By the same token, cultural assassins can be influential in a very negative way. Ronaldinho, for example, was formerly a cultural architect for Barcelona, but by 2007, he was partying often and training poorly. His physical decline did not lead to a decline in influence, though, and he became a cultural assassin, a person, in the words of Railo, "who is negative, who tells you why something cannot be done rather than how it can be done." Ronaldinho partied all night and slept on the massage table in the training room. He grew bored during games and faked injuries in order to be substituted. During his party years and decline, ten players on the Barcelona senior team got divorced. It was time for him to go in the eyes of Guardiola, before he derailed the careers of the new generation.[7]

Cultural assassins often bring an attitude of "What can I get?" to the team. In our self-centered world of selfies, Instagram, and a popular culture that says "look at me" every chance it gets, far too many athletes become cultural assassins. They want to know how they can

- Get to start;
- Get more playing time;
- Get to play their favorite position;
- Get to score all the points/goals;
- Get to work hard when they want to;
- Get to show up (physically and mentally) when they feel like it;
- Get to give less than their best because they are an upperclassman; and
- Get attention as the star player.

As a coach, I used to think that the most important thing was to have my best players be my hardest workers. But now I realize that isn't enough. Being a hard worker can still be a selfish pursuit. I now believe the most important thing as a coach is to have cultural architects that ask, "What can I give?" This is especially true when it comes to your captains, your upperclassmen, and your most talented athletes. You must teach them that a selfless attitude leads to excellence, celebrates the success of others, and makes you the type of athlete that every coach wants on his team. To do this, you must intentionally and relentlessly establish, promote, communicate, and reward the values that bring about this type of attitude. You must have a DNA. We have all probably coached cultural assassins, athletes with ability and influence that is used in a less than positive way. The list of "talented" professional athletes who have become cultural assassins within their teams would fill up a whole book. Our job as coaches is to minimize the effect the assassins have while, at the same time, creating an environment for the cultural architects to emerge and lead the group. So, how do we do that?

Reward Your Values

My two children went to a school called Bear Creek Elementary in Bend, Oregon. On paper, Bear Creek looked like a school that might struggle and at one point had over 70 percent of its students classified as Title One kids, meaning they got free or reduced lunches from the federal government due to economic status. Yet the school was fantastic, and I believe it was because they had three core values that everyone believed, promoted, and rewarded: Be Safe. Be Kind. Be Responsible.

You could find these three values on every wall and every school sweatshirt, written in both English and Spanish (over 50 percent of the students there are native Spanish speakers). They were in every classroom. There were assemblies throughout the year teaching students about these values and recognizing the children who exemplified the value of the month. But most important, in my mind, were the daily acknowledgments that children could earn. They were called Bear Hugs.

At any point of the day, if a teacher or staff member witnessed a student being safe, kind, or responsible, they could award them a sticker called a Bear Hug. Collect enough of these stickers and you got to go the office and pick a prize, usually some small bouncy ball that was perfect for tripping mom or dad in a dark room! In all the years at school, my children never failed to tell my wife and me when they received a Bear Hug, especially when they were very young and being taught about the culture of the school. Every student in the school knew the values. Every staff member knew what to reward. And if you paid even the slightest bit of attention, every parent could tell you what mattered most as well.

Be safe. Be kind. Be responsible. These were clear, concise, and believable values communicated every day and rewarded. It even works with five-year-olds!

Another example of how this can work with older athletes comes from a great school in Fort Wayne, Indiana, called The Canterbury School. Canterbury has high-quality academics and athletics, and its top student athletes regularly achieve All-American status, win state titles, and go on to compete for NCAA championships. But my long-time friend and athletic director at Canterbury, Ken Harkenrider, felt something was missing from their annual end-of-year sports banquets. The same athletes who received scholarships and all-state were, of course, winning MVPs and Athlete of the Year. In other words, the athletes who had already garnered tons of recognition were getting more of the same, and there was not much energy behind the awards event anymore. Harkenrider, a Positive Coaching Alliance trainer and AD for over twenty-five years, thought it could be so much more.

"The best advice I got when I started this job was that all my issues would come down to two things: playing time and recognition," Harkenrider told me. "Now, there are only so many roster spots and so many minutes in a varsity game to go around, so it's tough to deal with playing time in sports that are competing for state titles. But recognition is something that coaches have a lot of control over, and if they are intentional about it, they can make sure every athlete is a contributor and knows that she plays an important role. Our awards dinner was simply recognizing all the kids whose names were in the paper every week and who were already being recognized. We felt that we could do more."

In other words, Harkenrider and his staff realized that if you make athletes feel invaluable without being most valuable, great things would happen. "So, we got rid of the MVPs and Most Improved awards and came up with some that reflected our school values and were within reach of every student athlete," said Harkenrider. "And it has been incredible."

Canterbury got rid of the traditional awards and came up with five awards that each team could award, and then a male and female athlete from the school would win an overall award. The awards are as follows:

- Playing with Passion Award
- Best Impact Award (for a non-starter)
- Rise to the Occasion Award
- The Austin Hatch Grit and Persistence Award
- The Darby Maggard Attitude of Gratitude Award

How has changing the awards gone? Attendance at the award dinners is way up. Anticipation over which compelling athletic contribution will win is through the roof. More athletes are engaged and contributing because they know that they can be recognized, even if they are not the star player. "The stories that we have heard are incredible since the inception of these awards," says Harkenrider. "You don't have to be an All-American to play with passion or rise to the occasion or persist through an injury and contribute to your team." He then shared with me the story of Austin Hatch, for whom the Grit and Persistence Award is named. You may have heard of Hatch, who recently graduated from the University of Michigan and gained national attention when he stepped on the court for his final game there.

Hatch was in a plane crash in third grade, which killed his mother and two siblings. Unbelievably, following his sophomore year when he was named regional player of the year, he was involved in a second plane crash, which killed his father and stepmother. He survived but was in a medically induced coma for four months. He slowly returned to school, did intensive physical therapy, and returned to play basketball again. He played a final high school season and then again for Michigan, where Head Coach John Beilein honored the scholarship offer he had made to Austin one week before the second plane crash. He went on to finish his Michigan degree and now speaks as a motivational speaker on behalf of the Domino Pizza corporation. That is grit and persistence! "This," says Harkenrider, "is what sport is supposed to teach us, and this is what sport is all about."

Canterbury School developed their awards as an extension of the educational mission of the school. What if you don't have those values already in place? Here are a few simple ways to establish your DNA.

Activities to Develop Your Team DNA

Establishing your DNA can be done in many ways. Here are several ways to do this, whether you are coaching ten-year-olds or twenty-five-year-olds.

The Twenty-Minute Team Values Exercise

I learned this one from my good friend James Leath from Unleash the Athlete and have shared it at all my coaching talks for the last few years. I first tried this with a group of ten-year-old soccer girls I was coaching after I was asked to take over a struggling team whose coach had quit. The girls were placed in the wrong division and routinely losing games by eight or ten goals. We needed to learn how to practice well and compete in training first and then to start closing the gap with our opponents. I also realized that it was unlikely we would win a game that year, so we needed a new way to define success other than wins and losses.

Taking James's advice, I sat the girls down for twenty minutes before my first practice and asked them to give me some adjectives that describe a great teammate. They asked me what an adjective was, so I taught that first. And then they were on a roll. "Hard worker!" "Positive!" "Caring!" "Not afraid of mistakes!" "Focused!" they shouted out, and I wrote them down. Once we had compiled our list, I had them all sign the bottom of the paper, where it said, "I commit to being the type of teammate described above." I signed it, too. On the next page is that team values sheet:

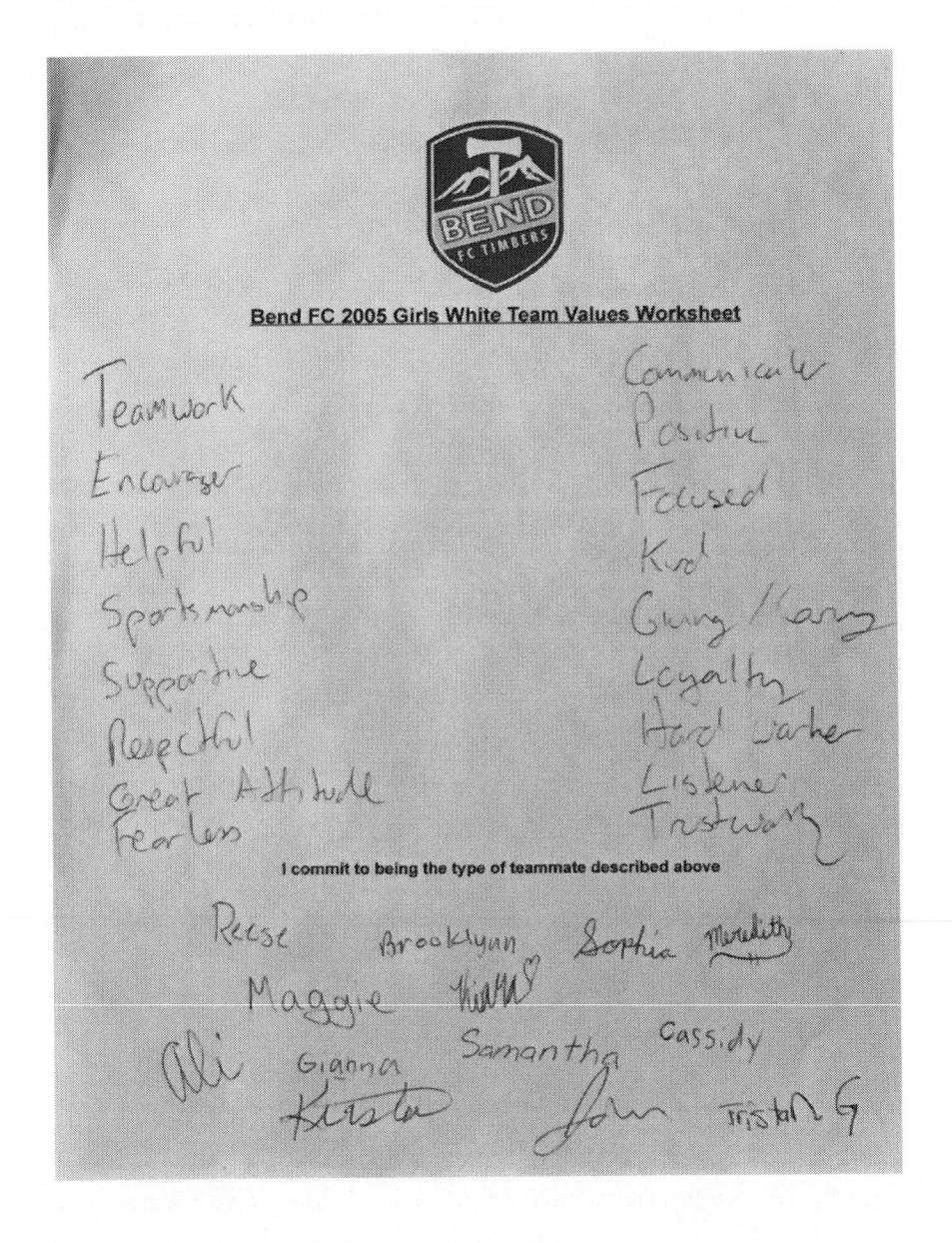

Bend FC 2005 Girls White Team Values Worksheet

Teamwork

Encourager

Helpful

Sportsmanship

Supportive

Respectful

Great Attitude

Fearless

Communicate

Positive

Focused

Kind

Giving / Caring

Loyalty

Hard Worker

Listener

Trustworthy

I commit to being the type of teammate described above

Reese   Brooklynn   Sophia   Meredith

Maggie   Kiana

Ali   Gianna   Samantha   Cassidy

Kirsten   Jane   Tristan G

"This is who we have all agreed to be when we come together," I reminded them. "Every practice I will pick one of these values to high-light. I don't care if you make a mistake or miss a pass or a shot. Just be this type of teammate, and we will get better every day." I then snapped a photo of the paper and sent it to all their parents, telling them the same thing and encouraging them to ask their daughter about the value of the day on the ride home from practice.

From that day forward, these values became our non-negotiables, the things we expected each other to bring. I did my best each session to introduce not only a technical or tactical element but also the value of the day. If we were doing something new, we might have said "fear-lessness." Throughout that session, I would do my best to catch them epitomizing that value. "I saw you try that turn, Reece; that's OK that it didn't work. That is being fearless. That is how we do things here!"

The real magic came at the end of each practice. After my debrief, I asked the girls, "Does anyone want to give one of your teammates a shout-out today for really exemplifying one of our values?" Many hands would shoot up. Many of the girls would get acknowledgment from one of their teammates for their effort or bravery or positivity that day. Myself and my assistant coach might throw in one or two as well. They would leave practice with their tank full, jump in the car and say, "I got a shout-out today for being fearless!"

At season's end, we had a team dinner. Inspired by The Canter-bury School, I did not give out an MVP or Most Improved. I went down our list of values and described to the parents and players what each one meant and which player exemplified that value the most. I watched their faces, and with almost every value, the players turned to the teammate who was about to get acknowledged as they recognized our values in each other. They all felt valued. They all contributed to our growth and improvement. After I was done and the kids scampered off to the hotel pool, many parents said that it was the best season in sports any of their kids had ever had.

Here is the kicker: we never won a game. We lost them all and tied one. But we got a lot better. That is how you redefine success, focus on your values, and embrace the process. That is how you make your athletes feel invaluable without being the most valuable.

The Ninety-Minute Team Values Exercise

The following season, I took over two teams of girls in my club and decided to take our twenty-minute values session to another level, much like the work I do with college teams. Thirty-two girls and two coaches, as well as a few interested parents, gathered together for ninety minutes. I started by asking the girls to write down three qualities of a great teammate. We then went around the room and shared each of our words, and I kept a running tally. Five values emerged as the most important to our group, the qualities that would drive our progress. We then defined what each of them meant and what we were willing to hold each other accountable for. The five values were as follows:

- Fun: we must enjoy ourselves and love what we are doing.
- Unity: we *all* work hard and compete every day together.
- Commitment: the willingness to do all the little things needed to be great.
- Sportsmanship: we respect our teammates, opponents, coaches, officials, parents, the game, and the opportunities it gives us.
- Accountability: we are all willing to be responsible to ourselves and our teammates.

2005 BEND FC GIRLS
TEAM VALUES

FUN: Love what you are doing

UNITY: We All work hard + Compete Everyday Together

Commitment: The Willingness to do all the little things to be great

Sportsmanship: Respect our teammates, opponents, coaches, officials, parents and the game + the opportunities it gives us

Accountability: we are all willing to be responsible to ourselves + our teammates

Again, all the girls signed our paper, seen here hanging on a window at our event, and the process began again: a value of the week; daily moments catching them being good; shout-outs at the end of practice for each other; timely reminders to the players when commitment, unity, or accountability was waning about how we all agreed to embody these values; timely reminders to the coaches, such as, "It was a crappy day at school. Can we make sure this is really fun today?" We lived these values together for two years. And guess what? We eventually won a lot of games.

Creating a Team Slogan

Come up with a team slogan like "Pound the Rock" that epitomizes what you value and your team's purpose. I have had teams with slogans such as "Inch by Inch" and "Rise to the Occasion." These went on shirts and the walls of the locker room. This simple reminder can be the difference between a team that knows its DNA and one that lives it.

Identifying Cultural Architects

This activity was inspired by the work of Damian Hughes in his book *The Barcelona Way*. He asked some top-level coaches what were the three most important things they needed from their cultural architects. Their answers centered around three key areas: talent, attitude, and behavior—what they called the "trademark behaviors," aka core values. Hughes suggests you grade your players in these key areas and see which players seem to score highly in areas that matter the most.[8] I would add the caveat that with youth and high school players, attitude and values would weigh more heavily than talent.

Player Name	Talent (A, B, C, D)	Attitude (A, B, C, D)	Values (A, B, C, D)
1.			
2.			
3.			

Ten Questions to Help You Establish Your Team/Club DNA

Try answering these ten questions recommended by Todd Beane to help you clarify what your organization's "do not alter" truly is:

- Why does our organization exist?
- What are we teaching?
- How do we define winning?
- How do we define losing?
- What are the characteristics of the ideal player?
- What are the characteristics of the ideal coach?
- What are the characteristics of the ideal parent?
- If the organization could accomplish one thing, what would it be?
- What do we want for our children?
- How do we have fun here?

Summary

Establishing your DNA is critical in building a program or team that will continually strive for excellence and uphold a high standard. In order to establish your DNA, you must

- Establish your core values, which will become the foundation of your DNA.
- Create a Shared Purpose Statement, a consistent phrase or reminder to go on your locker room walls and on your training shirts.
- Relentlessly communicate your values and assume that people *do not* know what they are—instead of assuming everyone is crystal clear.
- Promote your cultural architects, eliminate your cultural assassins, and shine a light on the people who bring it every day.

- Reward the things you value most by rewarding your values and not just your MVPs.
- Try the twenty-minute or ninety-minute core values activities with your team.
- If needed, take a quick DNA test for your team or club and learn what matters most.

Just like the New Zealand All Blacks, your DNA will promote improvement in the good times and, more important, keep you on the right path when the scoreboard is consistently not in your favor. It will tell you when you are on the right path and when you have veered. Most important, it will allow you to shape behavior and reward those athletes who epitomize all that your program is about. Culture comes first, and everything else follows.

LESSON 13

"PERFORMANCE IS A BEHAVIOR, NOT AN OUTCOME"

Establish Standards to Drive Excellence in Your Program

Playing to a standard is the biggest secret to our repeated success.

—DAVE BRANDT

Performance is a behavior, not an outcome.

—MARK BENNETT

Mark Bennett, MBE, is the founder of Performance Development Systems Coaching—PDS Coaching for short. He travels the globe working with sports teams and coaches, from the elite level all the way down to grassroots. One week he is working with an NBA team or the Cleveland Indians of Major League Baseball, and the next he is working with rugby coaches in Scotland and a group of eight-year-old players. Bennett got his start, though, doing much more serious work: training British Commandos.

Bennett joined the army in 1983, thinking he was going to be surrounded by fit, highly motivated people like himself, but he soon realized that was not the case. Frustrated, he attended the full British Commando course, and Bennett found a home. He described it this way: "I was surrounded by far more motivated and fit people that shared my enjoyment of pain." In the early 1990s, after serving in many over-seas operations, Bennett moved to the recruit training center, where he became an instructor. It was here that Bennett began to develop the framework for PDS Coaching.

At the end of every ten-week session, there were obstacle course marches, speed tests, and fitness tests. "For the first eighteen months I was there," said Bennett, "my platoon smashed it. They won every single competition and I thought, *I'm fantastic at my job.*" Then Bennett had a life-changing moment. At one of the graduation ceremonies, a parent of one of the soldiers told Bennett, "My son doesn't stop talking about you; you've really changed his life." Bennett was stunned. "A light bulb went out for me because, in that very moment, I connected with all the young soldiers and recruits that had not graduated." He looked around at graduation and noticed that all the other platoons were bigger than his and had not weeded out nearly as many soldiers. "I started to real-ize that actually where I thought I was a very good physical training instructor, I was actually quite poor. I was good working with people that had mental robustness, the desire to learn, and the tenacity to keep up with me. But I was not good enough in changing people's behaviors that didn't have those qualities. I realized I either needed to change jobs or change how I went about developing soldiers."

Over the next few years, Bennett began building out and testing his framework, and by the year 1999, he had become a senior instruc-tor. He also began working with elite sports teams and coaches while on leave. But there was a problem. "I started to realize that the system worked great when they were with me, but when they went back into their normal environment, they were reverting back to what they were doing. So, I realized I needed to come up with a way to train the trainers." Bennett eventually left the army to pursue PDS Coaching full time, and he not only works with elite teams and athletes headed to Olympic games and playing for world championships, but he also has become one of the top coach developers and mentors in the UK. As Bennett began working with more teams and coaches, he realized that we often evaluate performance based solely upon results. But as he dug deeper, he realized that those results were really a byproduct of behavior. Bennett's philosophy can be summed up in seven words: performance is a behavior, not an outcome.

"If you asked any coach," says Bennett, "'What if every single one of your athletes would turn up, make a decision, and commit to it 100 percent and were able to review both their commitment and their decision, what do you think would happen to your team, your play, and your athlete?' And everyone would say, 'My God, Mark, everything would go through the roof; it would be fantastic if that happened.' And I say, 'That's interesting. How much time have you invested in you becoming effective at that and how much time do you spend identifying that in the training session and working on it?' And normally the answer comes back, 'Well, I haven't really thought about it, so the answer's probably zero.'"[1]

The PDS Coaching framework is very person and athlete-centric, and that is why I am such a big fan. I have had the opportunity to see Mark work and have also had him evaluate and mentor me on some sessions. It is awkward at first, standing in front of your team with a GoPro on your chest, but eventually the players forget the camera and just play. You coach, and then you get to sit down and do a review with Mark as he looks at the places you intervene, how you conduct stoppages, how you draw the solutions out of your athletes instead of always providing them, and so much more. Bennett asks all coaches to review themselves using audio and sound before he makes any comments or suggestions. Why? Because a critical element to Bennett's principles is to develop effective self-awareness within the coach. "How can a coach make effective choices on any interventions and their style of communication," asks Bennett, "if they have poor self-awareness?"

As I have shared on the podcast often, working with Mark Bennett and implementing the PDS Coaching methodology has been the hardest thing I have ever done—and also the most effective. The methodology gives players more ownership and accountability and forces them to be fully engaged at all times, whether they are playing or off on the sideline injured. It has given them the permission and space to fix things on the fly, to hold their teammates accountable for being unfocused or unprepared, and to accept feedback from peers. They now do a lot of their own coaching during stoppages, and they are the first and last voices to speak at halftime. It has helped me sharpen the focus to training and to slowly but surely make myself a bit redundant, step back, and watch the players solve problems. PDS allows the intelligence and problem-solving to be on the field, not on the sideline. It has also allowed us to throw out a lot of team rules. In their place we now have standards.

This chapter is all about changing behaviors and implementing standards instead of rules in your program. A *rule* is a regulation or guideline while a *standard* is a level of quality. Rules can be demeaning in a way, as they are all about control, while standards can be inspiring. When young athletes encounter rules, they constantly test them to see how far they can go before they are held accountable for breaking them. Standards, on the other hand, are something to be strived for and attained. They result in stretch as athletes hold each other accountable for reaching higher, instead of sinking to the level of a rule. Endless sets of rules can be exhausting to enforce and can cripple a coach's ability to make decisions on an individual basis. Standards are levels of achievement that the whole group buys into and pushes each other toward and are usually policed within the group. In a nutshell, rules have a negative connotation—don't break me or else—while standards are far more positive: live up to me, and you will be your best self.

As legendary Duke basketball coach Mike Krzyzewski says, "When I was at West Point, we had a bunch of rules, all of which I didn't agree with. Usually when you're ruled, you never agree with all the rules, you just abide by them. But if you have standards and if everyone contributes to the way you're going to do things, you end up owning how you do things." In my research, the best programs seem to have as few rules as absolutely necessary and as many standards as they are capable of holding each other accountable for. I hope that is what you are seeking to create in your program as well, and my goal in this chapter is to give you some ideas on how to build a standards-based team. In it, we will cover

- How playing to a standard drives sustained success;
- How Riders, Elephants, and a roadmap are the key element of behavior change;
- Mark Bennett's "Rule of Three" for creating accountability in your team;
- A five-step process for engaging the "challenging" athlete;
- A simple activity for helping your athletes understand how ability and behavior work together to develop excellence; and
- Maintaining standards through a "legacy" notebook.

Many of us likely grew up playing sports and attending schools in rules-based environments, instead of standards based. And if you are like me, you did your best to stretch those rules as far as possible in your favor. At least once in your life, though, I hope you have been part of a culture that had standards to aspire to instead of rules to break because these are high-performing cultures. One such culture we have already visited in rural Pennsylvania, and the other is celebrated worldwide for their excellence. Let's revisit Messiah College men's and women's soccer and the New Zealand All Blacks.

What Messiah College Soccer and the New Zealand All Blacks Can Teach Us about Playing to a Standard

"Most people naturally play to one thing, and that is winning," long-time Messiah Head Coach Dave Brandt told author Michael Zigarelli for his book *The Messiah Method: The Seven Disciplines of the Winningest College Soccer Program in America.* That is not what they do at Messiah, though. "Playing to a standard," says Brandt, "is the biggest secret to our repeated success." Brandt, along with current Head Men's Coach Brad McCarty and current Women's Head Coach Scott Frey, likes to quote Will Durant: "We are what we repeatedly do. Excellence, then, is not an act but a habit." And all three know that a standard of excellence is not simply something you do in games; it is evident in everything you do.

When I speak with athletes who have played at Messiah, they speak about this high standard that permeates the program. They talk about the competitiveness of every single session. They speak about coming in for preseason and not wanting to let their teammates down by being unfit or not making the team's fitness standards. They talk about repeating activities in practice time again and again to get them right. They speak about training late nights in January, a full eight months before the season starts, and trying to stretch their advantage over other programs a little further.

Most important, they all speak about leaving the shirt in a better place by doing all the little things every single day to get better. That is why Messiah has set such a standard of excellence and year after year return to final fours and win national championships. Zigarelli was stunned when Brandt summed up his philosophy by quoting from an article called "The Mundanity of Excellence" in the academic journal *Sociological Theory*: "Excellence is accomplished through the doing of actions, ordinary in themselves, performed consistently and carefully, habitually compounded together, added up over time." High standards might not make you popular with everyone, but they will eventually attract the right kind of players and help you build the right type of program. As Zigarelli concludes, "If 'play to a standard' means anything, it means that the leader will be raising the bar—permanently—insisting on maximum effort, calling out non-adherents, quashing mediocrity, and unswervingly informing new thresholds of behavior."[2]

This same dogged pursuit of excellence is evident in the New Zealand All Blacks, and their unparalleled success can be traced to a statement that encapsulates that standard: "Better people make better All Blacks."

In 1999, Adidas made a commercial celebrating the high standards and legacy of the All Blacks. It began with the oldest living All Blacks captain, Charlie Saxton, standing in a locker room with his jersey on. As he pulled it over his head, he morphed into Fred Allen, another famous All Blacks captain and coach. One by one, the player pulls off his jersey to reveal another captain, all the way through to the current captain in 1999, Taine Randell. On the bottom of the screen, the caption reads, "The legacy is more intimidating than the opposition." As Coach Graham Henry told author James Kerr, "There is a big saying in the team, 'You don't own the jersey; you're just the body in the jersey at the time.' It's your job to continue the legacy and add to it when you get your opportunity."[3]

Much like Messiah College, the All Blacks never-ending quest to leave the jersey in a better place results in extremely high standards and accountability to your coaches, teammates, community, and all the players who came before you. But how do you go about beginning this process, of switching from a rules-based to a standards-based structure? Well, if you are going to change behaviors, first you must understand how to make that happen. To do that, let's talk about riding an elephant.

Riders, Elephants, and the Path Ahead

Our goal at Changing the Game Project has always been to help change behaviors around youth sports. Our speakers give hundreds of talks and workshops a year, all focused upon putting more play back in playing sports and helping coaches, parents, and youth sports organizations create a more athlete-centered youth sports environment. We are heavily invested in the behavior-change business, but for the first few years, I didn't realize that my efforts were largely ineffective because I did not understand how to motivate people to change. I was very good at providing data and studies to back up the reasons why children were quitting sports and getting injured; I could also articulate what they wanted from coaches. What I failed to do was engage my audience emotionally, to make sure they felt something that would compel them to change what they were doing. Then I read *Switch: How to Change Things When Change Is Hard* by brothers Chip and Dan Heath, and it altered how I went about my work.

In *Switch*, the Heath brothers use an analogy by University of Virginia's Jonathan Haidt to describe how our minds have two opposing forces that govern behaviors: our rational mind and our emotional mind. Haidt calls the rational mind the "Rational Rider" and the emotional mind the "Wild Elephant." "Perched atop the Elephant," write the Heaths, "the Rider holds the reins and seems to be the leader. But the Rider's control is precarious because the Rider is so small compared to the Elephant. Anytime the six-ton Elephant and the Rider disagree about which direction to go, the Rider is going to lose. He is completely overmatched."

When efforts to change fail, it is usually because our emotional mind overwhelms our rational one. Instant gratification almost always defeats long-term thinking. At other times, our Rider can cause us to overthink things and spin our wheels or, as the Heath brothers describe it, lead our Elephant in circles. To combat this and bring about sustainable behavior change, the Heaths recommend a three-step approach:

1. Direct the Rider: Provide crystal-clear direction and information since what looks like resistance to change is often a lack of information and clarity. We do this by pointing out our bright spots—our athletes who are upholding or exceeding our standards—and use them as examples. We also do this by setting goals and providing examples of what excellence looks like.

2. Motivate the Elephant: Since the Rider cannot force the elephant in any direction for very long, we must engage people emotionally and get their Elephants to cooperate. People don't fail to change because they are lazy; they are usually exhausted from the effort and give up. We motivate the Elephant by helping our athletes find that feeling change brings about and breaking the journey down into manageable and measurable steps.

3. Shape the Path: Often, it is not the people involved but the environment that prevents behavior change. When you shape the Path, you make change more likely to happen, regardless of what is happening with the Rider or the Elephant. We shape the Path by providing core values that lead to great daily habits and then constantly raising that standard in pursuit of excellence.[4]

Having high standards in our program is great for promoting behavior change because standards give the Rider some direction and also shape the Path and motivate the Elephant. They engage all three components of behavior change and make that change more likely. A great place to start is to circle back to Mark Bennett and PDS Coaching.

Defining Success and the PDS Rule of Three

Two of the most impactful things I learned from Mark Bennett are having your players define what success in an activity looks like and installing what Bennett calls the Rule of Three. Let's break those down.

Defining what success looks like for an activity every session has led to more ownership and accountability and engagement for my players. Bennett suggests that before starting an activity, call your players in and ask them to describe what acceptable, unacceptable, and exceptional looks like for that activity. "We're not telling them," says Bennett. "We're asking them to think about, based on where they are ability-wise, what would be unacceptable for us. What would be acceptable? In other words, what should we be working for every time? And when we have something to stretch for, what would be exceptional based on what we said was our definition of success for the session, not anything else?"

For example, I might be working on transition play in soccer. The players might define unacceptable transition as not spreading out when we win the ball and securing it with a pass or not sprinting to press the ball right away after a turnover. Acceptable might be defined as quick press after a turnover or for the team who won the ball to find the right pass to secure possession and for teammates to spread the field quickly and get into attacking shape. Finally, exceptional might be for a player to see the opportunity in transition to win the ball back high up the field and play a killer pass behind the defense. It is up to the team how they might define these things. (Depending upon the age of the players, perhaps a nudge from the coach as to what acceptable and exceptional might look like if they are not getting it is necessary, but try and resist the urge.)

Next, Bennett advises asking the team to answer a simple question: based upon what we now know is acceptable, how long can you maintain minimal, acceptable form? They might say five minutes, but more often it's about two minutes. "You set the parameter," says Bennett. "If it falls below the standard, I'll start shouting, 'Ten, nine, eight, seven!' I'll count down so that they're aware it's dropped to unacceptable." Bennett wants the players to fix the issues and keep the session going. If they cannot, he calls a reset.

In a reset, Bennett sends the players to work it out amongst themselves and figure out what they have to do differently. It is player directed, not coach directed. When I first tried this, I gave my players thirty second resets, eventually whittled them down to ten to fifteen seconds, and today they rarely need any time at all. During resets I call on one of the players to tell me what their plan is. I also use injured players to go help suggest changes and then share the plan. This keeps them engaged in practice instead of just attending but not being fully present. "All of a sudden," says Bennett, "what we see is that after a few blank faces, they start to realize, 'This is real; we've got to focus on this; we've got to work it out; and we've got to come up with the conclusions to be successful in this moment.' And that's the basic strategy to help get them engaged in something that's real, to help them bring it alive, and for them to own it completely. The final aim of the resets is to not have any; players recognize when something is unacceptable and either self-adjust or reach out to another player who accepts peer feedback and acts on it."

The other strategy that I learned from Bennett and implemented in my coaching is the PDS Rule of Three. Along with focus and competitiveness, the Rule of Three is one of my current team's non-negotiables, the three things that every player is responsible for and willing to be held accountable for at every practice and game. It is a simple framework that helps us as coaches create that athlete-centered environment that we want to create by giving players a pathway to hold each other accountable. And although Bennett calls it the *Rule* of Three, it is truly a set of *standards* to be upheld.

Rule One: Each player commits to excellence, which, in the words of Bennett, means, "Being the best I can with the tools I have in the present moment." It is the requirement of every player to be fully present, aware, and focused, to commit 100 percent to their choices in the game and then review those choices and their commitment level. It sounds simple enough, but it can be tough. "Until you start to live this as a lifestyle and a philosophy," says Bennett, "players can very easily regress and not even be aware that they are becoming disengaged. That is why we have Rule Two."

Rule Two: This is about teammates holding each other accountable for effective communication. "A lot of people, when they talk about effective communication, they say it's clear, loud, all this stuff, which, for me, is nonsense," says Bennett. "You may need some of those, but communication is effective only if it has the desired impact." Once you have agreed on what acceptable, unacceptable, and exceptional look like for a session, your team must agree that if one of them sees a teammate falling below the standard for too long, they will hold that teammate accountable. This can be tough, especially when junior players are calling out senior players. It can also be an avenue to help them understand each other and how they communicate. "Great communication is done in a way that allows someone to accept your feedback," says Bennett. "If someone's reaching out to you to give you feedback, they're doing it because they want to help you get better, so you must accept it. Even if you feel how it's being communicated could be better, their intent is honorable because they want to help you, so you must accept it."

I love Rule Two because of this scenario: Johnny does not like how Jimmy gave him feedback. Jimmy wants Johnny to uphold the standards. Rule Two gives us a chance to practice these conversations, which I think we all can agree are critical to team success. So when the team huddles up, the coach can mediate this interaction by asking Johnny why he didn't like the feedback. Then, he must remind Johnny that part of Rule Two was that he had to accept that feedback, but now is his chance to tell Jimmy how he would prefer to get feedback in the future. Then coach can ask Jimmy to state how he could have given feedback differently. They come to an agreement, fist bump, and off they go. "In a situation like that," says Bennett, "we know a disagreement is going to happen, so we stop everyone, and we do it in a positive and supportive way, and this becomes a learning opportunity. How critical is that to success? It's unbelievably critical. So, the question really is, 'How much time and energy do we need to put in at practice to actually develop that very skill that we know will give us phenomenal success in the game?'"

Rule Three: If a player fails to self-correct in Rule One, and his teammates fail to intervene in Rule Two, or the player does not accept or act upon the peer feedback, then and only then does Rule Three kick in, and the coach intervenes. You will likely struggle with this; I know I did. It is so hard to have patience and give players the space and time they need to intervene on their own. It is difficult to create an environment where they have the confidence and belief to correct each other. Most of our athletes have been raised in a youth sports environment where they look to the sidelines every time something goes sideways. But if you are truly a developmental coach, isn't this an incredibly important skill to teach? I would say that the ability to be fully aware and focused and be able to self-correct and help your teammates adjust might be one of the most important skills you ever teach them. When you practice this regularly, you will notice that the best teams rarely, if ever, get to Rule Three. "Behavior is a skill to develop," says Bennett, "and we have to put energy in training sessions to develop the skill. Don't expect magic to happen after one discussion."[5]

I have seen teams transform when using the Rule of Three to give them ownership and accountability. For example, Alan Keane was coaching the Great Britain basketball team, preparing for the U17 European Championships, while being mentored by Bennett. He was stunned when Bennett asked if he could take practice for a day, just a few days out from their first game. His staff was incredulous. But Keane agreed and let Bennett run the session. "It was the best practice we had in all our preparation," laughed Keane. "It's not about basketball. It was about people and behavior."[6]

"I've spent twenty-eight years developing applicational principles that can help coaches, teachers, managers, and organizations actually maximize the potential of the people they're working with," says

Bennett. "It is about giving people the tools to take their technical and tactical plans and actually engage people. How can they learn and understand? How can I develop ways to engage and increase learning to allow people to make effective choices, commit with intent, and evaluate the choice and the intent separately and effectively under any type of pressure without the need for the coach or the teacher? That is what we do." That is how we change behavior, slowly but surely, one day at a time. We relentlessly uphold the standard when our athletes fail to do so, but preferably we allow them to hold each other accountable. But this also begs the question, what do you do when you have that one kid who just won't buy in?

A Five-Step Process for Shaping Behavior Change

If you are reading this book, you have likely been in coaching long enough to have encountered a few athletes that won't get on board with the team standards. They are constantly falling below them, pushing the boundaries, and often testing our patience. It would be easy to quickly cut these kids loose; however, I believe our job as coaches is to shape behaviors—and not simply performance behaviors but moral ones as well. We should not continually give athletes with lots of ability a pass simply because they help us win. It is not our fault how they arrive to our team, but it is our responsibility to develop them and take ownership for how they behave when they leave. This is where shaping behavior comes in.

The ideas of shaping behavior have been around since the nineteenth century psychologist Edward Thorndike coined his Law of Effect, which basically stated that responses that produce a satisfying effect in a situation are more likely to be repeated, and those that produce an uncomfortable effect are less likely to be repeated. In other words, behaviors are modified by their consequences. Thorndike's work was expanded upon in the 1950s by psychologist B.F. Skinner, who used a process called shaping, which involved rewarding not simply the final, target behavior but also the small steps on the path to that behavior. Think of the concept "be on time." If you have an athlete that is chronically late and your desired outcome is to always be on time, perhaps you start by acknowledging that they showed up on time for a week. You catch them being good on the small steps toward your ultimate goal.

In a sporting realm, Bruce Brown and Rob Miller of Proactive Coaching have done tremendous work in this area of working with challenging athletes. As Miller told me on our podcast, "What *won't* happen over the course of the year when you are working with kids? You could have a rule for everything, and you still won't have a rule for everything that is going to happen!"[7] Brown and Miller outline a five-step process that I have used for many years. While we can publicly speak to our standards, Brown recommends this five-step process be done in a one-on-one setting with the athlete:

1. Identify the behavior/standard not being upheld: That which you do not condemn you condone, so call the behavior what it is immediately. Do not let it fester, or it gives a signal to others that this behavior is acceptable.

2. Help the athlete see the behavior through other people's eyes: Ask him, for example, "How do you think it makes your team-mates feel when you are constantly negative and screaming at them/always late/not working hard in fitness?" Many young athletes never think of their own behavior as seen by their teammates or coaches.

3. Ask, "Is that who you want to be?": Every athlete is a person first, and every person has a story, and often behaviors that manifest on the sports field are a result of other things in their lives that go far beyond sports. If you are a trusted coach and they truly love playing, you'll find that for most young athletes, their poor behavior is not whom they want to be. When they

tell you, "No, Coach, that is not the type of teammate I want to be," the door has now opened for change.

4. Ask, "How can I help you change?": This gives them ownership in the behavior-change process. Maybe you come up with a hand signal together, or you call them by their last name as a pattern interrupt when they are about to lose their temper. Work with the athlete to find a pathway of small changes on the way to a larger one.

5. Praise them when they exhibit the new, positive behavior: As Brown states, tell them, "Look at who you have become." Find small steps along this journey, such as the private acknowledgment that they just made five practices in a row on time. Or give them a quiet word about how in the past they would have lost their head when the referee made a bad call, but you noticed they just got on with the next play. The more you reinforce the behavior you want to see, the more likely they are to exhibit it.[8]

In my own coaching, I have found this process to be very effective. Nothing is more detrimental for a team than an athlete who has ability yet operates below the standard. Nothing can be as powerful as when that athlete gets on board, as it usually has the effect of raising the standard for everybody. Don't let young athletes with ability skate through your time with them without being held accountable. Instead, shape their behavior.

Activities for Creating Standards and Eliminating Rules

The Talent Quadrant

One of the best visual representations of the combination of behavior and ability I have seen was done by Wayne Goldsmith, the Australian high-performance coach who has worked with numerous Olympians and world champions across a variety of sports. He set up an X and Y axis grid with four quadrants. On the vertical scale, he listed "ability" from low to high, and on the horizontal axis, he listed "commitment" from poor to excellent. This gives four quadrants: average to below average ability and poor commitment, above average ability and poor commitment, above average ability and excellent commitment, average to below average ability and excellent commitment.

He then asked the audience which quadrant most elite athletes come from. The answer, according to Goldsmith, are athletes, especially young ones, who at first have average ability but develop excellent commitment and behaviors. "The top quadrant of high ability, exceptional behaviors is exceedingly rare in young athletes," Goldsmith told me. "Most coaches only come across a few of those in a lifetime. Most elite performers develop excellent habits and behaviors and from that develop their ability."

This visual representation got me thinking about creating this same grid and handing it out to a team. The athletes can put their name on it and then plot themselves on the graph. Where do they think they lie, not simply ability-wise but also behavior-wise? Our youth-sports culture celebrates ability while often ignoring behaviors, and yet we all know that the right habits, practiced daily, are far greater drivers of long-term sporting performance than a flash of ability in the absence of those behaviors. Try this exercise with your entire team or perhaps with a single athlete who is struggling to develop the behaviors that will lead to long-term success.

Create a "Legacy" Book

As we spoke about in the last chapter, when a player is selected to the New Zealand All Blacks, he is handed a black, leather-bound book. On the first page is a picture of the jersey of the 1905 "Originals" team and on the next page is a jersey of the 1924 "Invincibles" team. On each subsequent page are pictures of jerseys leading up to the present day.

The book then contains pages about the values, character, and standards of being an All Black. And then, the pages are blank; they are left to be filled by the player. He is charged with leaving the shirt in a better place, with writing his own story, and creating his own legacy.[9]

When my good friend James Leath was the head of leadership development at IMG Academy in Bradenton, Florida, he read James Kerr's *Legacy* and thought creating a legacy book might be a great idea for some of his teams as well. After all, many high school and college coaches are constantly trying to engage alums to remain connected with their program, as well as have the current players gain a greater understanding of what it means to be a part of this program.

Leath decided to start a legacy book of his own. For the football team, he had graduating players write a letter to the next player who would share their number. For swimmers, they could write to the next swimmers who would compete in their event. And over time, the goal would be to compile a binder of letters written from past players to the future ones, explaining the values, ethos, and meaning of this program. Leath left IMG and formed his own company after only two years of the program, but he already saw the powerful effect that voices from the past can have on the present.

I have recently started creating legacy books with the teams I work with. I think it is a great way for every senior to share their experiences, thoughts, and feelings with the next class of freshman. It is an opportunity to reach out to older alums and gain a little more life perspective and deeper meaning of the role of sports in the athlete's educational experience. It helps to connect new athletes to the legacy of the program and the shirt they are about to pull on. Watching someone reading a legacy letter and gaining a deeper understanding of the obligation they have undertaken is very cool. Writing a legacy letter to themselves or to a future teammate, putting pen to paper on their experience, can be a highly emotional and deeply moving experience for an athlete transitioning to her next stage of life. If you think this is right for your program, give it a shot and start your own legacy book with your current upper-classman and reach out to your alums to contribute as well. Start your own legacy.

When in Doubt, Implement My Favorite Team Standard

This section is short and sweet. There are lots of standards I have heard over the years, but my favorite one, heard from multiple sources, is a version of this one: don't let your teammates down.

That's it, simple and easy. Encourage your athletes to ask themselves, "Is this action letting my teammates down?" "Is my attitude letting my teammates down?" "Is this decision about to let my team down?" If there is a question, they probably should not do it.

Summary

Great programs have standards to be aspired to—not a lot of rules to be adhered to. They have the minimum number of rules needed in order to promote the health and well-being of their athletes and the maximum number of standards that they are willing to be held accountable for. In order to create a culture of standards, not rules, you can

- Learn from the All Blacks and Messiah soccer how playing to a standard drives success.
- Understand that in order to change behavior, we must direct our rational mind (the Rider), motivate the emotional mind (the Elephant), and provide a clear Path and environment that encourages the right behaviors and makes it uncomfortable to engage in the wrong ones.
- Use the PDS Coaching Rule of Three to give ownership and accountability of the non-negotiables over to your athletes.
- Try Bruce Brown's five-step process for shaping behavior when dealing with challenging athletes.

- Try out the Talent Quadrant with your team or with specific athletes who are not adhering to the program standards.
- Create a legacy book for your program and connect the past, present, and future in order to "leave the shirt in a better place."
- When in doubt, establish the standard, "Don't let your teammates down."

The tennis great Arthur Ashe once said, "You are never really playing an opponent. You are playing yourself, your own highest standards, and when you reach your limits, that is real joy." This is great advice for life and great advice for your teams as well. True joy will not come from simply adhering to rules; it comes from setting a very high standard and each and every day trying to live up to and even exceed the standards you have set. Your athletes might not get there every day, and some may never get there at all, but in aspiring to be something and someplace they have never been before, you help them achieve in both sports and life.

LESSON 14

"YOU ARE ENOUGH!"

Help Your Athletes Overcome Fear, Stress, and Anxiety

The whole goal isn't to get rid of the fear, necessarily. It's just to kind of change the way we interpret it and to work to stop it from making our decisions. Fear isn't driving the car. It doesn't mean it's not in the car. It's in the back seat, but it's not driving.

—TREVOR RAGAN

My job is not to create more pressure but to try to find ways to relieve the pressure and take the pressure off of them.

—NANCY STEVENS

Nancy Stevens understands pressure. You don't become the all-time winningest field hockey coach in NCAA history without understanding a thing or two about dealing with stress, anxiety, and pressure. In thirty-nine seasons of coaching, her field hockey teams have won nearly seven hundred games, and she has led her teams to thirteen NCAA Final Fours and three NCAA National Championships. So when the 2017 season came around and

Stevens looked at a roster with nine first-year players who were feeling a lot of pressure to uphold the University of Connecticut legacy, she was concerned. She knew the team had talent. She also knew that the stress caused by thinking they had to win or they failed could crush the team.

"When you come into preseason," says Stevens, "there's this high level of anxiety because they had all summer to train, and they're going to be like, 'Oh, my goodness. We're going to do the fitness test. How am I going to do?' So, before the team got here, I went into the locker room and put a sign on the mirror. The message was simple. It was three words."

"What did you write?" I asked, curious to learn these three magical words.

"You are enough," she replied. "You are enough."

You are enough. Three words that would change the dynamic of a season. In a world where people, especially young people, are always comparing how they feel on the inside to how everyone else portrays their "perfect" lives on Instagram, Facebook, and other social channels, it does not take much to make a person feel inadequate. Nowhere is this so true as in sports, where high school stars enter a program, such as UConn, and all of a sudden the spotlight is that much brighter, and the pressure is ramped up that much more.

"You could just see that level of anxiety just drop in half," said Stevens. "They were freed up to be who they are, and I thought it was so empowering." Three simple words reduced the fear and allowed their potential to shine through for the entire season. The Huskies made it back to the NCAA Final Four, and Stevens saw the stress return. "We go into the Final Four; we were twenty-one and zero. Again, of course, now the pressure returns. 'Oh, my goodness. We're the number one overall seed in the tournament.'"

Then Stevens said something that really resonated with me. "My job is not to create more pressure but to try to find ways to relieve the pressure and take the pressure off of them." UConn advanced to the final against eight-time champion Maryland, and the stories in the paper were all about whether the young Huskies could defeat the experienced veterans from Maryland. Stevens was worried that the pressure would be too much and that her players would listen to the stories others were writing about them, instead of writing their own story that day.

"The team's sitting around in the locker room at Louisville, getting ready to play for the national championship, and I could feel the tension. So, I just wrote on the board, 'You are enough.' And again, you could just see the whole anxiety level just drop," Stevens continued. "With this particular team, this helped free them to play for the joy of playing the sport they love with the people they care most about, and I think that contributed to our success. Obviously, there are probably another twenty-five factors why we were successful, but I think that did help a bit." The Huskies defeated Maryland on that day, two to one, winning their third title and finishing the season with a perfect twenty-three to zero record.

"You are enough" was the simple yet elegant mantra of the 2017 UConn Huskies and also demonstrated Stevens' great understanding of the people she was coaching. "There is a lot of insecurity in that age group," says Stevens, "unfortunately more so in women than men. So, you have to know this about the people you're working with, and what are the messages they're getting? Oftentimes, sadly, it is from their coach, 'You're not fast enough. You're not fit enough. You're not thin enough. You're not aggressive enough.' So, I just was trying to let them know that whatever's playing in their mind that they're not 'enough' of, whatever it is, that's not true. Those three words are so simple, but I do think they're powerful. And I'm hoping that some of the messages that we've imparted while the players are here with us for four years will carry forward so that they will feel like they're enough in a lot of different areas of their life."[1]

This chapter is about helping your athletes overcome the stress, anxiety, and outright fear that sports can induce. Whether they are young athletes simply trying to please a parent or coach, or collegiate and professional athletes competing for a high-stakes championship, stress can be the biggest negative influence on performance if we do not understand how to help our athletes strip it away. We will cover the following ways to understand, reframe, and reappraise stressful situations for our athletes:

- W. Tim Gallwey's "Performance Equation" as a model for understanding how stress limits performance
- How humans react to stress, fear, and anxiety
- How to reappraise those pre-match jitters, and why telling athletes, "Just calm down," does not work
- The RIVER Effect: how coaches can help with reappraisal
- A short note on working with perfectionist athletes

The world's most successful coaches understand that athletes cannot avoid pressure situations, but they can be taught how to reappraise and reframe them so that they sharpen the sword and help them perform better. Let's learn how this is done.

The Performance Equation

One of the most influential books in mental training for athletes is W. Tim Gallwey's classic *The Inner Game of Tennis: The Classic Guide to the Mental Side of Peak Performance.* The book was written in 1972, back when sports psychology was barely a profession and most athletes only sought mental training if they had been diagnosed with an illness. Mental training was for weak people, so went the thinking, and athletes were strong. Obviously, Gallwey tapped into something as today very few elite-level athletes do not engage in some level of mental training (as we saw in lesson 10 when we talked about training the inner game). But in the 1970s, the idea that you could train yourself to overcome stress and nervousness and approach your competition with more confidence and sharper concentration was a bit of a novelty. In his book, Gallwey laid out an equation that is incredibly helpful for athletes and those that influence them, such as coaches and parents:

Performance = Potential − Interference

Simple, huh? We can increase our performance by expanding our potential (through hours of practice, eating well, sleeping well, all the things we can see) and by stripping away all the things that interfere with that potential, most of which lies between our ears. If we first recognize that everything is a choice—and then train ourselves to remove self-doubt, fear, concentration lapses, and limiting thoughts and beliefs—then we can play up to our potential.[2]

Coaches can be huge contributors to stress and anxiety unless we are intentional about stripping it away (and educating parents on the Performance Equation to help them strip it away). The way we communicate and interact with athletes and the way we teach them to frame high-pressure situations is critical to how they will perform in the short term and oftentimes influences whether they continue with sport over the long haul. Before we can strip away that interference, it is probably good to understand why it exists in the first place and how the body's emotional responses to situations contribute to reduced performance.

How Humans React to Stressful Situations

Whenever humans encounter a situation that they perceive as a threat, or one with potentially negative consequences, it activates the sympathetic nervous system. You may have heard this called your "fight or flight" response. That threat can be the rattlesnake slithering across your foot, or it could be your boss coming down the hall looking for the report you failed to file. For athletes, it is often the approach of an important competition or event or a moment in the match, such as trying to score the winning penalty kick in a World Cup shootout or make a free throw in basketball with one second remaining and the game on the line.

The brain has a physiological response to perceived threats called arousal, which is actually a positive thing. Arousal is preparing your body to respond to the situation, including the release or suppression of hormones, a raising or lowering of the heart rate, and reduced blood flow to certain organs that will not be in use. We have all felt this arousal state, either through butterflies in our stomach, sweaty palms, or even nervous shaking during a big moment.

Along with our physiological arousal, our brain has an emotional response to threats. Since they happen at the same time, we often think they are one and the same, but they are not. For many athletes, this emotional response has negative connotations. (Remember the Rider and the Elephant in chapter 14.) Their increased physiological arousal leads to negative emotional appraisals of that arousal. This leads to what psychologists call maladaptive physiological responses. The body cannot process oxygen as efficiently; the brain becomes hyper-focused on other potential threats; you suffer a reduction in working memory; and, of course, performance is diminished. You become so hyper-focused on the negative potential threat that you lose sight of other opportunities. This fixation on the negative may be OK when you encounter a grizzly bear in the woods, but it does not help when trying to make a penalty kick in a World Cup shootout.[3]

Geir Jordet and Esther Hartman studied penalty kick takers in professional soccer. In tournament play, games that are tied at the end of regulation and overtime go to a best-of-five shootout, where teams alternate taking penalty kicks and whoever makes the most out of five shots wins. If still tied, they go to a sudden death shootout. A penalty kick is always taken twelve yards from goal, and the goal is always twenty-four feet wide and eight feet high. They were curious whether there would be a performance difference for penalty shooters if they were shooting to win or shooting not to lose. After all, it is still the same exact ball, the same size goal, and the same distance away. Remarkably, the results of that shot are incredibly different given two scenarios:

- If scoring a goal will result in a win for the team, the success ratio for shooters is 92 percent.
- If missing the shot will result in a loss for the team, the success ratio drops to 62 percent.

Remember, these are professional athletes, yet there is a massive improvement when the situation is perceived as a challenge (if I make it we win) versus a threat (if I miss we lose). There is a huge performance difference between playing to win and playing not to lose, and one of the most important things we can do as a coach is to help our athletes reappraise their stress and anxiety from a threat to a challenge.[4] And it's not that hard to do either.

Cognitive Reappraisal: Turning Threats into Challenges

Top athletes must learn to perform in threat scenarios as they can be unavoidable. You don't ignore the threat, though. The research says the best way to positively enhance performance is to reappraise it. Sadly, this is not what athletes are often told to do. Instead, they are told to ignore the arousal feeling or, worse, to calm down. Have you all seen the coach marching up and down the sideline yelling at his players: "Relax! Calm down, or I am taking you out of the game!"? Really? As Tim Gallwey says, "The instant I try to make myself relax, true relaxation vanishes, and in its place is a strange phenomenon called 'trying to relax.' Relaxation happens only when allowed, not as a result of 'trying.'"

When athletes try and suppress the anxiety and stress they are feeling, it can feel like a dam trying to hold back a swollen river. What they are being told is to suppress the body's arousal response to a situation and to shift the nervous system from a high-arousal state to a low-arousal state. Good luck with that on the eighteenth green at Augusta with a three-foot putt to win the Masters Tournament. How long are you supposed to stand there trying to calm down? Certainly not enough time for all that adrenaline to leave your bloodstream. Now, this is not in any way saying that mindfulness and meditation practices are not a critical component of athlete performance. Nor is this to say that taking a few deep breaths is not a helpful way to get re-centered on the task at hand; it is. But these are often accompanied by the advice to stop feeling the physiological response you are having, and that is poor advice. The research is demonstrating that training ourselves to reappraise our interpretation of our arousal state is more effective.

Remember above when I explained how the physiological and emotional responses to stress are two different things? In reappraisal, instead of trying to ignore the physical response, we reappraise the emotional response. Since the mind assigns meaning to those emotional responses, we can train our athletes to assign a better meaning. For example, researcher Jeremy Jamieson taught students at Harvard who were preparing for the GRE exam—a hugely stressful test that determines graduate school admission—how to reappraise their physiological responses to taking a practice exam. Half of the participants in the study were taught that their physiological responses, such as an increased heart rate or sweaty palms, predicted better performance on the test. They were taught to embrace these sensations as signs that their body was prepared for the task ahead. On the practice exam, participants who were taught to reappraise their responses outperformed those students in the control group who were not taught to do so.

Three months later, when these same students took the actual GRE, the appraisal group again outperformed the control group and reported that their feelings of arousal on test day aided their performance. Subsequent studies by Jamieson on public speakers found the following results: not only are speakers who are taught to reappraise their arousal in a positive manner more focused and effective in their speaking but they also return physiologically to their baseline state faster than those who are not taught to reappraise their feelings.[5]

So how do we help our athletes reappraise their stress? The answer is surprisingly simple. First, we can teach them that the responses they are feeling are actually the body's way of saying, "This is an important moment for me. I care about this! That tingling in my arms is my nerves getting primed for activity. These are not signs that there is impending doom; they are signs that this matters to me, and that is a great thing."

Second, according to Harvard researcher Allison Wood Brooks, when your athletes encounter a stressful situation and they feel the litany of physiological responses, such as butterflies, sweaty palms, or nervous shakes, they need to reappraise that feeling into one of excitement and opportunity instead of threat. In her studies of public speakers, karaoke singers, and math students, participants who reappraised their feelings as excitement performed better. How? All they needed to do was to say to themselves, out loud, three simple words: "I am excited!"

That is it. "I am excited," said a few times out loud, with the genuine belief that some part of you is actually excited for this opportunity and this challenge, can alter the emotional response to the situation. It does not mean that anxiety completely disappears. As Brooks writes in her research, "Imagine that anxiety and excitement are like the bass and treble knobs on a stereo. By reappraising anxiety as excitement, it seems individuals turn the excitement knob up, without necessarily turning the anxiety knob down." Those three words help the body and mind switch from threat to challenge mode, help increase cardiac efficiency, and help take the focus off the potential negative consequences of the situation.[6]

We often talk about fearlessness as an important value that great teams have. But what we mean by fearlessness is not necessarily the absence of fear. It is the absence of a negative emotional reaction to the body's physiological response to a threatening or stressful situation. Your athlete will feel it; they simply must be trained not to let it fuel their actions and responses.

"What are four things that create fear? Uncertainty, attention, change, and struggle," says Trevor Regan of Train Ugly, whom we met a few chapters back. "What are four things that happen a lot in sports? Uncertainty, attention, change, and struggle. As athletes, we're kind of signing up to do something that's just going to involve a lot of emotion and a lot of fear and the nerves. That's the fun part, but we have to be able to kind of take a step back and understand, I'm operating in an arena that involves a lot of uncertainty, which means there's going to be a lot of fear, and that's okay."

We do not need to eliminate all the fear, stress, and anxiety for our athletes. We simply need to help them reappraise these experiences. As Regan concludes, "The whole goal isn't to get rid of the fear. It's just to kind of change the way we interpret it and to work to stop it from making our decisions. Fear isn't driving the car. It doesn't mean it's not in the car. It's in the back seat, but it's not driving."[7]

An Activity to Remove Stress, Fear, and Anxiety in Your Athletes

Bathe Them in the RIVER

At the Way of Champions, Dr. Jerry Lynch and I speak about using what we call the "RIVER Effect" to help your athletes reduce stress and anxiety and strip away the interference that inhibits performance. RIVER is an acronym that we use to help coaches remember that athletes need the following things from us in order to feel confidence and belonging with our groups. And in typical Jerry Lynch fashion, each letter has a double meaning:

- Relevant and Remarkable: Our job as coaches is to help our athletes feel relevant, that they have a role and are important to this group. Whether they are a starter or barely play a minute, they must know that you see them. This makes them feel remarkable and unique.
- Important and Inspired: Great coaches inspire their athletes to reach for new heights and hold them accountable for standards,

not necessarily rules. They make their athletes realize they are important members of this group, and if they do not meet the standards, they are not just disappointing the coach; they are letting down the team.

- Validation and Value: The coach sees the contribution of each individual and values what the athlete is able to bring to the team. Great coaches make athletes feel invaluable without being the most valuable.
- Empowerment and Excited: The athlete feels excited to show up because Coach is excited and passionate about this team and puts the required energy and emotion into practices and games. This empowers our athletes to take more ownership and be more accountable.
- Revered and Respected: The coach treats the athlete with the respect and dignity he deserves as a human being. The athlete feels revered by her coach and goes all out.

"The RIVER is only as effective as your awareness and mindfulness as a coach. If you don't think the RIVER Effect works, then go ahead and try the opposite," says Lynch. Achieving thirty-nine NCAA titles and having worked closely with coaches such as Phil Jackson, Steve Kerr, Cindy Timchal, and Anson Dorrance, Lynch has seen the best coaches at work. And he knows they all work hard to bathe their athletes in the RIVER. "Go ahead," says Lynch, "don't value or validate your athletes. Don't respect them. Don't plan your practices ahead of time or come with the required presence and emotional energy to teach. Don't treat them like unique human beings. Let me know how that works for you."

I get a lot of emails about using the RIVER Effect from coaches, and it seems to be a sticky concept that is easy to remember. It provides a nice checklist when you see an athlete struggling or seemingly stressed and tight before a match. Does she feel valued, no matter what happens today? Does he know his role and how important it is that he plays his part? Is she empowered to take ownership, make decisions, and be a leader? And most important, is he excited? Because if he is, he will perform better.[8]

Summary

One of our most important jobs as coaches is to strip away the stress, fear, and anxiety that can inhibit our athletes' performance. We must help them turn the focus inward and not worry about outcomes. We help them to focus on the process and reappraise the fear, stress, and anxiety into something else. Write your own story. Do not let others write it for you. That is how you overcome fear. Every athlete, whether they are playing their first travel sports match or appearing on an Olympic stage, is going to have a physiological reaction to a situation they understand as important. They will view it as either a threat or a challenge. As coaches, our role is to help them frame these situations as challenges and opportunities to play to win. To do so, we must

- Teach them Gallwey's Performance Equation and understand it ourselves so that we are not a cause of cognitive interference.
- Understand that stress and fear causes both a physiological and an emotional response and that while we do not necessarily have a choice about feeling fear, we do have a choice about how to respond to it.
- Teach our athletes to reappraise their fear, stress, and anxiety, and their physical manifestations, and see them as a positive response. Teach them to say, "I am excited," and mean it. Communicate that viewing their physiological feelings as something to be excited about will help them perform better.
- Bathe them in the RIVER so that you, the coach, are not a source of interference.

When we teach our athletes to play to win, instead of playing not to lose, we are teaching them to focus on what can be gained by this endeavor, instead of how to prevent bad things from happening. As Ashley Merryman and Po Bronson write in their book *Top Dog: The Science of Winning and Losing*, there is a performance benefit to being gain-oriented: "Prevention-focused (people) are more likely to lose their motivation to compete along the way. Instead of persevering, they are perseverating—obsessing on their mistakes until they wonder if it's worth continuing on." On the other hand, they conclude, "gain-oriented people are more likely to persevere: as long as they have a fighting chance, they are never willing to admit defeat."[9] I am pretty sure that is the type of athlete you want to go into competition with.

LESSON 15

———

"TRUST IS LIKE THE AIR
WE BREATHE"

Build High-Trust Teams

*Good teams become great ones when the members trust each other
enough to surrender the "me" for the "we."*

—PHIL JACKSON

*Trust is like the air we breathe. When it's present no one notices and
when it's absent everyone can see it.*

—WARREN BUFFETT

The NBA season can be a long one, and basketball, to be honest, can often become a coach-centric sport. With preseason games, eighty-two regular season contests, and the possibility of twenty-eight more playoff games, the "season" can stretch to over ten months. That is a lot of coaching and a lot of time that athletes hear the voice of their coach. That is why in February 2018, on their way to their third NBA Championship, Golden State Warriors coach Steve Kerr decided to shake things up a bit. And boy did it cause an uproar.

Heading into a mid-February game against the Phoenix Suns, Kerr felt that the team was in a bit of a funk. "I have not reached [my team] the last month," Kerr said. "They're tired of my voice. I'm tired of my voice. I haven't been reaching them, so we figured this was a good night to pull something out of the hat." So what was this master plan Kerr and his staff decided to unveil? They decided to turn over gameday to the players. They let all-star Andre Iguodala run the morning shoot-around. They let JaVale McGee run the film session, and during the game, they let Iguodala, David West, and Draymond Green design the plays and run the huddle during timeouts.

The Warriors won the game that night, but afterwards there was a huge controversy. Some commentators thought it was disrespectful of Kerr to let his players run the timeouts and design plays. They said he was not taking the game seriously. When asked about it in the postgame press conference, Kerr stated the reasoning behind the decision. "It's the players' team," Kerr said. "It's their team, and they have to take ownership of it. As coaches, our job is to nudge them in the right direction, guide them. We don't control them. They determine their own fate. I don't think we've focused well the last month. It just seemed like the right thing to do."

On one level, what Kerr did that night was introduce a small pattern interruption for his players. He changed the daily routine to get them to refocus and think about what they were doing. But in my eyes, what he was really doing was demonstrating to his players, "I trust you; you've got this. This team belongs to you." And it amazes me that this shocked and insulted so many people. From my point of view, the idea that athletes making tens of millions of dollars per season, who had played basketball every day for twenty-plus years, were deemed incapable of drawing up a play or running a timeout was ludicrous. I could not imagine another industry where a leader giving the best people in the world in a given field some ownership and accountability and a voice would be deemed disrespectful. In fact, it would be disrespectful *not* to do this.

Kerr understands that the players he is coaching are highly capable and have a deep understanding of the game. He also knows that by demonstrating his trust in them—and by earning their trust—they will invest more in the team and in each other. Trust is the secret sauce.

Trust is the secret ingredient of great coaching and great teams. It is the foundation of all great relationships, and great relationships are the basis of winning teams. Players cannot consistently perform their best if they do not trust their coaches, their parents, and their teammates and, in turn, feel they are trusted. Parents cannot give their kids ownership and release their children to the sport unless they trust their kids and their coaches. Coaches cannot get the most out of their athletes and teams unless they trust them to perform and earn their athlete's trust in the process.

If we think about athletic development as a three-legged stool, the legs consist of the athletes, the coaches, and, especially in youth through college sports, the parents. Remove a leg, and the stool collapses. Remove trust, which is the glue that holds it all together, and you end up on your rear end.

Great coaches are trusted by their athletes when those athletes know that their coach has their best interest in mind. In youth sports, parents are far more likely to take a back seat and let the process of athlete development happen when they trust that the coach, the school, and/or the club have the best interests of their child in mind. However you look at it, trust is the glue that holds it all together.

In order to explore the concept of trust in the context of athletics, this chapter will

- Define trust and dispel the myth that trust is based upon solely upon ability;
- Outline the qualities of high-trust leaders;
- Explore the idea of the difference between high-trust and low-trust teams;

- Understand the power of vulnerability;
- Explore telling your athletes the truth and loving them to death; and
- Provide you with a great exercise to evaluate your trustworthiness in the eyes of your staff and your athletes.

What Is Trust?

The word *trust* is both a noun and a verb, and in both cases, it means to believe in the reliability, truth, ability, or strength of someone or something. To trust is to go all in, to fall and believe that you will be caught, to fail and believe you will be forgiven, to love and believe with all your heart that your love will be returned. It is the basis of all relationships. Yet it is often misunderstood, especially by coaches.

Many coaches believe that trust is based solely upon ability. If they have a lot of knowledge of a sport, if they have coached a long time, or if they have played at a higher level than their athletes, many coaches believe they should be trusted unequivocally. They could not be more wrong. Don't believe me? Here is a story that demonstrates my point.

Jean-Francois Gravelet was born in 1824 in St. Omey, Pas-de-Calais, France. From a young age, he showed great aptitude in balance, strength, and agility and at age five was sent to the acrobatics school in Lyon. After only a few months of training, he gave his first performance and was soon dubbed the "Boy Wonder." As he grew, so did his fame, and soon the world came to know him by a different name: the Great Blondin.

Gravelet, or Charles Blondin as he often went by, travelled from France to North America in 1855, where he became part owner of a travelling circus. Yet it was on June 30, 1859, when his fame and fortune took a turn for the better. On that day, Blondin crossed the 1,100-foot Niagara Gorge crossing from the US to Canada, balancing on a 3.5-inch tightrope and suspended 160 feet above the raging falls. The Great Blondin became a legend.

Blondin became world famous with his Niagara Falls escapades, so much so that tightrope walkers worldwide became known as different versions of Blondin (i.e., the Australian Blondin). Every year he would return to the falls and up the ante. He crossed blindfolded. He stood on a chair with only one leg balanced on the rope. He walked on stilts. He carried his manager Harry Colcord across on his back. One year, he even stopped halfway, sat down, and cooked and ate an omelet.

But for our purposes here, one crossing stands out. Blondin, ever the showman, showed up with a wheelbarrow that had a staff welded to it. You can picture the scene as the great showman revved up the crowd of ten thousand plus: "Who thinks the Great Blondin can walk across the falls on this rope?" Can you imagine the scene as the crowd cheered loudly, perhaps even chanting his name, "Blondin, Blondin, Blondin!"?

Then Blondin asked the crowd, "Who thinks I can push this cart across the falls?" They cheered louder still.

Then came the kicker: "Who wants to get in the cart?"

Crickets. Not a peep. Some nervous laughter and looks of, "Is he serious?" No one volunteered to get in the cart.

The entire crowd believed that Blondin had the ability to push the cart across the falls. But they still didn't trust him because trust goes way beyond ability. They had no connection. They had no idea about him as a person. They didn't know whether he was believable or reliable.[1]

Coaches, your players know you can push the cart across the falls without falling. That does not mean you have built enough trust for them to get in. Trust goes way beyond ability. Every one of your players needs something different from you, and it is your job to seek out how to serve them in order for them to be able to perform at their best ability.

Remember, you must coach the person, not the sport. Some of your athletes need technique; some need tactics; some need discipline; and some need encouragement. To build trust with each of them, you must first spend the time to get to know each athlete. Once you have gained their trust by giving them what they need, only then will those players play their hearts out for you, for their teammates, and for them-selves—not because they have to but because they want to.

The Qualities of Trusted Leaders

In the book *The Speed of Trust*, author Stephen M.R. Covey states, "Trust is equal parts character and competence ... You can look at any leadership failure, and it's always a failure of one or the other." In other words, trust either adds a dividend or extracts a tax from every activity we do and every dimension of our group. If you are going to build a high-trust team, first you must become a highly trusted leader. To do so, Covey recommends thirteen behaviors to be aware of.[2] The first five behaviors are character based:

1. Talk straight and tell the truth.
2. Demonstrate concern and genuinely care for others.
3. Be transparent.
4. Make things right when you are wrong.
5. Show loyalty and give credit to others.

The next five behaviors are what he calls competence-based actions:

1. Deliver results for individuals and teams.
2. Continuously improve yourself and be a lifelong learner.
3. Don't skirt the real issues, even the tough ones.
4. Be clear with your expectations.
5. Be accountable to your people.

Finally, he lists three behaviors that are equal parts character and competence based:

1. Listen before you speak.
2. Fulfill your commitments.

3. Extend trust in abundance to others.

This book is all about not just talking the talk but walking the walk. Being a trusted leader is the first step in building a high-trust team. Your athletes and your teams must believe in you, know you are all in, and know that you have the ability and the character to take them to where they want to go.

When it comes to trust, I encourage coaches to think of an acronym that should be easy to remember: COACH. Coaches will be trusted when you have

- Connection: Coaching is about winning the relationship game. It is about coaching a person, not a sport. Players remember how coaches made them feel, and when they feel the right things, they will run through a wall for a coach.

- Oneness: A great coach is all in with her team, and the players know it. Oneness is the unity of thought, belief, and spirit that all great teams have. A trusted coach is a part of that unity. She is a torch bearer, someone who walks along the journey with the group, shedding a bit of light on what comes next but still struggling and suffering the hardships with the group. A trusted coach is vulnerable; she looks at herself first and says, "That's on me."

- Ability: Trusted coaches know what they are talking about. They are curious, lifelong learners and can teach their players about the tactics, techniques, and physical preparation it takes to succeed. Having played at a high level, the coach has a certain amount of authority in this area, but playing the game and teaching it are not the same thing. If you want to inspire your players to continuously improve, then be open to new ideas and look to improve yourself every day as well. And you must remember that your players will model what they see, not what you say.

- Consistency: Are you clear and steady in your actions and judgment? Are you fair, and do you hold everyone to the same standards? Do you have clear values, standards, and expectations that you hold everyone accountable for? Do you treat everyone fairly based upon their unique situation? If you let your best player give 80 percent effort, you cannot call out others for giving 90 percent. If you want 100 percent effort all the time, then you have to hold everyone accountable for it.
- Heart-centeredness: A heart-centered leader is in it to serve others, to serve the greater good for all involved, and is not in it to be served by those they lead. Service to others is the filter through which all your actions are judged. Heart-centered leadership means that you take care of yourself—body, mind, and spirit—so you can take care of your team.

In my experience—and certainly this applied to me as a young coach—most coaches stop at ability. They believe that reputation, playing experience, and previous performance are the be-all and end-all of trust. They played the game. They know a lot about the game. Therefore, everyone should have complete trust in their coaching, their judgment, and everything they do. Those things may get a coach a job, but it won't be what makes the athlete trust him.

Think about it this way: if your accountant was great at math and knew all the accounting laws but filed your tax return late (lack of dependability), would you trust him? If your doctor stared at the computer screen the whole time during your visit, ignored your complaints, and didn't care or listen to you about your ailments (lack of connection), would you trust her?

Coaches, we must understand and accept that *we will not be trusted, no matter how much we know, until parents and athletes know how much we care.* We must treat athletes fairly, act with integrity, and follow through on the things we say we will do. COACH: connection, oneness, ability, consistency, and heart-centeredness. Those are the components of trust that we must display day in and day out. There is no way around it.

The Difference between High-Trust and Low-Trust Teams

The 2004 US men's Olympic basketball team had quite a legacy to uphold. Going into those games, since the 1992 Barcelona Olympic "Dream Team," the combined record for the US Olympic team was twenty-four and zero in Olympic competition. The general feeling was that any twelve players the United States threw together had a reasonable shot at gold.

Going into the 2004 Athens games, a few cracks had begun to emerge. A year prior, the team had dismantled the opposition in the Tournament of the Americas, yet there were quite a few distractions facing the team. By 2004, injuries, fatigue, and security concerns had led to a number of top players declining invitations to play for the USA that year. In fact, only three of twelve team members remained in Athens from the Tournament of the Americas qualifying side.

The games were disastrous by US standards as the team lost three games and only won a bronze. An imbalanced roster, far less preparation and time together than opponents, lack of unity among the players, and distrust of Head Coach Larry Brown demonstrated to the world that the United States could no longer put out any twelve athletes and dominate the world. ESPN reporter Chris Sheridan summed it up in an oral retrospective with NBC Sports years later: "The people in the federation were mad at the players. They were mad at the coaching staff. People on the coaching staff were mad at the federation and mad at the players. The players were kind of sick of the coaching staff. It was dysfunction all around."

The 2004 US men's basketball team shows that talent alone does not win championships; great teams do. One of the most important qualities of great teams is that everyone, from the athletes to the coaches to the support staff, all trust each other.

One of the things we teach at our workshops and conferences are the differences between high-trust and low-trust teams. This might not be a complete list, but take note of some of these items when thinking of your own team. High-trust teams have

- Common purpose and core values: Team members agree upon a shared set of core values and are willing to hold each other accountable for upholding those values on and off the field.
- Respect: High-trust teammates have a deep admiration for their teammates' abilities, qualities, and achievements, and they celebrate each other's excellence rather than get jealous of teammates' success.
- Commitment: High-trust teams are all in and committed to their shared goals through good times and bad.
- Resiliency: Every team faces adversity, and high-trust teams are far more diligent and dogged in the face of adversity, like losing, bad calls from officials, lousy weather, and angry fans. In contrast, high-trust teams seek out and fight through adversity.
- Fewer discipline problems: When teammates are all in, discipline issues are minimized or even disappear as teammates know that they are letting down each other, not just themselves or a coach. They are willing to hold each other accountable, help teammates make better decisions on and off the field, and become a team of high standards, not of rules.
- Intrinsically motivated athletes: Athletes on high-trust teams are focused on the process of continual improvement and rarely talk about winning. They talk about showing up and doing the little things every day. They are warriors with a burning desire to be the best they are capable of becoming, for themselves and for their teammates.
- The ability to celebrate each other's success: High-trust teams have an excellence mentality. They value and celebrate the

achievements of their teammates and recognize that their team-mates' individual accolades only exist because of the team. They focus on excellence.

In contrast, low-trust teams in sports are easy to spot because you consistently see

- Lack of a shared vision: Athletes on low-trust teams don't know where they are going or what they are trying to achieve. Without shared vision, when things go south, they usually go south quickly, and teams fracture. When they come up against a strong team culture, they often bicker and argue, pointing fingers instead of accepting blame.

- Lack of respect: Low-trust teams often have a lot more discipline issues on and off the field because teammates do not think about how their actions affect others. Lack of respect can be demonstrated many ways: players show up late, they miss practice, they give less than their best effort, or perhaps they do not pass to the open player. Upperclassmen mistreat younger players. They distrust their coaches and teammates, and when the chips are down, they often give up.

- Varying levels of commitment: Low-trust teams often have athletes who show up late, leave early, and train hard only when they feel like it. They come into the season out of shape and cut corners whenever the coach is not looking as they know their teammates won't hold them accountable. Star players give less than their best effort because they can still get by and succeed.

- Lots of finger pointing: On low-trust teams, when mistakes are made, everyone starts handing out blame. The coach blames the defense, who point to the offense, and the blame continues to cascade down to the point where nobody accepts any responsibility.

- Pursuit of individual goals over team goals: Low-trust teams often have athletes who give up on the team goal and go all in trying to make all-league, all-state, or All-American. They start chasing the individual accolades and, therefore, stop making the right pass or hustling on defense.

- A lack of team bonding and love, which creates fear: Fear and love cannot coexist, and fear-based teams often fall apart in the big moments. More often than not, when playing against teams of equal or even lesser talent, when things don't go their way, they turn on each other.[3]

Trust amongst athletes, parents, and coaches is something that first has to be earned, then cultivated, and then built upon. It is a self-fulfilling prophecy. High-trust teams consistently do the things that build more trust (and usually more success) while low-trust teams repeat the same mistakes over and over as the season falls apart.

It goes without saying that intentionally developing high-trust teams is a critical part of a coach's job each season. Yet, sadly, as we have seen numerous times in professional sports, high-talent/low-trust teams falter. Building high-trust teams is a process, not an event. It takes time, diligence, and belief in your culture. It takes great communication and the willingness to not simply look at an athlete's talent but his buy-in to your team. But ultimately, it starts with you, the coach.

How can you be more worthy of trust?

Be Vulnerable

A lot of coaches, myself included, were brought up on the idea that the coach carries the clipboard, the coach has all the answers, and the coach has all the knowledge. Any moment where we demonstrated that we did not have every answer was a sign of weakness. I remember being so frustrated as an athlete when coaches would not listen to a single word of feedback from the players who had solutions and ideas to make us more successful. Nothing turns a group of players off faster than a coach who week after week completely ignores any input from her athletes, especially as they become teenagers and adults.

Nothing is more frustrating than a coach who blames the athletes every time something goes wrong and never admits any responsibility for the problems. This is not about a coach abdicating all decision making to the players; it simply means that she creates a feeling of, "We are all in this together; let's come up with a solution that will work."

According to author Dan Coyle, in high-performing cultures, the smart leaders are the ones who radiate a sense of, "I don't have all the answers. I'm interested in what you think, and we have regular gatherings where you have the opportunity to use your voice to try to make us better." That is a powerful signal, says Coyle. "I think one of the things that [smart leaders] do is they send a signal early on of fallibility," he says. "They really open up the channels by giving permission to people to talk. They admit their own mistakes and feelings, and create the possibility for players to speak up, and have regular input. Great coaches have to be open enough to say, 'Hey, I want you people on the team to evaluate the last three practices, and tell me what's working, and what's not working, and let's make some adjustments. What am I doing wrong?' That idea is unconventional. But it is really powerful." The four most important words any coach or leader can use in front of his or her team, according to Coyle, are, "I screwed that up!" When leaders admit they do not have all the answers, your athletes do not suffer; they buy in even more.

"Tell 'Em the Truth and Love 'Em to Death"

Under Head Coach Gregg Popovich, the San Antonio Spurs of the NBA have established a culture of excellence and consistency, with five NBA titles since 1999, twenty-two overall division titles, and winning at least fifty games per season from 1999-2017. Chip Engelland, one of Gregg Popovich's assistant coaches at the Spurs, describes the legendary head coach: "Pop does two things. He tells you the truth, and he loves you to death." In other words, great coaches build a relationship that can bear the burden of truth. To do that, you need a lot of love in your coaching. But don't take my word for it. Take the word of John Wooden, one of the greatest coaches of all time, regardless of sport.

Wooden, the "Wizard of Westwood," won ten national championships, including seven in a row from 1966-1973. He mentored numerous collegiate and professional basketball hall of fame players and navigated the delicate balance and changing cultural landscape of the United States during some of the most tumultuous years of its history. Wooden's influence extends well beyond basketball as he is well known for his Pyramid of Success, a roadmap of values that leads to much more than better basketball; it leads individuals to become better people. It still adorns the wall of numerous locker rooms and boardrooms across the globe.

A little-known fact about Wooden is that in one of his final interviews, when asked by reporters the top reason for his success, he gave an answer that very few people expected. As the reporters waited for an answer about the drills he ran or his fitness regimen, he shocked them all when he said, "I had a lot of love in my coaching." The secret sauce of one of the greatest coaches of all time, the greatest competitive advantage of all, was love.

Wade Gilbert, currently a professor of kinesiology at Fresno State and a former UCLA professor, told me a story about doing a project with Wooden and former UCLA player Swen Nater. Gilbert was the lead author of a group tasked with creating an academic paper called the "Pyramid of Teaching Success in Sport," modeled after Wooden's Pyramid of Success, mentioned above. In a pyramid, the strongest points are the cornerstones, so Wooden and Nater decided that the cornerstone of the pyramid was "love." The editors of the academic journal did not take kindly to that term, and three different times sent it back to Gilbert, worried that the paper could not contain the word *love* and *coaching* or *teaching* together. "The editors said to me, 'You have some great ideas here and some powerful people, but you can't say coaching starts with loving your athletes; it's too controversial,'" chuckled Gilbert. "So I sent it back to Swen and Coach Wooden, and their response was, 'You know what, Wade? If you change the word *love*, take our names off it. It's love. We've lived this.'" The editors suggested a bunch of synonyms for *love*, thinking it's just a word and they could tweak it. "No, it's not just a word," Wooden and Nater replied to Gilbert. "It's really the essence of what we do and what we should do."

Love is acting in the best interests of your athletes. Love is being of service and acting in service of your athletes. It is the cornerstone of being a great teacher and a great coach, and without a lot of love in your coaching, you will not build a sustained culture of excellence. Whether in business or in sports, to get teams of human beings working well together, the leader must have a lot of love for his people. To quote Anson Dorrance from UNC women's soccer again, "The first principle of teaching is loving those you teach. No matter how brilliant you are, no matter how much you know in the topic you're teaching, no matter how much you know as a coach, the most powerful quality in connecting with these kids is for them to genuinely feel your care for them."

So, how do leaders demonstrate their love of their athletes? One way, according to Dan Coyle, is to establish a culture of psychological safety. "All coaches," says Coyle, "are trying to get people to get beyond what they think they can do and create extraordinary effort. How can people do that if they don't feel safe? How can people do that if they don't feel connected? To be really intentional about creating that platform of connection is the most powerful thing you can do as a coach. You can have all the knowledge you want; you can be the greatest coach on the planet; you can have all these right things to say; but if you don't create access by sending signals of safety, you're not going to succeed."[4]

"Safety," according to Coyle, "does not mean absence of conflict." The idea of safe spaces, as we hear about on many college campuses across the United States today, is actually not the type of safety Coyle is talking about. "In fact, it is almost the complete opposite," says Coyle. "Safety is an environment where people are more likely to be themselves and more likely to have the conversations that need to be had because they don't think they are going to get punished or made fun of for speaking up, being themselves, or being vulnerable. It's not about tamping down feelings or avoiding the tough conversations. It is not a sign in a locker room that says, 'Hey, you guys are psychologically safe here.' Safety is a series of signals that need to be sent all day, every day, helping people feel like they belong, feel like they matter, and know that they are that part of the team." Safety is a process, not an event.

Oftentimes, as coaches, we think that we can either be the nice coach or the tough coach, and according to Coyle, that is a false choice. "Nice or tough, it doesn't have to be a choice between the two, like I'm either the nice, friendly players' coach or I'm the tough task master. It's actually a false choice; you can be both. It's much stronger to be both." Coyle continued describing an experiment at Stanford where they looked at what feedback works the best, and it turned out to be a really simple form of feedback, where they said, "Hey, I'm giving you this feedback because we have really high standards here, and I believe you can make those standards. I believe you can reach them." Safety is about creating an environment where people are not afraid to disagree and speak their mind and where ultimately their respect for each other allows them to be completely open and honest without fear of retaliation. It is not the absence of fear; it is the healthy acceptance of it that keeps pushing you forward. [5]

Activities to Promote More Trust in Your Team

Evaluate Your Trustworthiness

Trust is the glue that holds it all together. Every time you think there is a trust issue between you and your team, or within your team, remember

COACH. Do your players want to get in the cart with you and with each other? That is always the million-dollar question.

In order to evaluate your trustworthiness, write down the following:

$$\text{Trust} = \frac{C+O+A+C+H}{SI}$$

We have already discussed the meaning of COACH: connection, oneness, ability, consistency, heart-centeredness. The SI stands for "self-interest." Are you in it for yourself, or are you in it for everyone else? Are you a selfish leader or a servant leader?

Score each one of those out of ten, a score of ten being a high score in that area and one being a low score. Do your best to honestly grade yourself in each of the COACH elements. Then score your self-interest. A low score for SI means you are an others-centered, servant leader; a high self-interest score means you are in it for yourself. Do the math, and that is your trustworthiness score.

For example:

$$\text{Trust} = \frac{C\ (3) + O\ (4) + A\ (8) + C\ (5) + H\ (5)}{SI\ (5)} = \frac{25}{5} = 5$$

In this example, a coach has a trust score of five. The higher that number, the more trustworthy a coach is. But do not simply score yourself. A self-evaluation is nice, but especially in high school, college, and beyond, why not have your staff score each other? Why not get some feedback from your athletes on your trustworthiness?

Authentic leadership is vulnerable, and when you lay something like this out to your staff and athletes and they know you are open to improvement and identifying weaknesses, they are old enough and mature enough to understand that you are making a real effort to get better. If you see scores you don't like in some areas, don't be afraid to ask them, "How can I be more consistent? What would make our connection stronger?" Great leaders are never done growing and learning.

Demonstrate Your Vulnerability

Remember Dan Coyle's advice regarding the four most important words a leader can say? "I screwed that up." If the Navy Seals can say this, we can, too, coaches. Start small and say it to an individual, and when the time is right, admit your imperfection in front of the team. If you point the finger first at yourself, you will be surprised how many of your athletes will be more accountable and accept responsibility as well.

Summary

Trust is the glue that will hold your team together. Lack of trust will tear it apart. You get to decide whether you will consistently and intentionally build high-trust teams and become a trusted leader for your athletes or whether you will leave it to chance. You would never leave physical preparation or tactical preparation to chance. Why would you ever leave trust to chance?

In this chapter, we have covered multiple aspects of trust:

- Trust is not based solely upon ability; it is based on dependability, connection, and not only talking the talk but walking the walk. Ask yourself, "Have I demonstrated trustworthiness in all these areas?"
- There are fifteen qualities of high-trust leaders, based upon competence and character or some combination of both. Look at your own leadership for areas where you are excelling and areas you can improve.
- We have explored the difference between high-trust and low-trust teams, so take a look at your team and see what areas

are going well and what areas need work.

- Be vulnerable and don't be afraid to say, "I screwed that up!"
- Tell your players the truth and love them to death by building a relationship that can bear the burden of truth.
- Do the two activities: one to evaluate your trustworthiness in the eyes of your staff and your athletes and the other to remind you to be vulnerable and admit when you messed up.

When you observe high-trust teams and trusted leaders in action, it not only looks different but it also feels different. Trust is not something that happens by accident; it is created through a series of actions that display competence, build connection, create accountability, and get everyone on your team moving in the same direction. There are many moments in every training session and game that will allow you to build trust, so do your best to take advantage of them.

LESSON 16

"THE RULE OF ONE"

Create Extraordinary Moments for Your Athletes

Every athlete is one relationship away from a successful life.

—JOE EHRMANN

Mark Wilson was living a young soccer player's dream. He was sixteen years old and a trainee for Manchester United during the heyday of the club in the 1990s. Every day he reported to The Cliff, United's legendary training ground where legends such as George Best, Denis Law, Bobby Charlton, David Beckham, Ryan Giggs, and others had cut their teeth as players. In those days, aspiring professionals did not just come to The Cliff to train and leave; they served an apprenticeship of sorts, cleaning locker rooms, polishing the shoes of senior players, and serving their senior clubmates while observing what it took to be a pro. Every Friday, as the trainees were cleaning the place after the first team left for the day, a special visitor would appear.

"My job was cleaning the showers and toilets," chuckled Wilson as he recalled his formative years at The Cliff. "Alex Ferguson (Manchester United's manager) would check in on us, and you could hear him coming down the stairs because he would carry this mini cricket bat with him and he would clink it on the railing. And he would grab me from time to time and say, 'Wilson, come with me!'"

Ferguson would lead Wilson to the first team locker room and bathroom and run his fingers along the tiles and behind the toilets, checking to be sure if they had been cleaned properly. He checked every nook and cranny, looking for a less than stellar effort on the part of his cleaning crew. And if he found some dust or dirt, you would get a talking to.

"He would look you straight in the eye," Wilson recalled, his face turning dead serious. "And he would say, 'Wilson, if I can't trust you to do this when no one is looking, how can I ever trust you to play in front of seventy thousand people on the weekend?' Then he'd give you a playful tap with the cricket bat and a smile that could make you feel ten feet tall. And you could do one of two things with that. You could say, 'I will get away with it; he only checks once a week,' or you could make sure you do it right every single day because you know it's going to serve you well on the soccer field."

Wilson went on to play for Manchester United and Middlesbrough in the English Premier League, as well as FC Dallas in MLS and other clubs in England, and that moment stuck with him throughout his career. It is what we call at the Way of Champions a "Rule of One" moment.

One person, one comment, one time can change a life. As coaches, each and every time we interact with our players, we have opportunities to create these "Rule of One" moments. We have the opportunity with just a few words to change the trajectory of a person's life. We have the ability to create extraordinary moments, if we are intentional about those moments.

In this chapter, we will

- Delve into the research around what makes certain moments in our lives memorable.

- Examine what researchers Chip and Dan Heath call EPIC moments and learn to identify those times so that you can be sure your words and actions in those moments have the desired effect.
- Understand multiple ways you can interact with your athletes and your teams to ensure the right message comes across at the right times.

If we are aware of what makes certain moments extraordinary and are intentional about our words and actions at those moments, we can change lives. Just like Sir Alex Ferguson. And just like my high school English teacher.

My "Rule of One" Moment

After many years in sports, I have had many of my own "Rule of One" moments in my life, but one in particular stands out as it is the reason you are reading this book today. It happened when I was in the eleventh grade at St. Anthony's High School in South Huntington, New York. I was always a good student, and good grades came rather easily to me, oftentimes without a huge amount of effort. And then I encountered Brother Jeff Pederson, my AP English teacher, who decided that my grade would be based not on the overall quality of my work but on the quality versus the potential quality if I actually put in some effort.

One day Brother Jeff handed me back a paper with a big red ink *F* on it. I was aghast, and I said to him, "Brother Jeff, there is no way this paper is an *F*. I know it's better than a lot of the papers in this class."

"I didn't give you a grade based upon what everyone else is capable of writing," countered Brother Jeff. "I gave you a grade based upon what you are capable of writing. And you put no effort into this at all. It's crap." Then he gathered up the books off my desk and threw them out the third-story window of the school.

Then Brother Jeff said something that changed my life forever.

"John, get out of my classroom," he said, staring at me with piercing eyes. "You can come back when you decide to put forth the effort to develop the gift you have been given to write. *Because you are a great writer!* Now, get out!"

I was angry. I was offended. I was humiliated as I stomped out to the jeers of my classmates and trudged outside to collect my books. *Who did he think he was? How dare he embarrass me like that! How dare he tell me…the truth? Am I really a great writer?*

Years later, I dedicated my master's thesis and my book *Changing the Game* to Brother Jeff. I didn't know it at the moment—and I certainly didn't appreciate it—but he is the main reason you are reading this today. Brother Jeff saw something in me that I did not yet see in myself. I was a writer. One person. One comment. One time. It can change a life forever.

How to Be Intentional about EPIC Moments

What Brother Jeff, Sir Alex Ferguson, and many other coaches and teachers instinctively know is that certain moments in life have the capability of being more memorable and more sticky than others. Sports, in particular, is filled with these potential moments, which researchers and authors Chip and Dan Heath call EPIC moments in their book *The Power of Moments*.

"A defining moment is a short experience that is both memorable and meaningful," write the Heath brothers. "Some moments are vastly more meaningful than others. But we tend to ignore this truth. We are not very good at *investing* in such moments."[1] In their research, the brothers have found that defining moments contain at least one or more of the following elements:

- Elevation: Most people's most memorable experiences are clustered in their teens and twenties and can warp their sense of time. Elevation moments rise above the everyday normalcy, they boost sensory pleasure, and oftentimes they come as a surprise. Think of winning the championship game or coming back in the bottom of the ninth inning. Not all wins are created the same.

- Insight: These moments give us a deeper understanding of ourselves, much like my interaction with Brother Jeff in eleventh grade. In a few short moments, we realize something that can influence our entire lives ("I am good enough," or "I am a writer," or "She is the one!"). While these moments may seem serendipitous, if coaches are intentional, we can lay the groundwork for insightful moments.

- Pride: Sports is filled with moments of achievement and courage, moments where our long hours of training pay off or a group accomplishes something they never thought possible. If our coaching plan consists of a series of milestone events that measure small achievements leading up to a big one, we can draw the attention of our athletes to the moments that matter most.

- Connection: Being a part of a team, even if you are in an individual sport, is all about oxytocin, the hormone released by a mother during childbirth that promotes immediate bonding with her child, despite the misery she may have just endured. Teams are all about connection, and, thus, defining moments are often social moments where athletes share an experience of achievement.[2]

You can probably think of multiple moments in your life that shared one or all of these characteristics. I was recently having coffee with a former player of mine, and we talked about one such moment for our group. The team was a fifteen-year-old girls soccer team, and we were at the western regional championships in Lancaster, California. We had just scored a late goal to come back and defeat a team we had never beaten before and had advanced to the knockout stage of the tournament. The team had almost dissolved six months prior due to a sudden coaching change, with players ready to jump to another club.

As the club director, I had stepped in as head coach to try and salvage the team, and we decided at the last moment to recommit and give it one last shot. The win provided *elevation* and *pride* as we had worked incredibly hard that year. We all gained *insight* into what we were capable of as the near-dissolution of the group was still fresh in our minds. And as we drove back to the hotel crammed in the team van, a very popular Taylor Swift song came on the radio. Our *connection* was forged as the team belted out the lyrics at the top of their lungs, toppling out of the van in the hotel parking lot and stunning a few guests. Every time I hear that song today, I relive that moment. It was EPIC!

All the metaphorical trophies we have in our lives, whether they be actual medals, love letters, inspirational quotes, or photos of our best friends, are what the Heath brothers call "relics of your life's defining moments." They carry us when times are tough and lift us when we are down. Sports is filled with opportunities to create and nurture these powerful moments, and coaches influence them in an extraordinary way.

"Being a coach comes with such a profound obligation because these moments are so magnified," Dan Heath told me. "For coaches, it is both unfair and absolutely an obligation to get these moments right. It's unfair in the sense that you have to fight that lizard-brain side of you that wants to shout them down, but you also have to realize that your influence is more profound than you may even realize ... Moments matter, and what an opportunity we miss if we leave them to chance!" Every moment matters.

Activities Coaches Can Use to Create Extraordinary Moments

This whole book is really about creating an environment that allows and encourages these EPIC moments, but I wanted to share with you a few ways you can be intentional about creating defining moments for your athletes.

The First-Day Experience

One idea that I implemented right away from *The Power of Moments* was the first-day experience. Think about what it is like to start a new job and how most people are treated that day (ignored, shallow introductions, your office is not ready yet, etc.). How often is a twelve-year-old's first practice with a new team similar? They get thrown into the fire, perhaps having just moved to a new town and not knowing a single person. Then, they go to a practice and are ostracized and treated like an outsider. And we wonder why they don't come back or don't perform well. What if we were intentional about the first-day experience?

When I have a new player coming to the team to try out or train with us, I pull aside two or three kids who are our cultural architects, the ones who live and breathe our values. I tell them, "We have a new player coming today. You are in charge of her. From the moment she arrives, she is in your group, and you need to introduce her to everyone. If we have partners or groups, she is with you. When we play at the end, she is on your team. It is your responsibility to make her feel welcome today." I have had the occasion to do this a few times now, and the results have been amazing. The parents often write me a note afterwards, telling me how nervous their daughter was before coming today and how she already feels like a part of the team. Twice I have been told it sealed the deal on their move to a new town as they were nervous about their children not having a good sports experience. I kick myself for neglecting the importance of this moment for many years.[3]

The Personal Note

A few years back, my friend and former Bucknell swimming coach Lynn Kachmarik told me that a big change in her coaching came from asking herself a simple question immediately after every practice or competition: "What did I miss today?" I have found this to be very helpful in my own coaching as each day I can usually think of a moment or two where I spoke to an athlete in an unnecessarily harsh manner or didn't take the opportunity to catch him being good. We often notice an athlete getting frustrated or down on herself, yet training moves on, and we don't get the opportunity to say something. I used to let these moments pass, but now, through technology, we have the opportunity to make up for missed moments with athletes.

In lesson 7, I mentioned the power of the personal note. Here is an example of one I wrote to a player who was transitioning to another sport but was still playing with great effort and commitment as our season was finishing:

Dear _____,

I just wanted to say how impressed I have been by you this week at practice. Your fitness and work ethic are extraordinary; your positive attitude is awesome, as always. Your will to compete and win has gone to a whole new level. I loved that you were begging me to get back in our scrimmage last night! I know that your path ahead may not include soccer, but I wanted you to know what an honor and privilege it has been to coach you these last few years and how much I appreciate your dedication to your sports and your team. Your growth and ability as a soccer player has been tremendous, and you are a true leader and one of the players that drives our team. Keep it up!

Notes such as these only take a few minutes, but they say to your athletes—and their parents—three critical words: "I see you!" You matter to me. I saw you doing well, or I saw you struggling. These notes can also say, "I screwed that up!" And I have certainly screwed up a lot:

Dear _____,

I wanted to talk to you last night, but we had a new player show up, and I ended up not catching you before you left. I have seen a big change in you, and it is down to your confidence level, I think, and that is on me. It is my job to find you the right environment and place to develop. I can see in the way you are playing that you are afraid to make a mistake, and as a result, you are not playing aggressively, and you are letting your player get the ball, turn, etc. You are a great player, and you have the speed, smarts, and skill to do so much better. This happens to every player. It certainly happened to me, and I hated how I felt when I was tentative and afraid. I was lucky that I had coaches who understood this, and I want to do that for you.

Coaches, it is OK to make mistakes—some of us more often than others. Just admit it and start moving on. So many young athletes never have a coach or teacher admit they screwed up, and this is sad. Showing vulnerability and admitting errors is one of the most important aspects of leadership, not a sign of weakness. I have found that my notes saying, "I screwed that up," are oftentimes more powerful than the ones that say, "I see you." I think you will find this true as well.

One important thing to note is that if you are working with youth and high school players, you must be SafeSport compliant. These types of notes, and all player communication, should be sent via a team messaging service such as TeamSnap, where there is a record of your correspondence. If I send something through regular email, I always copy the parents as well, both for SafeSport reasons and so they know that I am seeing what they are seeing as well. But in general, you should not directly text, email, or send messages to one of your athletes through social media. Don't put yourself or your organization in a situation where your communications can be misconstrued or misrepresented.

Send the Team a Johnny-Mail

You can call these whatever you like. I call them Johnny-mails because Dr. Jerry Lynch calls his Jerry-mails and my friends call me Johnny O, so it seemed to fit. Whatever you call them, just be sure to check in with the entire team once in a while (and their parents, of course, in youth sports) and let them know what you are thinking. If you are a podcast listener, you have certainly heard me talk about a great group of young soccer players I coached for three years. When we lost a heart-breaking game in the state championship tournament, I sent them this:

Ladies,

I just wanted to send you a note tonight about our game today and tell you how overwhelmed and proud I am of all of you. You were warriors today. You have been warriors this season. To watch you last weekend and again today, especially that first half, I have never had a team come so far in just two years. Our movement, passing, competitive fire, energy, it was all-time. I have never been more proud to be a coach of any team.

For fifty-five minutes today there was only one likely winner. And then it was snatched from us, and that hurts. It hurts a lot. You don't even have time to digest it emotionally, and, all of a sudden, it's just over. And you feel like you got kicked in the teeth. I had a team like this a few years back; we lost in the State

Cup semis three years in a row on penalty kick shootouts. I had not felt that way again until today.

But here is the thing. And this is not just a soccer lesson. This is a life lesson.

Two years ago, our group didn't collectively care that much whether we won or lost. We laughed it off. We carried ourselves in practices and games in a way that said, "I didn't try that hard anyway, so who cares?" But we have changed. We have become something so much more. We have invested deeply in each other and in ourselves. In the process, we have not only become better players, but we have also become people who take pride in who we are and how we do things. We care deeply about our group and about the result.

When you invest everything, when you care as much as we do, you risk feeling like you did today. You risk feeling worse than you have ever felt after a game. You can't laugh it off. You cannot say, "We didn't try," because we did. And when you do that, you risk it hurting. A lot.

But as you go on in life, if you have learned anything from me, I hope you have learned this: love what you do and care about it with all your heart. Risk feeling the lowest of the low because you will never know the highest of high achievement if you risk nothing. And I do promise you this. If you go all in, over and over again, you will eventually know the feeling of winning, and it will feel greater than anything else you have ever felt. Because you risked it all. Because you risked disappointment and tears like we felt today. Because you will know that you earned it.

I love you ladies with all my heart, and I am so proud of you all. Thank you for giving me your very best these last two years. Let's keep being warriors, have some fun these next few weeks, and finish strong.

Coach

Be authentic, be vulnerable, and use sport to fill your players' lives with a series of defining moments. Be intentional about those moments of elevation, pride, insight, and connection, and use them to shape the lives of your athletes. This is not hard to do, but it may be one of the most important things you ever do as a coach.

Summary

Sports is filled with defining moments and opportunities for athletes to experience life-changing words and deeds. Coaches who understand and are intentional about these life-changing moments will make a great impact on their athletes and create memorable team experiences. To do so, you should

- Gain an understanding of the research around what makes certain moments in our lives memorable. Look for those EPIC moments (elevation, pride, insight, connection).
- Learn how to identify those EPIC moments so that you can be sure your words and actions in those moments have the desired effect.
- Understand multiple ways you can interact with your athletes and your teams to ensure the right message comes across at the right times. Send them a personal note or a team note and continuously connect with your players and catch them being good.

The world's best coaches understand that sport is filled with moments of elevation, pride, insight, and connection, and they take advantage of those moments to coach up their athletes and their teams. One comment, one person, one time can change a life, so make those moments count.

LESSON 17

"JUST BECAUSE YOU'RE A GOOD PARENT DOESN'T MEAN YOU'RE GOING TO BE A GOOD COACH/PARENT"

Keeping It Fair When Coaching Your Own Child

Recognize that you wear two hats. Tell your child you need to treat her like everyone else on the team when you wear your coach's hat. It helps when your child calls you "Coach" during practices and games, not Mom or Dad. But when you put your parent hat on, she is the most important person in your life.

—JIM THOMPSON

Just because you're a good parent doesn't mean you're going to be a good coach/parent.

—FRANK SMOLL

The 2019 NCAA men's basketball tournament was known for many things: Virginia's historic first NCAA title, the exciting play of Duke's Zion Williamson, and much more. But during the tournament, one topic that did not get much mention was the common bond between three well-known coaches. Syracuse University's Jim Boeheim, Kentucky's John Calipari, and Central Florida's Johnny Dawkins all had their own sons on their roster.

When Brad Calipari told his father he wanted to attend Kentucky, his dad sat him down. As Brad wrote in *The Players Tribune* in 2016, "He asked if I knew what I would be getting myself into, how hard it would be—probably the hardest thing that I'd ever done. 'The way you work now, you'll have to take it to a completely different level, whether it's workouts, watching film, classwork.'" Or, as father John put it to ESPN's Dan Patrick, "Look, I coach everyone else's child. How about I get a chance to be with my own child?"[1] Brad walked on and redshirted in 2019.

For Buddy Boeheim and Aubrey Dawkins, the situation was a little different. Both players were highly touted recruits and are very capable players in their programs. Dawkins led the CFU Knights to the NCAA second round in 2019, and Boeheim was a significant contributor as a freshman. He also, wrote Danny Heifetz, led the nation in chants of "Daddy's boy" from opposing crowds.[2]

Coaching your own child can be one of the most joyful bonding experiences you can have as you get to share your mutual love of a sport and have a front row seat for your child's growth and development. It can also be quite a challenge as taking on and off your coaching and parenting hats can be confusing and even difficult. But every year, at every level—from youth to professional sports—there are examples of parents coaching their own children. Were Buddy Boeheim, Brad Calipari, and Aubrey Dawkins players who had earned their spots on top collegiate basketball teams, or was this the worst case of "daddy ball" we had ever seen? In this chapter, we will explore both the joys and pains of coaching your own child. We will cover

- The research around coaching your own child;
- The phenomenon of daddy ball, and how it affects both athletes and coaches; and
- Some tips, advice, and questions to help guide the parent/coach relationship.

Many Parents Coach Their Own Child

It is estimated that nearly 75–80 percent of youth sports coaches end up coaching their own children. And as was evidenced in the 2019 NCAA Tournament, this can even happen on the collegiate and professional levels. The opportunity to coach your son or daughter, and the time it affords you sharing an experience you both love, can be incredible. It can also be a source of stress and anxiety on your parent-child relationship and give others a cause to claim that you are abusing your position as a coach. Yes, coaching your own child can be the most rewarding and frustrating thing you ever do.

If you happen to be asked to be your child's designated coach, you are often in the difficult and unenviable position of having to balance the needs of your child with the overall needs of her team. On the one hand, you want to seem impartial, and on the other, it's really hard to not give your own child extra attention because it's your child. That's what you do.

I have worked with many mom and dad coaches who held their own kids to higher standards than everyone else in order to be "fair." Sadly, the child never gets to be "just a player" and be himself once in a while. For many kids, practice never ended, and these well-intentioned moms and dads never took off their coaching hat and put back on their parenting one.

When you coach your own child, let practice end. Do not discuss sensitive team information with, or in front of, your child unless it pertains directly to them. It is best to leave the coaching to practice time and just be a parent the rest of the time. If you do not, your child will never get a break from practice, and it will strain your relationship. This is hard, and I have been guilty of this many times myself. Just be aware of this and be intentional about what you say and when you say it.

On the opposite extreme, you must make sure you are being fair to your child and to his teammates. It is extremely important to be cognizant of, and deal with, other parents' and players' perceptions. Are you playing favorites, letting your child play more minutes or more coveted positions? In other words, are you playing daddy ball?

Avoid Playing "Daddy Ball"

I have to admit, *daddy ball* was a new term for me a few years back. Most commonly used in baseball and softball, but prevalent in other sports as well, the term daddy ball is used to describe situations where a coach favors their own child—or is perceived to favor their own child—over others, ultimately to the detriment of the team. Have you seen this: the coach's child plays more minutes, more important positions, bats at the top of the lineup, or takes all the free kicks while other, better players sit out? That is daddy ball in a nutshell.

The problems with this can be twofold. First, if daddy ball truly exists, and your child is one of the weaker players on a team yet is set up to be the star, playing her can have a detrimental effect on her relationships with teammates and your relationships with parents. When you volunteer to coach, you must be as impartial as possible. You must give every athlete attention. Pay attention to statistics to justify decisions. Sure, if every kid on the team gets to pitch, of course your son does as well. But if no one else gets to pitch and your son gets consistently battered by the opposing team, give someone else a chance. You are not doing any favors for your son or your ability to coach your group.

The second, far-more-potent face of daddy ball is the perception that it is happening, even when it is not. If you are perceived to favor your own child, despite your efforts to remain impartial, it can be equally destructive. Team politics can still rear its ugly head, and every mistake your own child makes will be used as fodder for the parents and, by extension, the players who will think that the deck is stacked. This is when coaching becomes not so fun. I have no perfect answer here because you cannot control others' thoughts and perceptions or how they will blame you for their own child's shortcomings.

So, what are we to do?

Some Tips and Advice for Coaching Your Own Child

While this is likely not a complete list, here are a few ideas to help you be the best coach for your own child and everyone else on the team.

Before You Coach

To start with, do not only ask yourself, "*Could* I coach my child?" Figure out, "*Should* I coach my child?" You can do this by answering these three questions for yourself, and if one of your answers raises some red flags, think long and hard about taking on a coaching role for your child:

- What is my relationship with my child, and how will coaching her affect that relationship? Are we already at odds in our relationship, or is it a good one that can withstand this situation?
- What is my relationship with the other children on the team, who may be my child's friends, and how will my coaching affect those relationships? If your child is very close with the kids on the team, you may have to be critical of them, even discipline them, and it could change the relationship between your child and her friends, which could ultimately change your relationship with your child.
- How will my coaching affect my relationships with the parents of my child's teammates?[3]

If you can comfortably answer these questions for yourself, then talk to your child and see what he has to say. Make sure he understands that when you are home you are Dad and when you are on the field you are the coach. The Positive Coaching Alliance recommends that you explain to your child, "I always love you, and you are special to me. But when I'm coaching you, I need to treat you like all the other players. And you need to respond to me as your coach, not your dad. Do you think you can do that?"

If your child is OK with this, then explain to her that she will be held to the same standards as everyone else, and this is not a free ride. Tell her you cannot play favorites and that she must work hard and earn her playing time, just like everyone else. Tell her that on the field you are Coach, and everywhere else you are Mom or Dad. Even have her call you "Coach" on the field to help keep the distinction.

During Practices and Games

The biggest issue you will face, in my experience, is how to treat your own child fairly. Sometimes, in an effort to ensure an appearance of fairness, coaches can be overly harsh and unfair to their own children. They can be more critical of mistakes or less likely to start or give extra minutes and responsibility to their own child, lest someone perceives favoritism. Or, since we know our own children the best, we may sometimes give them more opportunities because we know they can handle the situation. It's a tough one.

One piece of advice I often give is this: if you have an assistant coach, let him coach your child and you coach his child. Be responsible for the individual coaching points in training and games for the assistant's child, and let him be responsible for yours. That way, there really is a coach–athlete relationship at work and the perception of special attention is not as evident. Both athletes are also more likely to take feedback since it is coming from someone other than Mom or Dad.

After the Game or Practice

As soon as the game or training session ends, once you get in the car, put back on your parent hat. When my son or daughter asks, "How did I do?" I usually ask them, "Do you want me to answer as your coach or as your dad?" That way, I let them guide the conversation. And if I am feeling very emotional about the game or something that happened, I also will say, "This is probably not the best time to talk about this. Can it wait until after dinner?"

The car ride home after games and matches can often be one of the most toxic moments in sports, and its effect can be amplified when your frustrations are not just those of a parent but those of a coach as well. Emotions are high, and disappointment, frustration, and exhaustion are heightened for both player and parent, yet many parents and coaches choose this moment to confront their child about a play, criticize him for having a poor game, or chastise their child, their teammates, their coach, and their opponents. The ride home is often the least-teachable moment in sports, yet it is often the moment that well-intentioned parents and parent coaches decide to do all of their teaching.

The only exception to the above "ride home rule" is when your child engages in behavior that you would not accept at home, such as spitting, cursing, assaulting an opponent, or disrespecting a coach or authority figure. In these cases, you should initiate the conversation, not as a parent to an athlete but as a parent to a child. Even then, you must be careful and considerate of the emotions of the match and choose your words wisely. Deal with the issue and then put it to bed; do not use it as a segue to a discussion of the entire game.[4]

After the Season

At season's end, do not be afraid to revisit those first three questions of this section. How is your relationship with your child now? If you are thinking of coaching again, can your relationship withstand another season? Are you holding your child back because you are the coach? Are you affecting his relationships with friends because you are the coach? And what about your own friendships with the parents on the team?

And finally, and perhaps counter-intuitively, do not be afraid *not* to coach your own kid. This may sound silly, but part of releasing your child to the game is not being there every practice and game to micro-manage another part of your child's life. When your kids are young, even if you have expertise in a certain sport and get along great with your kids when you coach them, it is probably best if you are not the head coach season after season. Offer to run a practice or two, but remember that you can say I love you to your daughter just as easily by not coaching her as by coaching her. Ask your child if they want you to coach, explain to them why you will not coach them all the time, and give them the opportunity to say, "Thanks, Dad, but I want Billy's dad to coach basketball for us."

Summary

Coaching and teaching my own children about soccer, lacrosse, golf, volleyball, skiing, fly fishing, and so many other things that I love has been one of the greatest joys of my life. My kids are so different and respond in completely different ways to my coaching and my advice. I have looked forward to those seasons and sports where I can coach them and also to those sports where I cannot. I would not trade those memories for anything. I hope you get the chance to make your own memories with your sons and daughters. If you do, just remember:

- Avoid playing daddy ball at all costs as it does no one any favors.
- Have open communication with your children about whether they want you to coach.
- Draw clear lines between the times you are wearing your coaching hat and the times you are a parent.

- Reassess after every season and be prepared to step away if your child asks.
- Always remember that wearing both the coach and parent hat can be a challenge, not only for you but also for your child.

We can cast a big shadow at times, and we can also be a ray of light. Never forget that your job as a parent coach is not only to guide your own children and their teammates but also to be prepared for the day when you are asked to step out of the way.

PART IV

—

A NEW DEFINITION OF SUCCESS

Ask me in twenty years and we'll see how successful these boys are.
Then I'll be able to tell you if I succeeded as a coach.
—PIGGY LAMBERT

The only thing that will prevent you from getting better
is thinking that you know it all.
—FERGUS CONNOLLY

I f you have come this far in this book, thank you. We have covered a lot of ground together here, and it may be a bit overwhelming. It's even overwhelming for me, and I have been able to incorporate the things written about here over a few decades of coaching. Just remember what I wrote in the introduction: find your 10 percent, change that, and then add in new layers once you get comfortable or see the need. That is what I have done, and that is what all of these coaches, sport scientists, psychologists, and other experts interviewed for this book have done. We have all committed to taking small steps and making choices that, over time, add up to huge gains.

We have a serious problem in sports around the globe. Our children are dropping out or being priced out in many places. Our officials are getting run off, no longer willing to risk life, limb, or their own sanity to pursue their passion for refereeing or umpiring. And sadly, many of our great coaches are also walking away from sports, tired of the long hours, the politics, and the focus on outcomes over development, ultimately detached from their why and purpose for coaching.

Finding your why is what is going to get you out of bed in the morning. I think it is the question that we should ask at the start of every season because it is the question you are going to ask yourself every day. I think it is the question we should ask of every coaching candidate because the strength of their purpose is what is going to pull them through the stress, the long hours, and the time away from their own loved ones. If your answer to, "Why do you coach?" is, "To win a national championship," you might discover that you are looking for external validation for what you are doing. And if you are doing this for external validation, I might ask, "Do you really want to be living your life so that others will approve of you?" I have not found that to be a very solid foundation.

Back in 2011, I walked away from coaching because I had lost sight of my purpose. I was done with the politics, the parents, and the needs of the athletes constantly being trumped by the egos of the adults. I was tired of watching ten-year-olds playing eleven vs. eleven soccer on huge fields because the adults wanted to make more money. I was tired of the race to the bottom where children's interests were the last things considered by so many leagues and clubs. I began to rediscover my purpose by founding Changing the Game Project the following year, and when I returned to coaching in 2016, an incredible bunch of eleven-year-old girls helped me find my "why" again.

Those girls had been abandoned mid-season by a former coach. They were losing every game handily. They were struggling to find their place in sports and in the world. I reluctantly accepted the position, convinced that I no longer liked coaching and afraid that my travel schedule and work demands would make the situation untenable.

Yet day after day, their smiles, tears, boundless enthusiasm for life, and total trust that I would serve them and help them become better soccer players and better people helped me to rediscover my why. They helped me to fall back in love with coaching. They helped me realize that every moment matters. At the end of that season, the club coaching director pulled me aside and told me, "John, I know those girls really needed you this season, and I really appreciate you stepping up. But I think you needed them more than they needed you." Thanks, Keith, you were right. I definitely did.

My God, I love coaching. It is the best part of my day. I get excited about planning practices and cannot wait to spend a few hours outside with my players. It has brought me closer to both my daughter and son and has helped me seem, I think, somewhat cool in the eyes of their friends, which makes me at least tolerable for my early teenagers to be around. We will never win a national championship, but I really don't think that is the point anymore.

As Erin Quinn, a three-time NCAA champion lacrosse coach and current athletic director at Middlebury College, told me, "The feelings and euphoria of winning a national championship are really fleeting. Winning a championship is really *not* the most rewarding part of it. It is the process and it is the relationships and the love you feel for each other. Winning a championship without those things would be a hollow feeling, and it would never sustain you. But when you do it with integrity and values and love and you do it with each other and for each other, there is nothing better than that. The satisfaction of the national championship feels great but the depth of the experience comes from all the other things."

I love to win. I love to compete like crazy, but I have definitely come to realize that when I pursued only winning, I was extracting more from my athletes than I was pouring in. When I pursued the depth of relationships, became a more evidence-based coach, and became finely attuned to how it feels to be coached by me, I became a giver who serves his athletes and pours into them. I certainly remember the sudden-death winning goals and state championships, but what brings far warmer feelings to my heart are the bus rides with teams singing together, the inside jokes, and the long visits with former players years after coaching them.

Today, I am highly aware of the sacred trust I have been granted to guide my athletes, and if given one wish from a genie, I would not wish to win a national title. I would wish that these athletes in front of me could feel, deep down, how special and unique this time together is and also how fleeting. I would wish that they could be present in every moment and devour every second. Because being on the athlete's journey and being part of a team in pursuit of something one could never achieve on your own, with people you love, is the greatest feeling in life.

So, as we finish up this time together, I thought I would share a few final ideas with you. These were common traits amongst all the coaches I interviewed, and while not necessarily worthy of a chapter each, they are certainly worth mentioning. After all, if coaches who have won multiple World Cup and Olympic championships and dozens of NCAA titles all share some common traits, they are certainly worth emulating or at least considering. I feel confident in saying that every one of these high-performing coaches would advise you to

- Always be curious and ready to adapt; don't be afraid to kill the sacred cow.
- Plant trees you will never see grow.
- Find balance and create margin in your life.

Let's finish strong!

No Sacred Cows

I remember attending my first coaching course in San Antonio, Texas, back in 2001, and I was quite full of myself. I was convinced that everything being taught there was already in my tool box, and, thus, I sat in the back of the room and kicked my feet up as a sports psychologist began his lecture. After all, I had plenty of drills and *X*s and *O*s; this mental stuff was a bit fluffy.

As I sat in the back, half paying attention and half cracking jokes with my friends, I noticed something. There, in the front row, keenly attuned to the talk and furiously taking notes, were two of the top soccer coaches in the United States, Anson Dorrance and Schellas Hyndman. (Hyndman was fresh off a Final Four appearance with Southern Methodist University, soon to be a MLS head coach.) They were fully engaged. They were asking questions and challenging the speaker, curious how they could glean some tidbit to take back to their programs.

I am not sure the lightbulb in that moment was stronger than my ego. I certainly didn't change seats, grab my notebook, and hop in the front row, but I definitely took notice. If two coaches who had accomplished far more than I had in the sport were taking notes and learning, perhaps I was missing something. Perhaps I didn't actually know everything. Perhaps I didn't know very much at all.

I shared this story with my friend Rob Miller, the lead speaker for Proactive Coaching, and he laughed and shared his own story. He was watching his mentor Bruce Brown present to the National Association of Basketball Coaches when a thin, frail hand next to him tapped him on the shoulder. Rob looked over and, lo and behold, that hand belonged to ninety-three-year-old John Wooden. Yes, *that* John Wooden. "Rob, can you take some notes for me on this presentation?" Wooden asked him. Miller looked at him, decades removed from his last stint at UCLA, and said, "Sure, Coach, why?" Wooden smiled. "It's good stuff. I need it for the next team I am going to coach." When recalling the story, Miller smiled. "You talk about the essence of an intentional coach," said Miller. "Coach Wooden, at age ninety-three, was still learning his craft and his profession. That image, for me, is one of the most vivid images I have had because it tells me everything we should be as a teacher, a coach, and an athlete, constantly trying to learn our craft."

If you are standing still, someone will pass you by. So, keep exploring and moving forward. This certainly does not mean that you adopt every new idea or session that crosses your path. It simply means you must be open to the idea that there is something out there you have not yet learned that could improve your coaching and help your athletes get better. You must learn from within your sport but also from outside of it. Business has invested billions of dollars in studying leadership and highly functioning teams. You have become a specialist in one sport, and you are metaphorically looking down all the time, digging deeper into your current hole to find one extra gem. Don't be afraid to look up and out as well; there is amazing work being done all around you.

Coaches who model curiosity and vulnerability and freely admit they do not know it all are more likely to have athletes—and fellow coaches—who will do the same. Asking your athletes to be open to new things while being stuck in your ways is a path that is more likely to lead to frustration than excellence. "Never before have so many people had so much access to so much knowledge but been so resistant to learning anything," writes author Tom Nichols in his book *The Death of Expertise*. Don't be that person. Be curious. Be a lifelong learner. And don't be afraid to sacrifice that sacred cow.

Plant Trees You Will Never See Grow

One New Zealand All Black saying that I am quite fond of is, "Be a good ancestor: plant trees you will never see." In the All Black culture, this means to protect and enhance the reputation of the team for as long as you are chosen to wear the shirt and leave the shirt in a better place when you are done. For coaches, planting trees that you will never see grow means recognizing that you are coaching the next generation of coaches. Your influence over one athlete today may influence hundreds, if not thousands, of athletes a generation from now. They may be coaching their own five-year-old, or they may be leading their country to an Olympic gold. They say that success leaves clues, and I would add that successful coaches plant seeds of future coaches.

When Cindy Timchal led the US Naval Academy to the 2017 NCAA Final Four, a strange convergence occurred. The other three teams left standing—Maryland, Penn State, and Boston College—were all coached by former Timchal players. In 2017, 12 percent of NCAA Division I programs had a former Timchal player on the coaching staff, while countless others coached in lower collegiate divisions, not to mention high school and club programs. Her former players and assistant coaches have won many of their own NCAA titles in lacrosse and field hockey. [1]

I have had the opportunity to work closely with one of Timchal's former players, Karen Henning, at Colby College in Maine for the past three seasons. When I asked Henning, a former All American and national champion at Maryland, what made Timchal such a special coach, she recounted a story about going to Timchal with an issue that was dividing the team her senior year. "OK, I will be fifteen minutes late for practice today," said Timchal. "You guys figure it out." Timchal was already developing coaches while they were still playing for her by giving them ownership of their teams and demanding that the intelligence was on the field. "She gave us the space and time to find the answers instead of providing the solution for us," says Henning. "And most important, most of us left college still loving the game."

Many of us will never see those seeds germinate and grow as Timchal has because our platform is not as big nor is our stage the same as it is for many of Timchal's players. But if you look at the coaches mentioned in this book, they all have a coaching tree. Their influence on their athletes has spanned a generation or two, and those athletes are now influencing other athletes. When you start to think about how many human beings could be affected by what you say and do at practice today, does it change what you might say or how you might say it? When you realize that every moment matters and that your influence propagates and multiplies exponentially through the future coaches in front of you, should you become more intentional about your coaching? "A person only dies when the last person who loved him dies," says Jose Mourinho, the former Real Madrid and Manchester United manager about his late mentor Sir Bobby Robson. The seeds of your influence will last far beyond your lifetime. Sow them well.

Find Balance

I started this book off with a quote from Joe Ehrmann: "To be a better coach, you have got to be a better you." In order to be a better you, you must find balance and margin in your life. You must take time off, exercise, sleep, meditate, and eat well. You must read and learn, but more important, you must spend time with your family and loved ones as you may be the only father or mother, son or daughter, brother or sister they have. I have seen far too many coaches interviewed recently that have been asked what their biggest regret is, and the answer is usually painful for them. The answer is never about failing to win a championship. It is about the time they missed with their children or spouse during years of chasing after the big prize and the external validation.

I think it is extremely hard to coach at the top level and have much balance, and that is why we see many coaches taking time off to recharge. The stress, pressure, and relentless hours take their toll. If you don't take care of yourself, you will fizzle and burn out. You will lose sight of your purpose. You will lose the relationships with your children and loved ones. Most coaches will never coach at a level where they have to dedicate every single waking hour to their team or program, so be very careful if you are headed down that path. You may look back years later and realize that every moment matters, not only with your athletes but also with your loved ones. Don't forgo your own health and well-being chasing after something ephemeral and leaving human beings in your wake.

Make Every Moment Matter

I will finish up here with a final story from Anson Dorrance, who honors his senior players each season during the NCAA tournament by giving them a rose before each game. "The nice thing about having a rose honor our seniors during the NCAA tournament is, of course, pretty quickly the rose dies," says Dorrance. "It is a reminder that in athletics, that's about how long that glory should reign, the length of the life of a rose that you've clipped and put into a water jar."

That is about how long it takes to read a book as well, the lifespan of a rose in a jar. It's not the book that matters. It is the ideas contained within and what you take from it and apply in your own life. I have done my best here to collect wisdom from decades of coaching and research and distill it into something you can take with you and refer back to, finding ideas to implement in your own coaching. But if you take nothing from this book in terms of coaching advice and research on how to coach better or run effective sessions or establish a team culture and core values that drive excellence, I do hope you take one thing, no matter what: Every. Moment. Matters.

We do not get to determine what our athletes will remember and what they will forget. We do not get to choose whether we will win or we will lose. But we can be intentional about our influence. We can be intentional about our purpose. We can be intentional about how we coach. We can be intentional about how it feels to be coached by us. We will leave a legacy. We will plant seeds. We will leave a dent in the universe. And when we realize that we have been given the great privilege of being a coach and influencing more people in one season than most people get to influence in a lifetime, then we will realize that every moment matters. Every word matters. Every action matters.

What a privilege it is!

ACKNOWLEDGMENTS

Writing this book has been an extraordinary journey. When I wrote my first book, *Changing the Game*, my full-time job was simply to write. This go around, I had to carve out many early morning hours while running Changing the Game Project, the *Way of Champions Podcast*, coaching some soccer teams, travelling and speaking, and trying to find time to be a husband and a father. To make all that happen required some extraordinary people.

First to my wife, Lauren, who has given me the space and freedom to do the work I do. You are the most wonderful life partner and loving mom and my greatest supporter. Thank you. To my children, Maggie and TJ, who once again had to put up with Dad saying, "Give me five more minutes, and I will come outside," you both inspire me to be a better coach and a better person, and you remind me that I need to keep it all in balance. You have been the recipients of some of my best coaching and some of my worst, so thank you for putting up with me. I love you both to the ends of the earth.

To my brother, Desmond, my sister, Kat, and my mom and dad, thank you for encouraging me, inspiring me, and surrounding me with people who encourage me to do my best and then do a little bit more. You four have been my greatest coaches in life.

To my dear friends Darby Warmenhoven, Jerry Lynch, James Leath, Skye Eddy Bruce, and Glen Mulcahy, thank you for working side by side with me these last six years as we have built Changing the Game Project and the *Way of Champions Podcast*. Our influence is never neutral, and we have been able to influence millions of people through our work. Thank you for pushing me to get better every single day.

My amazing editor, Amanda Rooker, has her influence all over this book. This is our second book together, and she is incredible at helping me find my own words while making my writing clear, concise, and impactful. The book you are reading today is far better than the first one I sent her, and I consider myself privileged to be able to work with her and her team at SplitSeed.

To all the amazing coaches and guests from the *Way of Champions Podcast,* whom I was able to interview and learn from. Many of you are quoted in this book and many are not, but I have taken at least one thing from every single one of you, and it has made me a better coach, dad, and mentor. I cannot list you all here, but you know who you are. Thank you for your time, energy, and devotion to changing sport for the better.

To all the amazing kids I have had the opportunity to coach, especially the Bend FC Timbers 05 girls and 07 boys who have helped rekindle my love of coaching. Thanks for letting me try out so many things on you all. Some have been great. Some things, not so great. But your passion and spirit has never wavered. It has been a privilege to be your coach.

Thank you to all the amazing supporters of the Changing the Game Project and *Way of Champions Podcast.* Please know that I read every single email and blog comment you leave. You have turned me on to so many incredible ideas and stories, and you inspire me every day to keep changing the game for our kids. This book is for all of you because your influence has been so positive and affirming through many difficult times.

And last, but definitely not least, to Brother Gary Cregan and Jeff Pedersen, the teachers who many years ago saw more in me than I saw in myself. There would be no books, no Changing the Game Project, nothing without your belief and mentorship many years ago and your friendship that lasts to this day. Thank you!

ABOUT THE AUTHOR

John O'Sullivan is the founder of the Changing the Game Project and the host of the *Way of Champions Podcast*. He travels the globe providing coach education, parent engagement, and leadership training for athletes in sports as diverse as golf, soccer, lacrosse, Aussie rules football, rugby, swimming, and beyond. He is a sought-after consultant and presenter, having worked with organizations such as the US Olympic and Paralympic Committee, US Lacrosse, US Youth Soccer, USA Wrestling, USA Swimming, USA Football, Little League, Ireland Rugby, Australian Rugby League, US Sailing, US Ski and Snowboard, and many other schools and youth sports organizations.

John is the co-founder of the Way of Champions Transformational Coaching Conference and is on the National Advisory Board for the Positive Coaching Alliance, the National Association of Physical Literacy, and Blaze Sports. His work can be found on outlets such as CNN, ESPN, *Outside, The Boston Globe, The Washington Post*, and many of the world's most trusted news sources. His first book, *Changing the Game: The Parent's Guide to Raising Happy, High-Performing Athletes and Giving Youth Sports Back to Our Kids,* has been an international bestseller in the coaching and children's sports categories as has his booklet *Is It Wise to Specialize?*

John's TEDx talk, "Changing the Game in Youth Sports," has become mandatory viewing for many parents when they sign their children up for sports, and he is dedicated to giving youth sports back to our kids and putting a little more "play" back in "playing ball." You can find him at www.ChangingTheGameProject.com. If you cannot find him, it is because he is coaching or out skiing, hiking, biking, fishing, or camping with his two children, Maggie and TJ, and his loving wife, Lauren.

FURTHER RESOURCES

Do you want to be a better coach, parent, or youth sports administrator? Then visit www.ChangingTheGameProject.com and connect with our movement to transform youth sports and give it back to our children. If you want to join our movement, sign up at www.ChangingTheGameProject.com/freectgbook and get yourself a free PDF copy of my first book, the number one bestseller *Changing the Game: The Parent's Guide to Raising Happy, High-Performing Athletes and Giving Youth Sports Back to Our Kids*.

Here are some other great resources for aspiring coaches and administrators:

- Positive Coaching Alliance: www.PositiveCoach.org
- Soccer Parenting: www.SoccerParenting.com
- Proactive Coaching: www.Proactivecoaching.info
- National Alliance of Youth Sports: www.nays.org
- TeamSnap: www.teamsnap.com
- iSport360: www.iSport360.com
- The Aspen Institute Project Play Initiative: https://www.aspenprojectplay.org

I love podcasts and, as of the writing of this book, here are my favorites:

- *The Talent Equation* with Stuart Armstrong
- *The Learner Lab* with Trevor Ragan
- *The Real Science of Sport* with Professor Ross Tucker
- *The Perception & Action Podcast* with Rob Gray
- *Coach Your Best* with Jeremy Boone

- *Winning Youth Coaching* with Craig Haworth
- *Finding Mastery* with Michael Gervais

NOTES

Introduction: Why Coaches Matter

1   N. P. Barnett, F. L. Smoll, & R. E. Smith, "Effects of Enhancing Coach-Athlete Relationships on Youth Sport Attrition," *The Sport Psychologist* 6 (1992):111-127.

2   Amanda J. Visek, et al., "Fun Integration Theory: Towards Sustaining Children and Adolescents Sport Participation," *Journal of Physical Activity & Health*, 2014.

3   Trends in Team Sports, Sporting Goods Manufacturers Association, Fall 2012.

4   Simon Sinek, *Start with Why: How Great Leaders Inspire Everyone to Take Action* (New York: Portfolio, 2009). You can also view Sinek's Ted Talk "How Great Leaders Inspire Action" for a great overview of this concept.

Part I: Why Do I Coach?

1   Steve Kerr, "Steve Kerr, 8x NBA Champion Player and Coach, on Developing Your Culture and Being a Great Coach." *Way of Champions Podcast*, October 12, 2019, https://changingthegameproject.com/136-steve-kerr/.

2   Jerry Lynch, *Win The Day: Building and Sustaining a Championship Culture* (Monterey, CA: Coaches Choice, 2019), 10-14.

Lesson 1: "To Be a Better Coach, Be a Better You": Do the Inner Work First

1   You can find links to the entire Quality Coaching Framework here:
https://www.teamusa.org/About-the-USOPC/Programs/Coaching-Education/Quality-Coaching-Framework.
Dr. Wade Gilbert has written a fantastic book that expands upon the QCF. See Wade Gilbert, *Coaching Better Every Season: A Year-Round System for Athlete Development and Program Success* (Champaign, IL: Human Kinetics, 2017). I have also interviewed both Chris Snyder and Dr. Wade Gilbert on the *Way of Champions Podcast*. Here is the link to Chris Snyder: https://changingthegameproject.com/woc-podcast-6-usoc-coaching-education-director-chris-snyder/.

Here is the interview with Dr. Wade Gilbert: https://changingthegameproject.com/woc-33-best-selling-authors-wade-gilbert-jerry-lynch-discuss-quality-coaching-really-looks-like/.

2   Urban Meyer, *Above the Line: Lessons in Leadership and Life from a Championship Season* (New York: Penguin, 2015).

3   I first wrote about this on my blog: "Why We Rage: The Science Behind Crazy Parents and Over the Top Coaches," September 13, 2013, https://changingthegameproject.com/why-we-rage-the-science-behind-crazy-parents-and-coaches/.

4   See Gilbert, "Quality Coaching Framework," 19.

5   Seth Godin, "The Compass and the Map," https://seths.blog/2019/04/the-compass-and-the-map/.

6   Joe Ehrmann, *InSideOut Coaching: How Sports Can Transform Lives* (New York: Simon and Schuster, 2011), 110.

Lesson 2: "You Coach a Person, Not a Sport":
Be an Athlete-Centered Coach

1   Kris Van Der Haegen. "How Belgium went from #66 to #1 in The World Rankings with Belgian FA Director of Coach Education, Kris Van Der Haegen," *Way of Champions Podcast,* March 11, 2018. https://changingthegameproject.com/52-kris-van-der-haegen/.

2   Interview with Steve Kerr on *Way of Champions Podcast*, October 12, 2019.

3   If you want to learn more about athlete-centered coaching, see Lynn Kidman and Bennett Lombardo, Eds. *Athlete-Centred Coaching: Developing Decision Makers* (Christchurch, NZ: IPC Print Resources, 2010). I also found these online articles helpful and well sourced: Jason Drummond, "Why Athlete-Centered Coaching Is Better," https://athleteas-sessments.com/athlete-centered-coaching-research/. Jeff Mitchell, "Match-Day Coaching: Using an Athlete-Centered Approach," https://coachgrowth.wordpress.com/2013/07/21/match-day-coaching/.

4   There are more inspiring stories in her book. See Kyle Schwartz, *I Wish My Teacher Knew: How One Question Can Change Everything for Our Kids* (Boston: De Capo Press, 2016).

5   John Branch, "Karch Kiraly Now Setting Up US Women's Volleyball Team to Succeed," *The New York Times,* June 18, 2016.

Lesson 3: "The Goal Is to Win; The Purpose Is Something Much Deeper": Pursue a Higher Purpose than Winning

1 Michael Zigarelli, "The Seven Disciplines of the Winningest College Soccer Program in America," *Way of Champions Podcast*, March 18, 2018, https://changingthegameproject. com/mike-zigarelli/.

2 Dr. Matt Davidson, "Developing Performance Character and Moral Character in Youth," *The Fourth and Fifth Rs: Respect and Responsibility,* Volume 10, Issue 2, Winter 2004, https://ncyi. org/2017/09/14/developing-performance-character-and-moral-character-in-youth/.

3 Jody Redman and Joe Ehrmann, "Every Child Is One Relationship away from a Successful Life": A Lesson on Transformational Coaching from Joe Ehrmann and Jody Redman of the InSideOut Initiative. *Way of Champions Podcast*, February 3, 2019. https:// changingthegameproject.com/joe-ehrmann-and-jody-redman/

4 Nate Baldwin, "How to Transform the Culture of Your Youth Sports Program with Nate Baldwin, Appleton Parks and Recreation Sports Coordinator," *Way of Champions Podcast*, October 28, 2018. https://changingthegameproject.com/85-nate-baldwin/

Part II: How Do I Coach?

Lesson 4: "You Can't Practice in the 'Kind' World if You Compete in a 'Wicked' One": How to Turn Technique into Skill and Create an Effective Learning Environment

1 I first came across this great story in David Epstein's *The Sports Gene: Inside the Science of Extraordinary Athletic Performance* (New York: Current, 2013). You can watch Finch strike out Albert Pujols here: https://www.youtube.com/watch?v=gm9iZnqGMvY.

2 Andrew Wilson "Carving Nature at Her Joints: A Conversation with Andrew Wilson," *The Talent Equation Podcast* September 8, 2018. http://www.thetalentequa-tion.co.uk/single-post/2018/08/09/Carving-nature-at-her-joints---A-conversation-with-Andrew-Wilson.

3 For a summary of "kind" vs. "wicked" learning environments, see David Epstein, *Range: How Generalists Triumph in a Specialized World* (New York. Riverhead Books, 2019), 20-21. Also see Robin Hogart, et al., "The Two Settings of Kind and Wicked Learning Environments," *Current Directions in Psychological Science* 24, no. 5 (2015), 379-385, https://pdfs. semanticscholar.org/5c5d/33b858eaf38f6a14b3f042202f1f44e04326.pdf.

4   Peter Brown, *Make It Stick: The Science of Successful Learning* (Boston: Harvard University Press, 2014), 46-52.

5   The University of Arizona has a great website on learning called the Learning to Learn Series. Here is a link to material on spaced learning: https://academicaffairs.arizona.edu/spaced-practice. Also see Brown, *Make It Stick*, 203-205, and Epstein, *Range*, 79-99.

6   Brown, *Make It Stick*, 79.

7   Brown, *Make It Stick*, 19.

8   I first read about the Air Force study in Epstein, *Range*, 90-92. The actual study can be found at S. E. Carrell and J. E. West, "Does Professor Quality Matter?" *Journal of Political Economy* 118, no. 3 (2010), 409-432.

9   Epstein, *Range*, 96-97.

10   Ian Renshaw, Keith Davids, Daniel Newcombe, and Will Roberts, *The Constraints-Led Approach: Principles for Sports Coaching and Practice Design* (New York: Routledge, 2019), 86. Also, check out our interview with Ian Renshaw, "How to Design a Great Practice and Prepare your Athletes for Competition with Skill Acquisition Expert Ian Renshaw." *Way of Champions Podcast*, November 10, 2019.

Lesson 5: "Great on Paper, S#!% on Grass": Build an Engaging and Effective Practice

1   Wayne Goldsmith, "It's Time for Coaching Educators to Start Teaching Coaching and Stop Teaching Sport Science with Olympic Coaching Educator Wayne Goldsmith," *Way of Champions Podcast,* February 25, 2018. https://changingthegameproject.com/50-time-coaching-educators-start-teaching-coaching-stop-teaching-sport-science-olympic-coaching-educator-wayne-goldsmith/.

2   For more about the USOPC ADM, go here: https://www.teamusa.org/About-the-USOPC/Programs/Coaching-Education/American-Development-Model.

3   Excerpted from my blog: "The Incredibly Massive Importance of Play," *Changing the Game Project,* March 4, 2014. https://changingthegameproject.com/the-massive-importance-of-play/.

4   Ted Kroeten, "The Importance of Free Play in the Development of a Young Athlete with Ted Kroeten, founder of Joy of the People," *Way of Champions Podcast,* July 7, 2019. https://changingthegameproject.com/122-ted-kroeten/. For more on acquisition versus

structure in language learning, see the work of Stephen Krashen, *Principles and Practice in Second Language Acquisition* (London: Pergamon Press, 1982), and this article by Krashen, "The Right and Wrong Way to Learn a Language," *Washington Post*, June 16, 2012, https://www.washingtonpost.com/blogs/answer-sheet/post/the-wrong-and-right-way-to-learn-a-foreign-language/2012/06/16/gJQAK2xBhV_blog.html.

5   The HockeyHub at England Hockey is a great tool for coaches of any sport. You can learn more here: https://www.englandhockey.co.uk.

6   You can learn more about the Magic Academy and the work Earnshaw and Fletcher are doing at www.TheMagicAcademy.co.uk or in my interview with them, "Becoming a Coaching Wizard with Russell Earnshaw and John Fletcher of the Magic Academy," *Way of Champions Podcast*, November 11, 2018. https://changingthegameproject.com/87-magic-academy/

Lesson 6: "Win the Day": Don't Show Up to Win; Show Up to Compete

1   Mike Sager, "Big Balls Pete Carroll," *Esquire*, December 6, 2009, https://www.esquire.com/sports/a6245/pete-carroll-1009/.

2   James Clear, "Sisu: How to Develop Mental Toughness in the Face of Adversity," https://jamesclear.com/sisu-mental-toughness.

3   Lynch, *Win the Day*, 52.

4   Lynch, *Win the Day*, 19.

Lesson 7: "Make Your Athletes Feel Invaluable, Even if They Are Not the Most Valuable": Create a Positive, Inclusive Environment

1   Tom Farrey, "To Develop Champions, Norway Lets Children Be Children," *The New York Times*, April 28, 2019, D3, https://www.nytimes.com/2019/04/28/sports/norway-youth-sports-model.html.

2   Derek Thompson, "American Meritocracy Is Killing Youth Sports," *The Atlantic*, November 6, 2018, https://www.theatlantic.com/ideas/archive/2018/11/income-inequality-explains-decline-youth-sports/574975/.

3   Amanda J. Visek, et al., "Fun Integration Theory: Towards Sustaining Children and Adolescents Sport Participation," *Journal of Physical Activity & Health*, 2014.

4   Neeru Jayanthi, et al., "Sports-Specialized Intensive Training and the Risk of Injury in

Young Athletes: A Clinical Case-Control Study," *American Journal of Sports Medicine* (April 2015): 794-801. See also Dr. James Andrews, *Any Given Monday: Sports Injuries and How to Prevent Them for Athletes, Parents, and Coaches—Based on My Life in Sports Medicine* (New York: Simon and Schuster, 2013) and Mark Hyman, *Until It Hurts: America's Obsession with Youth Sports and How It Harms Our Kids* (Boston: Beacon Press, 2010).

5   David Epstein, *Range: Why Generalists Triumph in a Specialized World* (New York: Riverhead Books, 2019), 65.

6   Rasmus Ankerson, *The Goldmine Effect: Crack the Secrets of High-Performance* (London: Icon Books, 2015).

7   Jere Longman, "Tony DiCicco, Popular Coach of the US Women's Soccer Team, Dies at 68," *The New York Times*, June 20, 2017.

8   For more information on the USA Hockey ADM, go here: https://www.admkids. com/. For more information on the decline of youth sports participation, check out this article: https://www.socceramerica.com/publications/article/76121/new-study-finds-big-drop-in-soccer-participation-i.html.

Lesson 8: "Women Tend to Weigh the Odds; Men Tend to Ignore Them": Understand the Difference between Coaching Boys and Coaching Girls

1   Anson Dorrance, "22x NCAA and World Cup Champion Coach Anson Dorrance Discusses the Difference between Coaching Men and Women, Building the Competitive Cauldron, and the Keys to Building a Winning Culture with UNC Women's Soccer," *Way of Champions Podcast*, January 14, 2018, https://changingthegameproject.com/44-anson-dorrance-world-cup-and-22x-ncaa-champion-coach-and-jerry-lynch-discuss-the-keys-to-building-championship-teams/.

2   Nicole Zarrett, Cheryl Cooky, and Philip Veliz, "Coaching through a Gender Lens: Maximizing Girls' Play and Potential," *Women's Sports Foundation*, April 2019.

3   There are a variety of resources on the gender issues in sports and education. Two of the most comprehensive in sports are Michael Messner's *Taking the Field: Women, Men and Sports* and Po Bronson and Ashley Merryman's *Top Dog: The Science of Winning and Losing*. Other books I have found helpful on understanding boys are *Raising Cain* by Michael Thompson and *Boys Adrift* by Leonard Sax. On the girls' side, check out Lisa Damour's *Untangled* and *Reviving Ophelia* by Mary Pipher. Finally, Tim Crother's *The Man Watching* about Anson

Dorrance is excellent.

4   Quoted by Po Bronson and Ashley Merryman. *Top Dog: The Science of Winning and Losing* (New York: Hachette Books, 2013), 110.

5   Bronson and Merryman, 111.

6   Quoted by Bronson and Merryman, 90.

7   Bronson and Merryman, 96.

8   Terry Steiner, "Terry Steiner, Team USA Women's Wrestling Head Coach, 'You could be the last person with a chance to reach that kid!'" *Way of Champions Podcast*, September 8, 2019, https://changingthegameproject.com/131-terry-steiner/.

Lesson 9: "As Many as Possible, as Long as Possible, in the Best Environment Possible": Identify and Develop Talent, Not Simply Maturity

1   Stuart James, "Meet the Man Who Discovered Gareth Bale—in a Six-a-Side Aged Nine," *The Guardian*, May 14, 2014, https://www.theguardian.com/football/2014/may/17/man-who-discovered-gareth-bale-champions-league-real-madrid.

2   I wrote about this in the article "Help, My Child Is a Late Bloomer: 5 Tips for Overcoming the 'Relative Age Effect' in Youth Sports," May 29, 2015. This chapter contains excerpts from this blog: https://changingthegameproject.com/help-my-child-is-a-late-bloomer-5-tips-for-overcoming-the-relative-age-effect-in-youth-sports/.

3   Laura Finnegan, "Relative Age Effect in UEFA U17 Championships 2019," *Talent Development in Irish Football,* May 9, 2019, https://talentdevelopmentinirishfootball.com/2019/05/09/relative-age-effect-in-uefa-u17-championships-2019/.

4   Joe Baker and Nick Wattie, "Happy Birthday?" *The Psychologist* 26, no 2 (February 2013): 110-113, https://thepsychologist.bps.org.uk/volume-26/edition-2/happy-birthday.

5   I found this research in the article "How to Identify Young, Talented Tennis Players" at http://www.tennisconsult.com/identify-talented-tennis-players-juniors-play/. There used to be a link to the research by Unierzyski, but it is no longer available.

6   Sergej Ostojic, et al., "The Biological Age of 14-Year-Old Boys and Success in Adult Soccer: Do Early Maturers Predominate in the Top-Level Game?" *Research in Sports Medicine* (October 2014), https://www.researchgate.net/profile/Sergej_Ostojic/publication/266681325_The_Biological_Age_of_14-year-old_Boys_and_Success_in_Adult_Soccer_Do_Early_Maturers_Predominate_in_the_Top-level_Game/

links/54479a010cf2f14fb8120718.pdf.

7   Mark O'Sullivan interview with Johan Fallby, "Johan Fallby: As Many as Possible, as Long as Possible, in the Best Environment Possible," *Footblog-ball*, December 11, 2015, https://footblogball.wordpress.com/2015/12/11/johan-fallby-as-many-as-possible-as-long-as-possible-in-the-best-environment-possible/.

8   Stuart Armstrong, "The Difference Between Talent and Ability, a Discussion with Stuart Armstrong of The Talent Equation," *Way of Champions Podcast*, May 5, 2019, https://changingthegameproject.com/combining-the-art-of-coaching-with-the-science-of-coaching-a-discussion-with-stu-armstrong/.

9   Daniel Coyle, *The Talent Code: Greatness Isn't Born. It's Grown. Here's How* (New York: Bantam, 2009), 126. See also Karen Crouse, *Norwich: One Tiny Vermont Towns Secret to Happiness and Excellence* (New York: Simon and Schuster, 2018).

10   Aine MacNamara, Angela Button, and Dave Collins, "The Role of Psychological Characteristics in Facilitating the Pathway to Elite Performance. Part 1: Identifying Mental Skills and Behaviours," *The Sport Psychologist* 24, no. 1 (2010): 52-73. http://clok.uclan.ac.uk/4826/1/collins_4826.pdf.

11   Ibid., 74-96.

Lesson 10: "Most Sports Are Played on a Five-Inch Field": Succeed in the Outer Game by Winning the Inner Game

1   Johnette Howard, "How Sports Science Explains Greg Norman's 1996 Masters Meltdown," March 31, 2016, https://www.espn.com/golf/story/_/id/15091501/how-sports-science-explains-greg-norman-1996-masters-meltdown.

2   David Dobbs, "The Tight Collar: The New Science of Choking Under Pressure," September 27, 2010, https://www.wired.com/2010/09/the-tight-collar-the-new-science-of-choking/. Also see Beilock's book *Choke: What the Secrets of the Brain Reveal about Getting It Right When You Have To* (New York: Atria Books, 2011).

3   A large part of this section is quoted from my blog, "The Mindset of High-Performers," June 3, 2014. https://changingthegameproject.com/the-mindset-of-high-performers/.

4   Gregory L. Jantz, "The Power of Positive Self-Talk," *Psychology Today*, May 16, 2016. https://www.psychologytoday.com/us/blog/hope-relationships/201605/the-power-positive-self-talk

5   Amy Saltzman, *A Still Quiet Place for Athletes: Mindfulness Skills for Achieving Peak Performance and Finding Flow in Sports and Life* (Oakland, CA: New Harbinger Publications, 2018), 9-19.

6   The work of Csikszentmihalyi is referenced in Daniel H. Pink's *Drive: The Surprising Truth about What Motivates Us* (New York: Riverhead Books, 2009).

7   Quoted by Saltzman, 13.

8   Quoted by David Winner, "Beautiful Game. Beautiful Mind," *ESPN the Magazine*, May 16, 2012, https://www.espn.com/soccer/england/story/1071240/beautiful-game-beautiful-mind?src=com.

9   https://www.healthline.com/nutrition/12-benefits-of-meditation.

Lesson 11: "Some Parents Are Crazy, but Most Are Just Stressed": Effectively Engage Your Athletes' Parents

1   https://changingthegameproject.com/coaches-stop-dealing-parents-start-engaging/.

2   For a full list of parental answers to the five questions, check out the original article here: https://www.breakthroughbasketball.com/coaching/stopped-dealing-with-parents.html.

3   Urban Meyer, *Above the Line: Lessons in Leadership and Life from a Championship Season* (New York: Penguin Press, 2015).

4   Excerpt from John O'Sullivan, *Changing the Game: The Parent's Guide for Raising Happy, High-Performing Athletes and Giving Youth Sports Back to Our Kids* (New York: Morgan James, 2014), 122-124.

Part III: How Does It Feel to Be Coached by Me?
Lesson 12: "Don't Take Your Culture for Granted": Establish Your Team's DNA

1   Todd Beane, "What Is Your Club's DNA?" *Changing the Game Project*, January 24, 2016, https://changingthegameproject.com/what-is-your-clubs-d-n-a/.

2   James Kerr, *Legacy: What the All Blacks Can Teach Us about the Business of Life* (London: Constabe, 2013), 183-185.

3   Donald Sull, Charles Sull, and James Yoder, "No One Knows Your Strategy—Not Even Your Top Leaders," *The Strategic Agility Project*, February 12, 2018, https://sloanreview.mit.

edu/article/no-one-knows-your-strategy-not-even-your-top-leaders/.

4   This quote and the idea of cultural architects and assassins is taken from Damian Hughes, *The Barcelona Way: Unlocking the DNA of a Winning Culture* (London: MacMillan, 2018), 32, 193-235. The term "cultural architects" comes from the work of Norwegian psychologist Willi Railo. See Sven-Goran Eriksson and Willi Railo, *Sven-Goran Eriksson: On Management* (London: Carleton Books, 2002).

5   Erikkson and Railo, 145.

6   Jon Torine, "'If You Love the Process, the Process Will Eventually Love You Back': A Conversation with Super Bowl Champion Strength Coach Jon Torine," *Way of Champions Podcast*, March 24, 2019, https://changingthegameproject.com/podcast-107-jon-torine/.

7   Hughes, *The Barcelona Way*, 200-208.

8   Hughes, *The Barcelona Way*, 209.

Lesson 13: "Performance Is a Behavior, Not an Outcome": Establish Standards to Drive Excellence in Your Program

1   Mark Bennett, "Mark Bennett, Founder of Performance Development Systems, How Coaches Can Shape Behavior, Influence Training Habits, and Build Accountable Teams," *Way of Champions Podcast* October 15, 2017, https://changingthegameproject.com/woc-31-mark-bennett-founder-performance-development-systems-coaches-can-shape-behavior-influence-training-habits-build-accountable-teams/.

2   Zigarelli, *The Messiah Method*, 184-207.

3   Kerr, *Legacy*, 171.

4   Chip Heath and Dan Heath, *Switch: How to Make Change When Change Is Hard* (New York: Broadway Books, 2010), 7-19.

5   Mark Bennett, "Mark Bennett Returns! The Founder of PDS Coaching on Using the Rule of 3 for Coaching Excellence and Ways to Make Your Athletes More Accountable," *Way of Champions Podcast*, August 26, 2018, https://changingthegameproject.com/76-mark-bennett/.

6   Alan Keane, "How a Coaching Mentor Can Change Your Life with Alan Keane, England U18 Basketball Head Coach," *Way of Champions Podcast,* December 2, 2018, https://changingthegameproject.com/90-alan-keane/.

7   Rob Miller, "Turning Confrontation into Communication, Not Conflict," *Way of*

Champions Podcast, June 2, 2019, https://changingthegameproject.com/117-rob-miller/.

8   This five-step process, as well as other suggestions about working with challenging athletes, can be found in Bruce Brown, "Teach Attitude First: Developing an Attitude of Gratitude in Your Athletes." This is a self-published booklet that can be found on their website here: https://proactivecoaching.info/shoppac/product/teach-attitude-first/.

9   Kerr, *Legacy*, 183.

Lesson 14: "You Are Enough!":
Help Your Athletes Overcome Fear, Stress, and Anxiety

1   Nancy Stevens "'I Like Recruiting Farm Kids': How 3x NCAA Champion Field Hockey Coach Nancy Stevens Builds Championship Teams," *Way of Champions Podcast*, April 29, 2018, https://changingthegameproject.com/nancy-stevens/.

2   Tim Gallway, *The Inner Game of Tennis: The Classic Guide to the Mental Side of Peak Performance* (New York: Random House, 2010).

3   I found the article "How to Overcome Anxiety with Cognitive Reappraisal" to be very helpful in understanding the concept: https://themotivationmindset.com/cognitive-reappraisal/.

4   A summary of the research of Jordet and Hartman can be found in Ashley Merryman and Po Bronson, *Top Dog: The Science of Winning and Losing* (New York: Hachette, 2013), 135-137.

5   Jeremy P. Jamieson, Wendy Berry Mendes, and Matthew K. Nock, "Improving Acute Stress Responses: The Power of Reappraisal," *Current Directions in Psychological Science* XX (X) (2012): 1-6. I first learned of Jamieson's work through Trevor Ragan's podcast *The Learner Lab*, "The Science of Being Better When You Are Nervous."

6   Allison Wood Brooks, "Get Excited: Reappraising Pre-Performance Anxiety as Excitement," *Journal of Experimental Psychology* 143, no. 3 (2014): 1144-1158, https://www.apa.org/pubs/journals/releases/xge-a0035325.pdf.

7   Trevor Ragan, "How to Learn Like a Jungle Tiger with Trevor Ragan from TrainUgly. com," *Way of Champions Podcast*, June 9, 2019. https://changingthegameproject.com/118-trevor-ragan/.

8   "Jerry Lynch and John O'Sullivan Discuss How We Use the RIVER Effect to Connect with Our Athletes," *Way of Champions Podcast*, August 5, 2018. https://changingthegameproject.

com/73-jerry-lynch-john-osullivan-discuss-use-r-v-e-r-effect-connect-athletes-can/.

9   Merryman and Bronson, 144.

Lesson 15: "Trust Is Like the Air We Breathe": Build High-Trust Teams

1   I first heard this story from author Chester Elton, who has written about it in his book *All In: How the Best Managers Create a Culture of Belief and Drive Big Results* (New York: Simon and Schuster, 2012).

2   https://saom.memberclicks.net/assets/SAM_unpublished_links/13-Behaviors-Hand-out-CoveyLink.pdf.

3   For more on high- versus low-trust teams, a great read is Pat Lencioni, *The Five Dysfunctions of a Team: A Leadership Fable* (San Francisco: Jossey-Bass, 2002).

4   Dan Coyle, "#61 Dan Coyle, NYT Bestselling Author of *The Talent Code* and *The Culture Code*, on The Four Most Powerful Words a Leader Can Say and Other Secrets of Highly Successful Teams," *Way of Champions Podcast* May 13, 2018, https://changingthe-gameproject.com/woc61-daniel-coyle/.

5   One of the top companies in the world, and one which heavily invests in discovering ways to perform better, is Google. Google did a project called Project Aristotle where they looked for the most common elements of high-performing teams, and the answer surprised them: psychological safety was the number one quality. You can learn more in this article: Charles Duhigg, "What Google Learned from Its Quest to Build the Perfect Team," *New York Times Magazine,* February 25, 2016, https://www.nytimes.com/2016/02/28/magazine/what-google-learned-from-its-quest-to-build-the-perfect-team.html.

Lesson 16: "The Rule of One":
Create Extraordinary Moments for Your Athletes

1   Chip and Dan Heath, *The Power of Moments: Why Certain Moments Have Extraordinary Impact* (New York: Simon and Schuster, 2017), 11-12. As a side note, the two brothers choose not to use the EPIC acronym as they acknowledge that many of these moments are not epic but are very difficult, painful, and transformational in ways that are not benign.

2   Heath, *The Power of Moments*, 13-14.

3   You can read more about "first-day experience" in Heath, *The Power of Moments,* 17-39.

Lesson 17: "Just Because You're a Good Parent Doesn't Mean You're Going to Be a Good Coach/Parent": Keeping It Fair When Coaching Your Own Child

1   Brad Calipari, "What I Know," *The Players Tribune*, July 15, 2016, https://www.theplayerstribune.com/en-us/articles/brad-calipari-kentucky-basketball.

2   Danny Heifetz, "The Wins of the Father," *The Ringer*, March 20, 2019, https://www.theringer.com/2019/3/20/18273759/buddy-jim-boeheim-brad-john-calipari-coach-son.

3   I first wrote about this in 2014 as part of a chapter on how to unconditionally love your child in sports. See John O'Sullivan, *Changing the Game: The Parent's Guide to Raising Happy, High-Performing Athletes and Giving Youth Sports Back to Our Kids* (New York: Morgan James, 2014), 169.

4   John O'Sullivan, "The Ride Home," May 1, 2014, https://changingthegameproject.com/the-ride-home-after-the-game/.

Part IV: "The Only Thing That Will Prevent You from Getting Better Is Thinking That You Know It All": A New Definition of Success

1   Dan Steinberg, "'She's Our Pat Summitt': A Remarkable Coaching Tree Blooms at Women's Lacrosse Final Four," *Washington Post*, May 25, 2017.